D0982949

BEYOND BROADCASTING

Patterns in Policy and Law

Don R. Le Duc

University of Wisconsin-Milwaukee

Longman

New York & London

COMMUNICATIONS

George Gerbner and Marsha Siefert, Editors
The Annenberg School of Communications
University of Pennsylvania, Philadelphia

Executive Editor: Gordon T. R. Anderson
Senior Production Editor: Ronni Strell
Text Design: Steven August Krastin
Cover Design: Steven August Krastin
Production Supervisor: Judith Stern
Compositor: Best-Set Typesetter Limited
Printer and Binder: R. R. Donnelley & Sons Company

Beyond Broadcasting: Patterns in Policy and Law

Longman Inc., 95 Church Street, White Plains, N.Y. 10601

Associated companies: Longman Group Ltd., London; Longman Cheshire Pty.,
Melbourne; Longman Paul Pty., Auckland; Copp Clark Pitman, Toronto;
Pitman Publishing Inc., New York

Library of Congress Cataloging in Publication Data

Le Duc, Don R.
    Beyond broadcasting.

    Bibliography: p.
    Includes index.
    1. Broadcasting—Law and legislation—United States.
2. Broadcastng policy—United States.   I. Title.
KF2805.L4   1987   343.73'09945   87–2654
ISBN 0–582–29039–2   347.3039945

87 88 89 90   9 8 7 6 5 4 3 2 1

CONTENTS

PREFACE

Not too long ago, enlightened politicians viewed regulation as the proper remedy for all inequities created by the marketplace. Today equally enlightened politicians see the marketplace as the proper remedy for all inequities created by regulation. As usual the truth appears to lie somewhere in between.

The trend toward deregulation may well be a healthy reaction against the ponderous and repressive restrictions federal bureaucracy has imposed on economic advances. Yet the bureaucratic process of a privately owned conglomerate can be fully as ponderous and repressive as the bureaucratic process of government and equally as constraining on innovative thought or action.

No one can claim that the Federal Communications Commission's (FCC) regulatory record during the past half-century has been a particularly outstanding one. Established by Congress to encourage diversity and local orientation in American broadcast service, the FCC has failed to achieve either objective. However, the FCC's regulatory record reveals no effort on the part of the broadcast industry to offer the public a broader range of programming alternatives or a greater number of community-oriented features than it has been required by law to provide.

A regulated American broadcast industry may not have fulfilled the hopes once held for it, but is there any reason to be more optimistic about the performance of an unregulated electronic mass media industry in the future? Those who favor deregulatory policies claim that the communication needs of the public can be served more efficiently within the marketplace of media offerings the industry will be able to provide in a competitive environment. Perhaps this is true; but if it is not, will public law be capable of making a less-than-competitive mass media industry responsive to the needs of the society whose values its services shape?

As we progress beyond broadcasting, what patterns in policy and law are likely to emerge to determine the nature of the universe of electronically portrayed myths and legends that have become our common cultural heritage? Although it is impossible to foresee all the political, social, economic, and technological changes that may act and interact to influence the decades ahead, it does appear that certain trends reflecting characteristics inherent in the private legal and policy structures of American mass media may foreshadow future production and distribution strategies during an era when the public policy role of government in this field has all but disappeared. Thus, to isolate more precisely the specific mass-cultural issues that media deregulation is likely to raise and to predict how diminishing the governmental role is likely to alter the probable shape and scope of future strategies, it is useful to understand as completely as possible how public policy and law have influenced the nature of past production and distribution strategies.

My interest in studying this fascinating area of law, where continuous conflict between public and private policy forces shape the nature of an industry's service, was stimulated both in law school and in my history and political science courses at the University of Wisconsin. There, Professors Calvin Corman, Gaines Post, and John Phelan were eager to guide me beyond the specific statute, administrative rule, or published opinion to isolate the conflicting social and economic interests the statements of law sought to reconcile.

In addition, Professor Phelan nominated me for the Ford Fellowship, which allowed a novice attorney to view his newly memorized principles of American law and process in the context of other national legal systems and to gain from this perspective a clearer sense of how the structuring of a policy process may affect the policies it produces. At the same time, the opportunities offered to me to practice law with the firm of Arnold, Murray and O'Neill in Milwaukee and with the Kaftan law firm in Green Bay and to serve as staff counsel for the State of Wisconsin's Department of Insurance gave my research its human dimensions.

During this early period of my career, when communications law research was only a hobby rather than a professional interest, Professor Lawrence W. Lichty encouraged me to pursue doctoral studies in the field of broadcast law at the University of Wisconsin, acted as my advisor and major professor, and through his dedication to scholarship, served as a continuing inspiration to me.

In 1972 I wrote a book, *Cable Television and the FCC*, that urged that cable TV be liberated from the repressive broadcast protectionist policies of the FCC so that the marketplace could determine which medium best served the public. At that time, as now, I had abundant faith in the capacity of American business to offer, through a competitive marketplace, a far more efficient and effective means for distributing goods and services than any bureaucratic plan could achieve through rules and regulations. However, as Lord Acton, a true conservative, once observed, "Power tends to corrupt and absolute power corrupts absolutely." As cable TV and other electronic delivery systems have evolved since the early 1970s, it has become increasingly clear that media deregulation may be less effective in stimulating a marketplace of ideas than in stifling consumer choice and vesting in our mass-cultural industry an awesome power over the hearts and minds of our citizens, a force that is frightening in its degree of First Amendment absolutism. It was this sense of lack of balance in the trend toward deregulation that led to my decision to write this book.

For the past decade, the book within these covers has existed as an ever-mounting pile of clippings, notecards, and papers, patiently awaiting their author. What finally began transforming this collection of materials into a manuscript was the unique opportunity to accept an endowed research chair appointment as the first Ronald Reagan Professor of Broadcasting at the University of Alabama. I am grateful to my former colleagues in the School of Communication at the University of Alabama, in particular, to the word processor staff, headed by Elizabeth Southwick, for their help and support in the preparation of this manuscript.

At the same time, it is only fair to admit that an extra incentive to complete this work came from an invitation to serve as a senior scholar in the revitalization of the Mass Communication Department of the University of Wisconsin-Milwaukee. I want to thank Dean William Halloran and Professors George Bailey and Ruane Hill of the University of Wisconsin-Milwaukee for offering me the opportunity to return to a school that has always held a special place in my heart.

I want to express my appreciation to Ronni Strell, senior production editor at Longman, for her skill and dedication in imposing upon this manuscript whatever degree of polish and precision it has ultimately attained.

I would also like to thank Marsha Siefert, associate editor of the *Journal of Communication*, for all that she has done to encourage my research efforts and for her faith in this work.

I owe my gratitude to all these individuals, but there is one other person I wish to thank. More than two decades ago, an attorney in northern Wisconsin decided to abandon his law practice and return to graduate school. His wife understood and put aside her dreams for his as they sold their newly furnished home, left family and friends, and brought two small children to Madison, Wisconsin, to live on a graduate assistant's salary.

It was not the first time she waited patiently for him to find himself; there was law school, the Ford Fellowship in comparative law, the district attorney's office—

But the lure of graduate school was too great for him to resist; the lure included a newly established doctoral program in electronic mass media, with a host of bright young scholars and their eager graduate students searching the horizon for the dawn of a new day in mass communication study when no hope for future scholarship seemed too extravagant or extreme.

But graduate school days came to an end, and the attorney and his wife left—first for the University of Maryland, next for Ohio State University, and then back to the University of Wisconsin to settle in among family and friends for a lifetime of teaching and research in that state that had always been home to both of them.

Then one day he asked her to abandon it all again, and once again she was willing to put aside her dreams for his and leave everything that was dear to her simply because he asked her to.

It is for all of this, then, and for so much more that this book is dedicated to my wife. It is one small gesture reflecting my love, admiration, and wonder for what she has freely and lovingly given to me.

And it is for this reason, then, as well as many others, that I am happy now that we have finally returned to the school where we met and married, the place where it all began.

Don R. LeDuc

TO ALICE

INTRODUCTION

Why shouldn't American broadcasting be deregulated? Why shouldn't the marketplace be allowed to decide what programming services the public will receive? Why shouldn't electronic mass media be granted the same free speech rights exercised by all other forms of communication in the United States? No one can claim that broadcast regulation has been particularly effective in achieving the public-interest objectives established for these media in the past; therefore, why not end the remaining vestiges of bureaucratic interference and allow all communication services an opportunity to operate freely and competitively?

These are certainly reasonable questions to raise, especially during an era when most other forms of direct federal control over industry trade practices have already been abolished. Yet, electronic mass media are unique in so many respects that what may be reasonable in the context of airline or trucking industry deregulation may have little or no relevance to the particular public policy problems involved in efforts to deregulate American electronic mass media service.

For example, although other industries seek total freedom from federal control, broadcasters must remain dependent on federal supervision to protect the integrity of the electromagnetic spectrum channels of frequencies essential for the delivery of their programming services. The chaotic interference that caused the broadcast industry to call for federal regulation in 1927 would almost undoubtedly return if spectrum allocation and assignment were once again based only on voluntary compliance with a set of general spectrum-use guidelines.

Understood in this context, broadcast deregulation means, not total independence from government control, but only the rescission of the special federal requirements now imposed on broadcasters and others who seek the privilege of spectrum usage. Those favoring this type of deregulation contend that federal licensing and programming standards have inhibited creativity and competitiveness and thus have denied the public the marketplace of electronic mass media services that can emerge only in an unregulated environment.

How accurate is this assessment of the impact of public policy and law on the competitive tendencies of broadcasting and other electronic mass media? Perhaps more significantly, how accurate is this description of the natural tendencies of these media in the absence of such regulatory constraints in the future?

To answer these crucial questions, we must examine how these public and private processes have interacted in the past to define the characteristics of American broadcast service. *Public*, in this sense, refers to the standards of conduct imposed by governmental statutes, administrative rules, and judicial interpretations of their legal consequences, as well as to the tactics governmental bodies use to realize the policy objectives reflected in the legal standards. *Private*, in the same sense, describes the elaborate structure of legally enforceable contractual relationships formed through industry negotiations, strategies to use the public law process to achieve private objectives, and political maneuvers to enhance the competitive position of the industry or of one segment of the industry in its conflicts with regulatory or other industry opponents.

In following this approach, the broadcast regulatory process will be examined in order to consider not only what the Federal Communications Commission has been able to achieve through its licensing and programming policies during the past half-century, but also to consider how each of these commission policies appears to have affected the natural competitive tendencies of the industry being regulated. In other words, this analysis will extend beyond the traditional assessment of how public and private policies have interacted in shaping the nature of American electronic mass media service in order to isolate the fundamental characteristics of the industry's economic strategies and tactics that the patterns of policy accommodation reveal. In this way, then, it should be possible to understand far more clearly how such industry strategies are likely to shape the nature of future electronic mass media service during an era when the balancing influence of regulation may have all but disappeared.

If this examination of long-term industry economic strategy provides little or no evidence to support the hope that a vigorously competitive marketplace in mass media services will naturally emerge during an era when the industry's policies reign supreme, then a new set of questions will arise. Under those circumstances, is American antitrust law adequately designed to discourage anticompetitive mass media mergers? Is our system of free speech law sophisticated enough to recognize and consider the interests of citizens in the quality of their mass-cultural environment? Do our federal courts have the capacity to resolve the wide range of complex, media-related controversies that have heretofore been settled within the broadcast regulatory process?

This study will focus primarily on the policy issues raised by the delivery of mass entertainment through electronic mass media channels, because it is through this process that we come to share the same myths and legends each evening. These myths and legends provide us with a common cultural experience that is far more pervasive than any traditional bond of community, kinship, or religion. Although media news obviously exerts an extremely important influence on American society, the unique qualities of the shared mass-cultural entertainment experience, as well as the equally unique qualities of the industry's production and distribution structure, seem to justify concentrating greatest attention on this most popular form of electronic mass media usage.

Unfortunately, viewing this vast process from the distance necessary to see its various patterns in proper perspective may tend at times to obscure details that a more focused work would reveal. Thus, terms such as *industry*, *Congress*, *federal courts*, and *FCC* obviously cannot convey the degree of diversity existing within each general institutional category during any single era, much less over an extended period of time. Designations of this type are used in this work simply to establish basic legal and policy relationships among the major forces in electronic mass media. To correct for the problem of generalization, references have been listed at the end of each chapter in order to furnish more specific information about each of the broad patterns described in that portion of the book.

On the other hand, the broader perspective has significant advantages as well. Looking beyond broadcasting to trace its relationships with program suppliers, feature-film distributors, and rival media delivery systems should reveal the areas of private media policy that will be most instrumental in determining not only the ultimate fate of broadcasting, but also the basic qualities of all future electronic mass media service in the United States. From this vantage point, it should be possible to raise broader and more profound questions about the proper and legitimate role of public policy in electronic mass media service than were apparent during an era when industry research in broadcasting was confined mainly to studies of the practices of broadcast stations and their networks.

It may be too soon to propose any final answers to these questions, but it is certainly not too soon to begin developing a rational, comprehensive philosophical foundation for answers we must either formulate for ourselves in the near future, or delegate once again to be formulated, on our behalf, by the impersonal forces of technology and historical accident. To understand more clearly what remains to be done to prepare this foundation for use, it seems logical to begin by surveying what we already know about the broadcast regulatory process in order to determine more precisely where the boundaries of our knowledge still need to be extended.

CHAPTER ONE

POLICY AND LAW
IN PERSPECTIVE

Broadcast Law in Theory and Practice

It all seemed to be so simple once, not too long ago. The American broadcast industry and its regulator, the Federal Communications Commission (FCC), were natural enemies. Any expansion in the FCC's authority diminished broadcaster autonomy to the same extent; therefore, every new policy initiative of the commission was certain to be challenged by the industry it sought to dominate.

American broadcasting was a closely supervised commercial activity. The FCC had the power to determine who could become a member of this industry and to decide, at the time of license renewal, whether the privilege of remaining in this field of business would be extended or revoked.

Acting under authority delegated to it by Congress in the Communications Act of 1934, the FCC compelled each applicant seeking a broadcast license to establish not only its technical, legal, and financial qualifications to operate a station in the public interest, but also its commitment, as evidenced by its programming proposal, to serve specific local-audience needs that its community surveys had isolated and defined.

If an applicant's documentation satisfied the commission in all these respects and there was no indication that its approval would result in an undue concentration of media control in the applicant's hands, a license was granted. This license specified the exact allotment of radio spectrum frequencies, maximum operating power, transmission hours, and call letters to be conveyed by the assignment.

Broadcast licenses were generally issued for a three-year period. License renewal for additional three-year periods depended on a station's performance during the previous three years being in conformance with its programming promises and in accordance with its broader legal and technical responsibilities as defined by commission rules and the Communications Act of 1934. The FCC, however, could revoke a license at any time or impose a forfeiture of up to $20,000 during a license period if it found a station to be violating any specific federal rules or regulations.

Among these rules and regulations was the requirement, under the *Fairness Doctrine*, that a station actively seek out controversial issues of public importance and present them in a balanced, impartial manner. In addition, each licensee was compelled by section 315 of the communications act to grant equal opportunity for broadcast time to all legally qualified candidates for political office and, under the Political Spending Act of 1971, to keep comprehensive records of all requests and payments for such access.

Broadcasters were also required to ascertain the programming needs of the communities they served and to keep records of all programming and advertising they broadcast. This included features designed to meet the community's needs. In addition, stations were prohibited from transmitting certain types of content, such as lotteries, advertisements for lotteries, or obscene programming.

To avoid concentration of control over broadcasting, the commission limited any individual or corporation to owning no more than seven AM, seven FM, and seven TV stations, of which a maximum of five could be VHF television facilities. Beyond this, no individual or corporation could operate more than one commercial station of the same type within any single service area.

Although the FCC was not empowered to license broadcast networks, it did formulate rules to guide a number of network practices, such as station affiliation agreements, program ownership rights, and the extent of affiliate station usage of network-television prime-time programming.

The FCC's authority in the field of broadcasting was extensive; however, it was by no means limitless. Every regulatory activity of the agency had to be based on powers clearly delegated to it by Congress and had to conform to the constitutional constraints imposed on all governmental agencies by U.S. federal courts. Because of these limitations, FCC regulatory programs were often vulnerable to legal challenge. Strategies for the skirmishes between the industry and the commission had been refined through decades of negotiation and litigation. Generally, before risking confrontation in the courts, the industry reacted to any new FCC policy position by trying to weaken the agency by undercutting its congressional support.[1] Even if this political maneuvering failed, the commission might ultimately have decided on its own to abandon the policy position rather than face the possibility of being ordered to do so by a judicial decision that could jeopardize other similar regulatory programs.[2]

When the agency refused to withdraw from a position the industry could not allow it to maintain, the industry almost inevitably appealed to the federal courts. Through the years, the legal conflicts between the commission and the broadcast industry began to create a substantial body of law capable of drawing rather precise distinctions between authorized and unauthorized regulatory activity in virtually every area of broadcast operation. In time these decisions seemed to provide a pattern of principles so predictable in nature and stable in form that publishers could begin to package them in "broadcast law" texts within their casebook lines, designed for courses devoted to the study of "broadcast regulation."[3]

The purpose of these studies was to define the exact dimensions of federal broadcast regulatory power by determining how courts had construed each FCC regulatory responsibility in the context of those more fundamental constitutional considerations that these responsibilities were to reflect.

During this same period, other studies were evaluating the effectiveness of the FCC's regulatory supervision by assessing the impact of various commission policy positions on a wide variety of industry practices. These "broadcast policy" studies, as they were called, invariably found the agency to be deficient in its performance as a regulatory body; but the nature of the deficiency seemed to depend on the type of scholarly training the policy analyst had received.

The analysts employing a political-systems approach generally found the commission to be incapable of shaping broadcast service in response to public-interest needs because of defects in the agency's structure that denied it the capacity to control industry conduct.[4] On the other hand, analysts trained in the traditions of classic economic theory found the FCC to be at fault precisely because it *was* controlling industry conduct, but in a manner that prevented competitive marketplace forces from furnishing the public with a far broader array of innovative services than any FCC edict could produce.[5]

Yet, whatever the particular orientation or methodology, this entire body of research and analysis rested on a common base of shared assumptions about the nature of the American broadcast regulatory process. The most fundamental assumption, derived from over a half-century of experience, was that the relationship between the FCC and the broadcast industry was and would continue to be an adversarial one with each party striving to extend its area of influence over American electronic mass media services at the expense of the other. Implicit in this assumption was the belief that the commission would remain the aggressor in these regulatory clashes and would constantly attempt to coerce the industry into making a greater commitment toward public interest in its broadcast services than economic incentives alone would dictate. From this perspective, the commission was seen as being the primary force in the broadcast and telecommunications policy arena. The nature of these services reflected the commission's successes and failures in the field of regulation. Similarly, predictions about future patterns in electronic mass media evolution were based primarily on an assessment of the commission's ability to shape new industry practices to conform to its policies.

During the mid-1970s, however, the commission announced its intention to follow a new policy that few of these studies had foreseen, a policy rebutting the presumption on which all these studies had rested. After more than a half-century of attempting to monitor and supervise nearly every aspect of American broadcast operation, the FCC decided to begin to withdraw as far as was legally possible from its traditional regulatory role and to relinquish to its former adversary, the industry, as many areas of responsibility for broadcast service as broadcasters themselves were willing and able to assume.

Free-market economists and "public-interest" advocates reacted predictably to this new policy of deregulation. As economists hailed the lessening of the commission's anticompetitive influence over broadcast service, public-interest supporters charged that the agency was attempting to escape its historic role as defender of audience rights in the field of broadcasting.[6] Perhaps the only point of agreement between these rival factions was that the fundamental nature of American broadcast regulation had been altered radically by the new commission policy. In this one area of consensus, however, it was entirely possible that they both were mistaken.

The traditional view of broadcast regulation provided in the preceding pages, although reasonably accurate, is also incomplete. Its narrow perspective distorts by concentrating only on the governmental, or public, portion of the policy process while overlooking the far more influential private, or industry, area of this process. Thus, to understand how the FCC's decision to deregulate broadcasting may affect broadcasting, competing electronic mass media, and audiences served by these media, it is essential to begin by understanding as fully as possible the characteristics of that regulatory relationship that are being modified by the decision to deregulate.

The Limitations of Public Policy and Law

Researchers have generally focused on governmental, or public, policy and law simply because it is the most visible and uniform portion of the regulatory process. A congressional enactment, an administrative ruling, or a judicial opinion is far more accessible and easy to interpret than the body of informal agreements, contractual obligations, and business practices that reflect private policy and law. Yet the very uniformity and absolutism of the public portion of the policy process limits its effectiveness in responding to the flexible, adaptive qualities of private policy and law. Thus, for example, the congressional legislation enacted in 1927 to assert dominion over broadcasting in the United States was outmoded at the time it was adopted; but it was virtually impossible to modify later to conform to the realities of American broadcast practices. The Radio Act of 1927, reenacted almost word for word in the Communications Act of 1934, was actually drafted in 1922, when broadcasting was dominated by hobbyists and radio-receiver manufacturers operating individually without networks or advertising revenues and transmitting sporadically on one of two broadcast frequencies assigned for their use by the secretary of commerce.

An obsolete bill became law five years later because legislative bodies seldom anticipate the need for law and instead react in haste to crises they have been unable to foresee. In this case, chaotic inter-ference resulting from the collapse of voluntary broadcast-frequency assignment and use agreements compelled Congress to act without delay to satisfy public demand for a solution.[7] Lacking the time necessary to consider carefully how the nature of broadcasting in the United States might have evolved during the intervening years, Congress simply decided to adopt existing legislation for this purpose.

Although the public might have complained about the quality of broadcast service under the existing voluntary-compliance plan, their interest in the particular orientation of the new law that would regulate broadcasting would obviously be minimal, because radio listening was, for them, only a diversion. In contrast, investors in a broadcast station were obviously deeply concerned about the orientation of the legislation and employed all their political influence as broadcasters to ensure that the privilege they already exercised would not be diminished under the Radio Act of 1927.

When the radio act became law, broadcasters licensed under its provisions could argue from that point onward that any amendment in its terms would be unfair and inequitable because their practices, business agreements, and long-range planning relied on the con-tinuation of those legislative conditions as stated in the act. Adding to the potency of these arguments, of course, was the fact that the broadcasting industry, with its deep and abiding commitment to the preservation of the interests that the radio act had created, was in daily contact with Congress and the FCC. These contacts were made through the industry's lobbying organization, the National Association of

Broadcasters (NAB), and the members of the Federal Communications Bar who represented specific broadcast groups.

Under these circumstances, then, it is not surprising that when a liberal, "New Deal" Congress revised the radio act in 1934, the basic regulatory provisions of the communications act that replaced it were little more than renumbered restatements of earlier provisions from a more conservative era. Even four decades later, as television, cable TV, pay-TV, and communications satellites, in turn, emerged to change many of the fundamental characteristics of American broadcasting, Congress again failed in its efforts to revise this legislation to conform to those changes, thus leaving a substantial number of its provisions much as they had originally been drafted in 1922.

The FCC, as the Federal Radio Commission (FRC) before it, was charged with the responsibility for realizing these outdated public law principles through the policies it formulated. This mandate, demanding enough in itself, was made even more difficult to follow because of the standard Congress provided for directing the regulatory agency's conduct in broadcasting. The federal broadcast regulatory agencies were told to base their policies and administrative actions on what would best serve the "public interest, convenience or necessity," a phrase borrowed from an 1887 Illinois railroad statute and later adopted in the Federal Transportation Act of 1920. Yet, whereas it would seem relatively easy to decide when the extension of a rail line or an increase in shipping tariffs might ultimately serve the needs or interests of its customers, it was far more complex and less precise in outcome to make a similar determination, in terms of audience requirements, about factors as sophisticated and subtle as programming balance or local orientation.

Looking to the past for legislative language in order to resolve future controversies has been the traditional approach of public law. There is obvious merit in such an approach, because an existing law has almost invariably been subject to litigation and is thereby defined through case law. In this way, a degree of predictability can be immediately transferred to new legislation as it is enacted, rather than having its application delayed while those affected by the new provisions test the extent of their obligations under its terms.

Unfortunately, however, seeking guidance from the past can seriously undermine the effectiveness of public law. If the similarities perceived as linking the present with the past are superficial in nature, a provision that has been taken out of its historical context can be totally inappropriate for the situation it has been adopted to control. In broadcast regulation, the vagueness of this public interest standard constantly inhibited the commission's broadcast policy formulation through the years; and the standard's lack of precision made the agency vulnerable to both legislative and judicial critics who validly questioned whether or not any position the agency adopted was clearly justified by the standard's requirements.

On a day-to-day basis, however, what actually inhibited meaningful FCC policy making far more than its nebulous public-interest standard was the agency's limited jurisdiction over broadcast service. The commission was authorized by law to license local broadcast stations, but these stations were little more than outlets for the national network program sources the FCC had no legal right to regulate. From the Radio Act of 1927 onward, public law coupled the acceptance of the privilege to use broadcast spectrum space with the imposition of an obligation to be subject to federal regulation in the use of that spectrum space. However, because the networks employed leased telephone circuits rather than spectrum space to deliver programming to affiliated stations, they needed no broadcast license for this distribution function and therefore incurred no obligation to be regulated.

In essence, then, although the FCC's Broadcast Bureau workload increased substantially with each passing year, the decisions it made with regard to awarding, renewing, or revoking the licenses of individual broadcasters had little effect on the overall quality of broadcast service in the United States. The approximately 1000 radio licenses the bureau processed during each three-year licensing period before World War II became more than 9000 licenses as the 1970s ended. But this increase in paperwork did not result in a similar increase in FCC influence over the practices of the industry the FCC was supposed to regulate in the public interest.

Whenever the FCC attempted to break out of the public law constraints that restricted its policy efforts, it faced a federal judiciary that was mindful not only of First Amendment and anticensorship barriers to its program-regulation activities, but also of the limitations on its authority that were imposed by Congress as it delegated powers to the commission through the Communications Act of 1934. Restraints of this magnitude encouraged the agency to seek to achieve its objectives through indirect means such as threats or attempts to offer the broadcast industry a reward for adopting some course of conduct that the FCC lacked the legal capacity to compel.

Although the menace inherent in the prospect of a particularly rigorous license-renewal proceeding or the advantages apparent in FCC support before Congress may have motivated short-term compliance with a specific commission directive, these tactics were certainly not capable of compelling any major or meaningful changes in the basic private policies of American broadcasting. In this respect, though, strategies such as these clearly exemplified characteristics shared by virtually all public policy efforts in the field of broadcasting during the past half-century; a sporadic set of pragmatic responses to specific crises created various industry practices this policy process could neither prohibit nor direct.[8]

Under these circumstances, it is obvious why policy research focusing almost exclusively on congressional actions and FCC activities offers such a poor perspective for those seeking to understand how legal and policy processes affect American broadcasting. Lacking from this vision are the industry policies that not only determined the nature of the service but that also created the conditions to which public policy had to respond.

The Scope of Private Policy and Law

The greatest tactical advantage that broadcast-industry policy makers have held in each skirmish with the FCC has been the far greater flexibility and adaptability of that private law system that they could employ to establish or modify terms and conditions of broadcast operation. Restraints imposed by federal due process standards required the commission to give adequate notice of any major rule change it planned to consider, to allow all interested parties an opportunity to be heard during the commission's deliberations, and often to defend, in federal court, any policy position the agency ultimately adopted before the measure could be enforced.

As the FCC was forced to move ponderously from issue to issue, the industry, fully forewarned of the commission's intentions, could set up the necessary negotiations among the parties involved and even draft the new contract provisions that would avoid or at least minimize the effects of a proposed rule on industry practices if the agency ultimately decided to adopt it.

Thus, for example, each of the rule-making proceedings that the commission initiated through the years to consider restraints it might impose on the capacity of affiliate stations to delegate programming authority to their broadcast network provided the parties with months or even years during which they could plan private legal strategies capable of reducing the impact of any type of regulation the FCC might eventually adopt. Working for the most part through a small group of attorneys specializing in broadcast law, the broadcast industry could negotiate terms and conditions for new arrangements and could have contracts containing these modifications ready to be signed long before the FCC's proposed regulations were to take effect. In addition, the attorneys, because of their continuous contact with FCC staff members,

were able to advise their broadcast clients of any subtle shifts in commission regulatory position that might require changes in the provisions
of these contracts as they were being negotiated and drafted.

Considering the strategic disadvantages the commission faced in its
efforts to adopt rules with the legal force necessary to achieve its
regulatory objectives, it is perhaps not surprising that nothing the
commission formulated in the field of public policy was capable of
transforming either the radio or the television stations it regulated into
the locally programmed entities that public law favored.

In theory, of course, the FCC did have the legal authority to end the
practice of networking at any time by simply enacting a regulation
barring the licensing or the license renewal of any station that agreed to
transfer any portion of its own programming responsibilities to any
other party. In practice, however, it was clear, virtually from the
inception of broadcasting in the United States, that basic economics
would make this simple act of public policy impossible to implement.
The creation and widespread dissemination of polished mass entertainment depended on a large commitment of capital, which only a large
organization could afford. Federal law limited the number of broadcast
stations that any single organization could own; therefore, mass
distribution of this programming required that independently owned
stations throughout the United States agree to act as local outlets for
this programming service. This affiliation not only furnished the independently owned stations with attractive, audience-building programming free of charge, but also allowed them to share in the national
advertising revenues that the shows generated.

Had either the FRC or the FCC tried to curtail this circumvention of
public law intent, they would have faced not only the political
opposition of the broadcast industry, but also the wrath of citizens
suddenly denied access to their favorite programs because of this action.
Instead, the FRC and the FCC had to content themselves with simply
limiting the extent of affiliate-station subservience to the programming
judgment of its network and had to accommodate to a structure of
private mass entertainment law that they lacked the political support to
challenge.

In one sense, it could be argued that this adaptation of private policy
and law actually allowed the federal government to escape a very
difficult dilemma it would otherwise have had to face. Rather than being
forced either to deny the American public its popular network
programming or to approve domination of broadcast service by a
handful of corporations, the affiliation agreement offered government a
means for avoiding either distasteful position. The affiliation process
allowed networks to function and yet preserved the federal govern-

ment's theoretical commitment to a locally oriented, diverse, and competitive broadcast service for the American public.

In another sense, the domination of broadcasting by a triumvirate of corporate powers probably allowed the FCC to exert more influence over the general quality of program content than it would otherwise have been able to do under the narrow constraints of the First Amendment. The networks were quite responsive to any broadly based public criticism of the cultural or moral values reflected in their programming. As in the era of the Hollywood studios, the high visibility of this trio of corporations shaping American cultural values made them extremely vulnerable to a wide range of private and public pressures, Having so much to gain by avoiding controversy whenever possible, the broadcast networks, as the film studios before them, carefully monitored the political climate and imposed on the creators of the mass entertainment that the networks financed and distributed a far more restrictive set of standards than any governmental body would have dared to require.

In situations where even those rigorous private codes failed to prevent public attack or political challenge, the FCC played dispute arbiter, a role that greatly enhanced the FCC's short-term authority over networks' practices. By announcing its intention to launch a full investigation of a controversy, the commission could divert the attack while negotiating with the networks for some compromise in program policy that might divide or at least weaken the coalition of opponents they faced.[9] Ironically, the very concentration of control that Congress had directed the FCC to prevent in the field of broadcasting made compliance with any agreement that the commission negotiated easy to achieve, because to change any element of American television service that the public found to be objectionable required concerted action by only three organizations.

As the 1980s began, however, the total domination of television service, which formed the foundation for the networks' private content-control structure, began to crumble. The networks' share of prime-time television viewing began diminishing as pay-TV and other cable-delivered services competed for viewers with programming and feature films often more daring or suggestive than anything the networks had scheduled. In response, the networks themselves became slightly more venturesome and included, among the themes treated in both mini and regular series, programming topics that would have been summarily rejected only a decade ago. At this point, the television industry's self-regulation system, which responded to both actual and potential public concerns about the cultural values reflected in its programming, no longer operates with the same degree of vigor as it had for the past quarter-century and will probably become even less active during the years ahead as the proportion of the audience watching network television each evening continues to diminish.

Because of the private content controls, the federal judiciary has had few opportunities during the broadcast era to decide how responsive this industry should be to citizens' concerns about the nature of the programming that the industry has provided. Even in the few instances when the FCC's rigorous controls failed to prevent controversy, the courts have generally refused to intervene and declared the FCC to have the exclusive right to protect the public's interests in all matters relating to program content. Now, however, as private controls are being relaxed and the FCC is seeking to reduce its responsibilities in this field, will the American judicial system have the capacity to fill in any gaps in policy and law that these changes may create?

The Status of Public Communication Law

Unfortunately, the American judicial system is even less capable of responding rapidly and effectively to change than is the legislative process. This is because the Common Law tradition provides only one method for developing and refining new legal principles—through judicial opinion, issuing on a case-by-case basis over an extended period of time.

In the absence of *ruling case law*, the courts are even more prone than Congress to look to the past for precedents to resolve current controversies. This practice tends to force newly emerging social or political issues into categories much too narrow and confining for their future growth. This is what has happened in the field of mass communication law, where jural principles still are little more than philosophical abstractions derived from an era of soapbox orators and hand-set printing presses.

It is important to realize that the Supreme Court's first major decision relating to freedom of expression was not rendered until the year 1919 and that federal intervention to safeguard citizens from state or local abridgments of free-speech rights began only in the year 1925.[10] Even more significant, perhaps, is the fact that nearly all the major mass media–related free-speech cases of American law were decided since 1950 and for the most part by divided courts. The courts were often unable to find a simple majority of justices for any single opinion to explain the basis for a decision.

It was not until the film industry's major studio content-control structure collapsed in the early 1950s that the first significant controversies could emerge in this field as the newly independent theater owners began importing more daring feature films from Europe. State and local film-licensing boards, which were dormant during the decades of private self-regulation, suddenly became active once again, and the Supreme Court was forced to establish the permissible boundaries of state police power in the area of mass entertainment.

Precision and sophistication in judicial analysis arise from an opportunity to consider over an extended period of time the relative priorities that should be accorded various legally recognized interests when different combinations of these interests are in conflict in a given field of law. With the sudden collapse of film's private content-control system, the Supreme Court was compelled to find an immediate solution to a major legal problem in a field where none of this development had yet taken place. Lacking such a jurisprudential foundation, the Court ultimately decided to follow standards it had recently established for state police power in the supervision of "adult" bookstores. The standards required these public law bodies to satisfy specific federal legal requirements before limiting or prohibiting public exhibition of a feature film.[11] Two decades of nearly continuous review of local and state film-board decisions imposed such a heavy administrative burden on the federal judiciary that the Supreme Court finally decided to end the massive workload it had created for itself. In 1973 the Supreme Court declared that it would presume the efforts to exercise state police power to be valid if they seemed to be reasonable and were based on a set of legislative standards prescribed by the Court.[12]

In the end, the judicial system left this area of mass media expression much as it had found it, with no clearer sense of the larger principles that determined the scope of permissible state control over film content than had existed when the courts began their intervention in the early 1950s. The problem was not lack of competence but simply the judicial process's lack of capacity to resolve a major public policy issue on its own in a rapid or precise manner.

In the area of broadcast law itself, the judicial system has been only slightly more effective in providing both the FCC and the industry with clear, consistent guidance. Operating within the constraints of the typical federal administrative process, the United States Court of Appeals for the District of Columbia simply reviews the record of any hearing in which the FCC's decision is being appealed. If the judge or group of judges finds that the record supports the FCC, the court will affirm the action and will generally include a discussion of the principles of law that support the FCC's position. On the other hand, if the court feels that the commission is in error, the matter will generally be remanded to the agency providing instructions on how additional proceedings should be conducted to avoid such an error.

Unfortunately, the system has seldom worked this smoothly or easily in practice. Remanding a case to the commission does not guarantee that the agency will interpret or apply the court's instructions as the appealing party expects they will be understood in determining the outcome of the controversy. In numerous instances, a single broadcast regulatory dispute required three or more appeals for its ultimate resolution; and one celebrated clash between two broadcast stations over the assignment and use of a particular broadcast frequency eventually resulted in the parties' making seven separate appeals during the 35-year period that it required to end this proceeding.[13]

The situation could become even more complex if the Supreme Court agreed to accept an appeal from the lower court decision either affirming or reversing a commission ruling. Occasionally, the high court would issue a concise, clearly worded opinion that would clarify some complicated broadcast regulatory issue; but in the more typical instance, the wide-ranging, broadly stated sets of majority, concurring, and dissenting opinions drafted by jurists with only limited knowledge of day-to-day broadcast regulatory process have operated to obscure what the court intended to establish as the ruling principle to be followed in subsequent FCC actions.[14]

In reality, perhaps the single most important influence that the federal judicial system has exerted on broadcast law during the past half-century has been to encourage all parties to seek some voluntary resolution of their differences whenever possible, rather than risk the lengthy, costly, and uncertain relief that litigation ultimately might provide. To ask more of the courts than this would be to impose a demand for mass-produced, generalized solutions on an individualized, hand-crafted art of adjudication, a demand the judicial process is incapable of satisfying.

Patterns in Policy and Law

Policy is a word much in vogue at the moment. The "broadcast regulation" text of decades past is now the "telecommunications policy" treatise, even though it is still typically confined only to broadcasting and focused primarily on the bureaucratic behavior of the FCC. No one can blame the scholar for invoking a trendy term to transform a rather old-fashioned field into a glamorous new area of inquiry. By investing routine regulatory activity with the aura of high-level public law planning, however, this ploy has tended to blur crucial distinctions that must be drawn between mundane administrative actions and sophisticated legal tactics if the functions of the regulatory and policy processes are to be clearly understood.

Broadcast regulation is, in one sense at least, to broadcast policy what the pawn move is to the chess match. The regulatory process, as the pawn, is rather modest both in scope of movement and in influence. The primary function of broadcast regulation is simply to monitor the performance of those within its jurisdiction while ensuring that all licensees adhere to minimum standards of conduct as defined by public law. A successful regulatory program demands nothing more than bare compliance with the dictates of a particular legislative or rule provision and compels those subject to its terms to act or to refrain from acting as the provision specifies.

In terms of the chess analogy, many regulatory actions of the commission have resembled the pawn moves of a novice reacting tentatively and defensively to threats only dimly perceived. In contrast, regulatory activity that is part of a policy process is neither a tentative nor a defensive reaction but rather a carefully coordinated portion of a broader, bolder strategy to achieve a specific long-range communications objective.

Thus, for example, despite all noble pronouncements to the contrary, locally oriented broadcast service has never been a true commission communications policy, because the agency has refused to restructure its regulatory guidelines so as to make this single element of licensee promise or performance the primary factor consistently determining the outcome of each licensing proceeding through the years. On the other hand, the FCC's equally unsuccessful attempts to reduce the degree of network domination over broadcast programming can be described as aspects of a basic policy, reflecting, as they have a rather consistent strategy on the part of the agency, to diminish this influence through a wide variety of different regulatory tactics. As in chess, stalemate or even defeat does not necessarily indicate a lack of strategic planning but may only reflect the fact that an opponent has been capable of responding to each tactical maneuver with equal or greater skill.

Yet in reacting to an opponent's movements, even the most skillful chess player must make certain accommodations, such as abandoning a favorite gambit or sacrificing a powerful piece, simply to avoid facing a more serious loss later in the game. It is here, however, where parallels between chess and the policy process end. Although the pieces lost are restored to the chessboard before a new match begins, the continuous nature of the policy process tends to make any strategic sacrifice a permanent one that, once offered in sacrifice, is difficult to reclaim for the next round of negotiations.

American broadcast policy studies have often failed to draw this distinction and have judged the success or failure of a proceeding solely on the basis of whether the commission's announced public-interest objectives have been realized in the end through formal rules or regulations. As a result, this literature, focusing only on "victory" or "defeat," has tended to overlook the extent to which the industry itself, in responding to the commission's challenge, has reshaped the practices that the FCC sought to reform through the public policy process.

Thus, examining the constantly interactive process more closely may reveal certain patterns of private accommodation emerging from the industry's tactics to protect the most vital or vulnerable elements of its operation from public policy pressures. From this perspective, then, it should be possible to view the full dimensions of industry responsiveness to public criticism or concern during the half-century period when the word *industry* was virtually synonymous with the word *broadcasting*.

As cable TV and other new electronic mass media delivery systems begin to alter the nature of this traditional regulatory relationship, it is important to note that the telecommunications policy and electronic media policy issues they raise are in no sense recent ones. Broadcast policy has always been just one aspect of telecommunications policy, whose spectrum allocation, technical standards, and communication common carrier tariff proceedings have affected broadcast service profoundly through the years. The only thing that the new media have done is to emphasize the significance of these areas of the policy process that have generally been ignored by researchers.

This is particularly true of that area now called *electronic mass media policy*, where what has been seen as a two-way struggle between industry and government has always been a more complex process intimately involving the mass entertainment industry, on which broadcasting has always relied for its programming. Although changes in public policy have attracted most of the attention during the past decade, the simultaneous changes in the private policy structure linking electronic mass media distribution systems with their massentertainment program suppliers may ultimately be recognized as having had a far greater impact on the specific qualities of future American mass communication services.

Broadcast policy seemed less complex in the past simply because our knowledge of its form and functions was so limited. Only by expanding the scope and sophistication of our analysis can we see the FCC in proper perspective, standing as just one of several public law institutions and influencing just a portion of the entire process that shapes the nature of American electronic media operations. Only in this way can we become aware of the direct and indirect effects of the public policy process on industry practices and thereby gain the capacity to project probable future patterns of practice during an era when public policy pressure will have all but vanished. Only in this way can we fully understand the implications of broadcast deregulation for emerging media, American audiences, and other public law structures suddenly drawn into the vacuum created by the disintegration of the federal broadcast-regulatory process.

After more than a half-century of regulatory experience, it now seems rather clear that the FCC lacks the capacity to exert a comprehensive and consistent policy influence on electronic mass media services in the United States. What is now far less clear is how responsive the electronic mass media services will be to various societal needs and interests in the absence of such a policy process in the future.

Despite its limitations, broadcast regulation has allowed for some degree of public participation in the establishing of standards for broadcast programming. In addition, accommodations that broadcasters made to policy pressure through the years have resulted in such obvious benefits as the production and scheduling of more programming designed for children, more educational series, and more cultural features than economic considerations alone would have dictated.

Those who support total deregulation of all electronic mass media operation contend that every societal need and interest can be met and satisfied more efficiently and effectively within the marketplace of mass communication service that the industry will provide on its own initiative in response to public demand. Yet, if this assumption is too optimistic, will public law have the capacity in the future to make a narrowly controlled, less-than-competitive system of mass media services accountable to, or at least responsive toward, the needs of the society whose values these services shape?

Although it is true that no projection of competitive tendencies within the electronic mass media industry can be made with absolute confidence, it seems equally true that patterns in the private policies that these media have been following during the past six decades could foreshadow strategies that are likely to continue even after the American public law structure has been altered substantially. In that event, then, the most important questions to be answered will be how public policy and law have affected or influenced these strategies in the past and how diminishing the scope of that policy and law will affect the nature of industry planning in the future.

An effort of this type can be far more than just an abstract exercise in historical parallelism because these long-term trends in industry policy seem to reflect equally long-term economic objectives of media interests, objectives unlikely to be significantly modified simply because of a lessening in federal regulatory activity. In addition, many industry policies operate within private legal structures that are nearly as elaborate in form and permanent in nature as the structures that have shaped public policy through the years.[15] As a result, these forms and structures themselves will tend to perpetuate the continuation of such industry policies in the future.

Ironically, as private law processes operate to preserve existing industry practices, the FCC is moving to abolish the processes that have provided the agency with the capacity to supervise these industry practices in the past. It is in the area of procedural law that the commission's deregulatory campaign has focused thus far, an area of public law too mundane to attract scholarly attention but one that could ultimately achieve the agency's current policy objectives far more effectively than any frontal assault it might mount on its congressionally mandated regulatory responsibilities.[16]

Therefore, to gauge how the gradual withdrawal of the federal regulatory agency from the field of broadcast regulation will affect future electronic mass media services in the United States, it is essential to know exactly what the term *deregulation* now signifies and what it may eventually mean in this vital field of public policy.

Notes

1. See, for example, the industry's response to the FCC blue book of public-service responsibilities of broadcast licensees as described in Frank J. Kahn, ed., *Documents of American Broadcasting*, 4th ed. (Englewood Cliffs, N.J.: Prentice-Hall, 1984), 148–149.
2. This was always a particular concern in cross-media holdings, where the commission's authority to prohibit or restrict media ownership combinations was not clearly delineated under the communications act. As Christopher H. Sterling and John M. Kittross indicate in their book *Stay Tuned: A Concise History of American Broadcasting* (Belmont, Calif.: Wadsworth, 1978), 190–192, one reason that the FCC was reluctant to include any limitation on newspaper ownership of broadcast facilities during its chain broadcasting proceedings of the 1930s was the fear that a successful challenge of the agency's power in this area might establish a precedent that would inhibit the FCC's entire effort to exert some regulatory control over ownership concentration in the field of broadcasting.
3. Two of the most popular of these recent broadcast law "great-case" packages are Douglas H. Ginsburg's *Regulation of Broadcasting* (St. Paul, Minn.: West Publishing, 1983) and William K. Jones's *Electronic Mass Media* (Mineola, N.Y.: Foundation Press, 1979).
4. Examples of this type of approach include *Selected FCC Regulatory Policies: Their Purposes and Consequences for Commercial Radio and Television* CED 79–62 (Washington, D.C.: General Accounting Office, 1979); this author's *Cable Television and the FCC* (Philadelphia: Temple University Press, 1973); and Barry G. Cole and Mal Oettinger's *Reluctant Regulators:*

The FCC and the Broadcast Audience (Reading, Mass.: Addison-Wesley, 1978).

5. Studies of this type include Roger G. Noll, Morton J. Peck, and John J. McGowan, *Economic Aspects of Television Regulation* (Washington, D.C.: Brookings Institute, 1973); Bruce M. Owen, Jack Beebe, and Willard G. Manning, Jr., *Television Economics* (Lexington, Mass.: Lexington Books, 1974); and Harvey J. Levin, *Fact and Fancy in Television Regulation: An Economic Study of Policy Alternatives* (New York: Russell Sage, 1980).

6. For a sense of this feeling of concern by those who viewed deregulation as a direct threat to all public-service–oriented functions of broadcasting, see former FCC commissioner Nicholas Johnson's comments relating to the deregulatory features of the Van Deerlin bill of 1978 in Timothy Haight, ed., *Telecommunications Policy and the Citizen* (New York: Praeger, 1979), 1–8.

7. For an excellent description of the chaotic conditions that compelled the passage of the Radio Act of 1927, see Marvin R. Bensman, "The Zenith-WJAZ Case and the Chaos of 1926–27," *Journal of Broadcasting*, 14:4 (Fall 1970): 423–437.

8. Examples of such pragmatic responses are illustrated in five case studies of broadcast policy in Erwin G. Krasnow, Lawrence D. Longley, and Herbert A. Terry, *The Politics of Broadcast Regulation*, 3d ed. (New York: St Martin's Press, 1982), 145–270.

9. Examples of the FCC's use of this tactic in the area of children's-television policies and the prime-time access rule are described in Chapter 4 of this book.

10. This first major federal free-speech case was *Schenck v. United States*, 249 U.S. 47 (1919) in which the clear-and-present-danger rule was advanced by Justice Holmes as in this case justifying conviction. In *Gitlow v. New York*, 268 U.S. 652 (1925), the federal courts recognized that citizens of each state should be protected from abridgment by the state of their rights to free speech through the privilege-and-immunity and due-process sections of the Fourteenth Amendment.

11. Although the Supreme Court overturned a state film-censorship law in *Joseph Burstyn v. Wilson*, 343 U.S. 495 (1952), it did so on the narrow ground that the term *sacrilegious* was too vague in meaning to be used to limit film exhibition. It was not until *Roth v. United States*, 354 U.S. 476 (1957), which upheld the conviction of Roth under federal charges of dealing in obscene books, that a divided court established a federal definition of obscenity that it would thereafter apply in determining whether or not state film laws abridged individual free-speech rights.

12. *Miller v. California*, 413 U.S. 15 (1973).

13. This 35-year controversy began in 1941, when KOB, an Albuquerque, New Mexico, station was shifted to WABC New York's clear-channel frequency of 770 kilohertz (kHz) on a temporary basis. The initial action of ABC to regain exclusive use of this frequency was rejected in *ABC v. FCC*, 191 F. 2d 492 (1951); but it would be another quarter-century before the matter would finally be resolved.

14. Thus, for example, *Red Lion Broadcasting v. FCC* 395 U.S. 397 (1969), the classic affirmation of FCC fairness-doctrine authority, was drafted with such a broad oratorical tone that it was far more widely quoted than actually followed in day-to-day commission practice.
15. This elaborate policy pattern is traced effectively in Joseph Turow, *Media Industries: The Production of News and Entertainment* (White Plains, N.Y.: Longman, 1984).
16. See, for example, "Reduction of Information Required by Specific Application Forms" (FCC 82–557), 47 Fed. Reg. 58539 (30 Dec. 1982); "Postcard Renewal, Memorandum Opinion and Order in BC Docket 80–253," 46 Fed. Reg. 55116 (6 Nov. 1981); and "Radio De-regulation, Memorandum Opinion and Order in Docket 79–219," 87 FCC 2d 797 (1981).

Tracing the Patterns: Primary Sources

There is nothing particularly startling about the revelation that public regulatory policy and law in the United States lacks the capacity to influence the conduct of industries subject to its jurisdiction. The structural weaknesses in the policy process described in this chapter were pointed out almost a half-century ago as flaws that eroded the strength not only of the FCC but also of all other independent commissions operating under similar mandates.

For example, Merle Fainsod, in a study published in the classic Carl J. Friedrich and Edward S. Mason *Public Policy* (Cambridge, Mass.: Harvard University Press, 1940), observed that vaguely defined legislative authority, coupled with overzealous judicial review, would deny a federal agency not only its authority but its very independence and would force the agency to rely on its client industry for the political support it needed to survive. In 1959, Bernard Schwartz, in Samuel Grislov and Lloyd Musolf's *The Politics of Regulation* (Boston: Houghton Mifflin, 1964), put it even more bluntly by declaring

> The present crisis in the commissions arises from the fact that these agencies have, for years, been disproving the basic assumptions which have led to their creation. Set up to regulate the public interest, they have...tended to equate that concept with the private interests of those being regulated. Intended to promote competition, they have fostered monopoly (p. 25).

Similar criticisms were voiced by Robert E. Cushman in *The Independent Regulatory Commission* (New York: Oxford University Press, 1941); by Thomas F. Robinson in *Radio Networks and the Federal Government* (New York: Columbia University Press, 1943); and by Samuel F. Huntington in his widely quoted "The Marasmus of the

Interstate Commerce Commission: The Commission, the Railroads and the Public Interest," Yale Law Review 61 (April 1952): 467–509.

This criticism continued through time; and scholars such as Marver Bernstein, in his Regulating Business by Independent Commission (Princeton, N.J.: Princeton University Press, 1965), and William Carey, in Politics and the Regulatory Commission (New York: McGraw-Hill, 1967), provided ample evidence that the process had not become more effective during the intervening years.

Although researchers such as James M. Landis, in his Report on Regulatory Agencies to the President (Subcommittee on Administrative Practice and Procedure, 86th Cong., 2d sess. [Washington, D.C.: Government Printing Office, 1960]), sought from time to time to make federal regulation more effective, it was generally assumed that some supervisory role in certain crucial areas affecting public interests would be preferable to no federal role at all.

Studies such as Roger G. Noll, Morton J. Peck, and John McGowan's Economic Aspects of Television Regulation (Washington, D.C.: Brookings Institute, 1973); Bruce Owen and Ronald Braeutigam's The Regulation Game: Strategic Use of the Administrative Process (Cambridge, Mass.: Ballinger, 1978); George J. Stigler's "The Theory of Economic Regulation" (Bell Journal of Economics and Management Science 2 [Spring 1971]: 3–21); Harvey J. Levin's Fact and Fancy in Television Regulation: An Economic Analysis of Policy Alternatives (New York: Russell Sage Foundation, 1980); among others, challenged this assumption and evaluated the performance of the FCC and other federal regulatory agencies solely in terms of cost-benefit relationships; but the influence such research actually had on federal policy makers was a clearer reflection of a drastic shift in political philosophy than a major increase in understanding based on this evidence alone.

What these studies did provide was a useful foundation of empirical evidence to support a move toward deregulation, which had already become popular as a political doctrine. What made this approach ideal for this purpose was that its dollar-derived projections, as this author has pointed out in "The Plight of 'Public Interest': A Principle Lost in the Process" (Journal of Media Law and Practice 4 [Sept. 1983]: 130–143), allowed analysis to avoid any consideration of the nonempirical public-interest social objectives sacrificed in order to realize the monetary benefit.

Unfortunately, private policies and legal practices in the field of broadcast production and distribution have received far less scholarly attention. A number of insightfully written descriptions of particular network practices have been published, such as Sterling Quinlan's Inside ABC: American Broadcasting Company's Rise to Power (New York:

Hastings House, 1979); Robert Metz's *CBS: Reflections in a Bloodshot Eye* (Chicago: Playboy Press, 1979); and more academic works such as Stewart Long's *The Development of the Television Network Oligopoly* (New York: Arno Press, 1979); Barry Littman's *The Vertical Structure of the Television Broadcast Industry* (East Lansing, Mich.: Michigan State Graduate School of Business, 1979); and Muriel G. Cantor's *The Hollywood TV Producer: His Work and His Audience* (New York: Basic Books, 1977) and *Prime Time Television: Consent and Control* (Beverly Hills, Calif.: Sage Publications, 1980). However, only Joseph Turow's *Media Industries: The Production of News and Entertainment* (White Plains, N.Y.: Longman, 1984) has viewed this process from the broad perspective necessary to sense its complexity and sophistication.

Thus, the problem with this literature is that it provides no solid basis for projecting how private mass media policy and law processes are likely to operate during an era in which government regulation no longer has any significant effect on industry practices. The flaws of public policy and law have been described in massive detail, but similar flaws in the private policy process have not been isolated or evaluated. In essence, then, we are now in a position to point out quite clearly structural deficiencies of federal mass media policy making without any clear sense of the specific characteristics of private media policy that will determine the nature of our mass-cultural services in the absence of such public policy structures in the future.

CHAPTER TWO

THE DIMENSIONS OF DEREGULATION

From Reregulation to Unregulation

In retrospect, it appears that the FCC's assault on its broadcast service monitoring and enforcement procedures may have begun as early as 1972, when then–Commission Chairman Richard Wiley instituted a campaign to *reregulate* the field by eliminating as many burdensome administrative procedures from licensees as possible.[1] However, this gradual reduction of reporting processes became much more rapid during the Carter era, as the next FCC chairman, Charles Ferris, followed the general approach of the Carter administration by making industry deregulation the policy of choice. During Ferris's term in office, the commission issued an order deregulating radio and began similar proceedings to deregulate television as well.[2]

Mark Fowler, the Reagan administration FCC chairman, pushed the agency beyond deregulation to what he called *unregulation* and dismantled every portion of this monitoring and enforcement structure his agency could rescind without violating the public interest responsibilities imposed on the commission by Congress.[3] Fowler completed the television deregulation proceedings, abolished FCC supervision of program formats, and began a crusade to convince Congress to end fairness and political access requirements under the Communications Act of 1934 as well.

Yet, this flurry of rhetoric and bureaucratic activity should not obscure the fact that despite all the claims that have been made about this era of broadcast deregulation, there has as yet been no substantial modification in the fundamental legal obligations that bind those who accept a broadcast license. In 1981, Congress amended the communications act to extend the length of a broadcast license from three years to five for television stations, and from three to seven years for radio. But these licenses remain subject to public challenge and commission revocation and require the same adherence to public-interest standards as those that existed prior to the beginning of the commission's deregulatory efforts.[4]

Thus, for example, in its orders to deregulate radio, television, and public broadcasting, the FCC was limited to offering its licensees procedure relief. It abolished the "community ascertainment" and "maintenance of a broadcast log for public inspection" requirements for all broadcasters and furnished commercial stations relief from its nonentertainment and advertising guidelines. However, fearing congressional criticism, it attempted to balance this relief by imposing on the broadcasters a new requirement to submit annually to the commission a list of 5 to 10 issues of public importance and to include a description of programming scheduled to address each of these issues.[5]

Even in the area of station ownership, where Congress has imposed no specific regulatory requirements on the FCC, the agency was forced to withdraw, under congressional pressure, from its original position that all ownership restrictions would end in 1990 and to move to a more modest revision that increased the number of stations each entity could own from 7 each of AM, FM, and television facilities to 12 of each. Also included in the new position was the additional limitation that the 12 television stations could not serve a combined market of more than 25 percent of the nation's audience.[6]

During the past decade, the FCC has consistently tried to convince Congress to amend the communications act to allow the agency to grant broadcasters greater relief from regulation. As a congressional agency, the commission can only rescind rules it has enacted pursuant to the communications act; but it can neither rescind nor refuse to enforce the provisions of the act on its own. However, instead of acting on the FCC's recommendations, Congress attempted to revise the act and delayed any action while the Van Deerlin committee struggled to balance the various conflicting interests affected by each proposed revision. In the end, Congress followed its usual policy tactic of doing nothing, thus preserving the act basically as it has existed since 1934.

Members of Congress do have a vested interest in protecting at least one major provision of the act, the equal political access requirements of its section 315. Operating only during official political campaign periods, this provision limits congressional challengers to the same terms and conditions for access to broadcast airtime as the incumbent while allowing the incumbent access to local broadcast audiences at all other times as a public service feature of a station's programming. The station is not obligated, however, to provide similar access to any potential challenger. In contrast, the fairness doctrine is neither as directly related to political self-interest nor as clearly protected by existing legislative language as "equal time"; thus, there is a possibility that the FCC could be successful in simply refusing to enforce the doctrine at some point in the near future.[7]

However, even if Congress insists on maintaining these public-interest–related broadcast licensee obligations just as they were originally enacted in the Communications Act of 1934, it is important to remember that the provisions of the act are neither self-policing nor self-enforcing. In other words, despite the declared public policy intentions of Congress, broadcasters may operate as they wish unless some process exists for monitoring compliance with these statutory provisions and for imposing penalties on broadcasters who violate the terms or conditions of these provisions.

Pursuing yet another tactic to avoid its obligation to enforce the fairness doctrine, the commission issued a report in 1985 that admitted that it had no legal alternative but to follow the dictates of Congress but declared that such a congressional requirement infringed upon the broadcaster's constitutional rights. In issuing this report, the agency was obviously appealing to the broadcast industry to win relief from this doctrine for itself and the agency in the federal courts.

Industry leaders were not slow to follow the suggestion implicit in the FCC's declaration of position. Almost immediately after the report was approved by the commission, the Radio-Television News Directors Association, financed and guided by CBS, brought an action in the U.S. Court of Appeals for the District of Columbia to have the agency's finding that it must continue to enforce the doctrine set aside on the basis of its tendency to abridge a broadcast licensee's right of freedom of expression. A second action, brought by Meredith Corporation, a broadcast-group owner, appealed to the same court for relief from an FCC decision that one of Meredith's stations, WTVH-TV, Syracuse, New York, had violated its fairness-doctrine obligations.

The court of appeals has already held that the fairness doctrine is not a statutory obligation imposed by Congress. If the holding in the recent *Telecommunications Research and Action Center* case should be extended by the court in either the *News Directors* or *Meredith* case to deny the FCC authority to enforce programming standards not established for it by Congress, the commission will have moved much closer to its ultimate objective of escaping all fairness doctrine regulatory responsibilities. Yet, even if the fairness doctrine is ultimately found by the federal judiciary to be an appropriate requirement to impose on those seeking the privilege of a broadcast license, the commission will, in the meantime, have provided itself with a justification for limiting its activities in this field pending a final determination of the constitutionality of this doctrine by the courts.

As the commission works feverishly to clear away what it often describes as the "regulatory underbrush" of traditional station reporting requirements, it is at the same time quietly undercutting the foundations of the monitoring process that is essential for future agency supervision of broadcast-station practices. Equally, and somewhat more deviously, the commission is employing the "reduction of bureaucratic burden" argument to deny citizens' groups throughout the nation the type of detailed information about station operations on which they have relied in the past to challenge the renewal of certain broadcast licenses.

At the moment, then, the broadcast deregulation movement has reached an impasse. Congress refuses to release the commission from its obligation to regulate American broadcast service, while the agency refuses to discharge this obligation with any more diligence or dedication than that absolutely required by law. In essence, public law and public policy are in direct conflict; the law is providing standards the commission has made a policy decision not to monitor or enforce with any degree of vigor.

Under these circumstances, then, it is less than accurate to say that American broadcasting has been deregulated, for those dormant public law principles governing the issuance and renewal of broadcast licenses may still be invoked and enforced through the courts, if necessary, by citizens' groups capable of documenting their own cases of violation. In addition, it is still possible, though not likely, that a future administration might appoint to the FCC members eager to reclaim the broadcast regulatory domain that has been preserved for them by congressional inertia.

Yet, even if Congress decides that it is no longer sensible or equitable to single out broadcasting for supervision in an otherwise unregulated field of electronic mass media services, rescinding the communications act or even abolishing the FCC itself will in no way end the influence that federal policy and law exert on broadcasting and its electronic mass media rivals.

Residual Regulatory Requirements

The most obvious role that some federal agency must continue to play is in the allocation and assignment of electromagnetic spectrum frequency, because international law obligates the United States to manage the use of this spectrum space in conformity with the rules and regulations of the International Telecommunications Union (ITU). Every member of the ITU is responsible for making certain that each transmitter operating within its borders is using the proper band of frequencies for the service it is providing, is not exceeding the designated power it has been assigned by license, and is not interfering with transmissions from legally authorized communication services in other nations. In addition, a federal agency or office must also monitor use of spectrum space to ensure that American broadcast facilities do not violate the more specific regional agreements in force with neighboring nations. Thus, for example, in August 1985, the commission achieved, in principle, an agreement with Mexico that in many respects paralleled one previously worked out with Canada. These agreements authorized more extensive spectrum usage for the AM services of the three countries.[8] Under the terms of these agreements, broadcasters who were granted a secondary usage of a *clear*, or protected, channel allocated to one of the other nations could now operate on that channel on a 24-hour-a-day basis as long as full-time operation did not materially interfere with the transmissions of protected foreign stations. At the same time, stations previously limited by law to daytime-only operation would now be allowed to continue transmissions until two hours after local sunset.

Although such technically oriented amendments to regional accords at first glance may not seem to be particularly meaningful, it is important to realize that through these provisions alone the FCC has opened up new broadcasting opportunities for some 125 unlimited-time AM stations as well as allowing for more extensive operation by FM stations located near national borders.

In similar fashion, the competitive position of existing American AM broadcast stations will obviously be affected by the degree of success American negotiators had at the Regional Administrative Radio Conference, where newly authorized channels between 1605 kilohertz and 1705 kilohertz were scheduled to be allocated among the nations of the Western Hemisphere. In the meantime, the commission, through its docket 80-90 proceeding, has decided to add about 1000 new commercial FM stations to its existing licensed broadcasters within the next few years.

In the area of television, the commission recently backed away from earlier plans to authorize additional VHF (channels 2–13) stations in a number of markets where engineering surveys indicated that the stations could operate without adversely affecting existing service; however, the commission has already granted construction permits for more than 1200 low-power television transmitters to balance this retreat from competition.

The FCC is presently responsible only for nongovernment spectrum-use supervision, whereas the National Telecommunications Information Agency, with the Interdepartment Radio Advisory Committee acting as coordinator between the two agencies, is responsible for government use of spectrum space. Whether this dual system continues or is supplanted by one in which a single organization is granted total jurisdiction over all spectrum use, the influence such federal spectrum management will continue to exert over private electronic mass media policies will not be reduced by any change in administrative structure.

For example, the decision to space American domestic satellites only two orbital degrees apart, rather than the four-degree spacing originally specified, doubles the number of satellite services possible and thus tends to reduce, through competition, the costs of mass media interconnection and networking operations. This decision will also increase the costs of services previously using those frequencies now required by the additional domestic satellites for their up-link and down-link channels. Similarly, domestic spectrum-management decisions that have allocated channels for new low-power television (LPTV) service and multichannel multipoint distribution services (MMDS) and created additional AM, FM, and television channels to be inserted within existing allocations obviously have had and will continue to have major impact on competitive patterns in electronic mass media service.[9] Each of these spectrum-management decisions resulted from advances in telecommunications technology that ultimately were recognized by those responsible for allocating and assigning use in the most effective and efficient manner. There is no reason to doubt that such advances will continue to be made; therefore, it seems equally reasonable to expect that the mandatory federal role, even in a totally deregulated broadcast environment, will remain an important force shaping private media policy in the foreseeable future.

A second federal function, regulating the rates and services of communication common carriers, will also continue as an important factor in electronic mass media service policy decisions, not only in the area of domestic satellite interconnection, but also in the control of more traditional terrestrial microwave and coaxial networking operations. Despite the alleged deregulation of these services at the time of the AT&T divestiture, the FCC remains responsible for supervising these communication common carrier practices to prevent discriminatory tariffs or charges in the field of interstate commerce.[10] The open-entry common carrier policy, which the commission pursued for the past two decades, has stimulated the development of cable TV–delivered networks whose pay-TV and advertising-supported programming now competes with broadcast network programming. In addition, broadcast networks themselves have recently begun switching to domestic satellite interconnection in response to the greater economy and flexibility such channels provide. Here again, whether this role continues to be exercised by the FCC or is transferred to some new federal entity, the policy decisions made with respect to communication common carrier operations will, of necessity, continue to exert a substantial influence on private electronic mass media planning.

Until the beginning of the 1980s, the FCC, on behalf of the federal government, played an important role in stimulating audience support for technological advances in telecommunications by establishing uniform technical standards for such services. Thus, for example, the FCC's approval in 1941 of an industry-proposed 525-line-per-frame, 30-frame-per-second transmission mode for television service made it possible, for the first time, for the prospective purchaser of a television set to be certain that the set would remain technically compatible and thus capable of receiving any future television programming transmitted in the United States. Until that time, the purchaser of each television set could only hope that the reception standards chosen by its manufacturer would be the ones ultimately adopted by American broadcasters; the purchaser facing the prospect of no television reception if that were not the case.[11]

Similarly, in 1953, with the commission's final decision relating to color television standards, a demand for color receivers began to emerge because of the confidence consumers could have in the fact that the set would not be made obsolete by future changes in these standards. In other instances, the FCC established similar technical standards for FM broadcasting in 1941, for FM subcarrier transmissions in 1955, and for FM stereo in 1961.

However, after having initially made such a technical standards decision in the field of AM stereo broadcasting in 1980, the commission reversed its position in 1982 and declared that it would let the market-place decide which of the rival and mutually incompatible systems for transmission and reception would ultimately become the universal one in the United States.[12] Similarly, and perhaps more significantly, the commission adopted the same position with regard to American teletext standards in 1981. It refused to adopt a universal standard for the manufacture of this equipment and thus issued to every prospective purchaser a clear caveat emptor of the risk of obsolescence involved in becoming a teletext-equipped household.[13]

It is possible, as the agency contends, that both the AM-stereo and the teletext-standards decisions of the FCC can be explained on a basis of legal and political, rather than philosophical or competitive, grounds. In neither instance did the commission have general support from the industry for a single standard; in other words, there was not a consensus among the dominant forces in the electronics field that could protect the FCC from political attack or legal challenge. Teletext divided its supporters into two equally powerful and mutually antagonistic coalitions; whereas in the AM-stereo case, the industry consensus collapsed soon after the FCC's original decision to adopt the Magnavox standard as the universal one for this service. The commission thus was forced to face a hostile industry opponent eager to test the validity of the agency's decisions in the courts. This is a position the FCC attempts to avoid at any cost, because the agency must either rely on its own meager technical resources to establish the wisdom of its decision or be forced to rely on the industry faction it has favored in its decision to protect itself from reversal.

However, if these recent decisions truly reflect a permanent change in the federal government's positions in the field of technical standards, future advances in telecommunication service are certain to be retarded as substantially as teletext and videotex have already been delayed in the United States. Although the commission admittedly has no jurisdiction over nonspectrum compatibility standards for devices such as videocassettes, it clearly has been empowered by Congress to encourage the most effective and efficient use of spectrum space by adopting uniform technical specifications that will allow the public to become part of the market for a new service and to do so without unnecessary concern about investing in a device that may soon become obsolete.

Some argue for a marketplace approach to technical standards by pointing out that the commission's adoption, in 1941, of the industry's television standards resulted in the United States' being saddled today with a far less-clear television picture than that provided by European advances after World War II.[14] Yet this argument must assume that the consumer reacts only to engineering considerations in making the purchase of electronic equipment and is unmoved by pricing or promotional strategies. It also overlooks the fact that technological advances are as likely to make a marketplace selected standard obsolete as a governmentally established set of standards and that, in either case, massive investment in existing equipment makes modification virtually impossible at that point. Most of all, however, it ignores the fact that efforts to introduce substantial technological advances, such as high definition television (HDTV), will be discouraged in a marketplace environment by public reluctance to purchase what may soon be out-moded, useless equipment. This reaction can only retard the progress that the federal government claims to be dedicated to promoting. During an era of aggressive global marketing of telecommunications equipment, such a policy of regulatory neutralism can have other unfortunate consequences as well. Thus, for example, the recent decision of the FCC not to dedicate any portion of the frequencies being allocated for direct broadcast satellite usage to the development of an HDTV, enhanced-definition transmission service did nothing to enhance American electronics-industry advances in this promising area of telecommunications technology. In one sense it could be argued that the agency was simply trying to remain impartial in this field by refusing CBS's application for a special satellite delivered HDTV channel assignment that could have resulted in CBS's gaining such an engineering advantage over its rivals that the particular transmission system it perfected would ultimately have set the *de facto* standards all others would have been forced to adopt.

Yet, although this policy might have been sensible and equitable only a quarter-century ago, it is no longer realistic in a world where nations such as Japan, France, West Germany, Canada, and the United Kingdom, among others, actively encourage their own national industries to advance as rapidly as possible to perfect devices and techniques capable of allowing them to capture a world market for their systems and standards. At the moment, for example, members of the American electronics industry generally support a Japanese developed HDTV transmission standard but face powerful opposition from a number of West European nations favoring an incompatible HDTV transmission mode much more closely related to their own 625 line PAL or SECAM systems of color television reception. The International Radio Consultative Committee (CCIR) is trying to reconcile these opposing national industry coalitions, but it is entirely possible that the world will once again be divided by different television standards and that the American television industry will be relegated to a secondary role in this division.

In this particular situation, it is highly unlikely that any single policy action of the FCC could have altered these circumstances. However, what the FCC's HDTV decision does illustrate is that national regulatory neutralism in the development of telecommunications standards is no longer a "colorless" policy but rather one almost certain to have damaging, if unintended, consequences in the broader arena of world politics and trade. By the same token, a refusal to establish technical standards for new telecommunications services does not remove the FCC from the domestic policy arena either but rather places it in the middle of the process, protecting the interests of those who wish to see these advances delayed to avoid their competitive impact. The question that must ultimately be faced in this field, then, is not simply whether the FCC should or should not deregulate the technical standards process but whether it is in the interests of the American public and the American electronics industry itself to shift the risk of technological development to the individual consumer while at the same time discouraging the demand that could finance industrial growth or advances that could create international sales opportunities.

Deregulation: Federalism versus Localism

From the Radio Act of 1927 onward, the federal government has asserted its sole and exclusive jurisdiction over all use of broadcast spectrum space in the United States. Even if a transmission were so limited in power that it could not possibly extend beyond the borders of the state in which it originated, the use of the federally allocated and assigned spectrum resource preempted or denied a state or a municipality any authority to regulate the terms or conditions of a broadcast station's operation.

The basic right of federal preemption was affirmed by the courts as early as 1928 but was given its clearest expression in *Allen B. Dumont Laboratories v. Carroll*, 184 F. 2d 153 (3d Cir., 1950), in which a broadcaster asked a federal court of appeals for a declaratory judgment to prevent a Pennsylvania motion picture censorship statute from being applied to require every feature film scheduled for broadcast by a television station located in Pennsylvania to be approved by a state board before its transmission. In defending its action, Pennsylvania pointed out that the FCC was prohibited by section 326 of the communications act from censoring broadcast content. This, state officials argued, created a gap in federal power, a vacuum that could be filled by a state or local agency performing this function. In granting broadcasters of Pennsylvania relief from this statute, the federal court declared that "Congress had occupied fully the field of television regulation and ... that field is no longer open to the States."

However, a decade later, in *Head v. New Mexico,* 374 U.S. 424 (1963), the Supreme Court upheld a New Mexico injunction preventing a station, located in that state, from accepting, in violation of New Mexico law, broadcast advertising from a Texas advertiser. Here the Court pointed out that federal regulation of broadcasting was not intended to supplant all state authority over broadcast stations, only state regulation that infringed in some way on lawful federal authority in this field. Although this Supreme Court decision provided state and local authorities with at least a limited area of legal jurisdiction over broadcast stations operating within their boundaries, there was little incentive for any state action as long as the FCC supervised and controlled broadcast programming, aided and abetted by the industry's private self-censorship code, which was far more rigorous than one that any locality might impose.

While broadcasting remained firmly under the control of the federal government, the emergence of the modern cable-TV systems of the 1960s provided states and local governments with their first opportunity to become deeply involved in the process of electronic mass media regulation. Because these coaxial networks had to extend across municipal streets, roads, and other public property, no system could be constructed without the granting of *easements* by local authorities. These easements gave cable applicants the right to use municipally held land for this purpose. During the 1960s, this privilege began to be packaged within a franchise, which offered a cable applicant the right to use municipally held land in return for the applicant's pledge to provide the city with public-access channels, educational services, and other similar features to be supervised by a local regulatory body that often also had authority to approve or disapprove proposed subscriber rate increases and to hear complaints about system service.[15]

During this era, federal cable regulatory policy was concerned only with protecting broadcasters from cable competition by restricting the number of broadcast channels that major-market cable systems could import. As a result, local and state governments remained the dominant force in this area of regulation until 1972, when the FCC began to assert its right to review and either approve or disapprove each cable-TV franchise to be granted or renewed after that time.

In its exhaustively detailed *Cable Television Service: Cable Television Relay Service* report and order of 1972, the commission thrust itself into what had been a predominantly local process and claimed the right not only to certify or to refuse to certify local cable-TV franchise agreements but also to set basic terms and conditions for these agreements in the future.[16] Although its authority to compel states and localities to follow its orders when drafting private contracts with cable-TV operators was questionable, the FCC used its control over broadcast transmissions to achieve the same result. Operators who were party to a franchise agreement that did not meet the commission's specifications would be denied the right to import broadcast signals and thus effectively prevented from operating a commercially viable system.

Through this technique, the FCC was able to undercut, if not preempt, local control of such cable-TV regulatory features as the franchise fee to be paid the franchising authority to defray the costs of supervision, the dedication and use of locally programmed channels, and other services the franchise applicant had agreed to provide. The federal incursion into the cable-TV regulatory area was completed in 1984 when Congress enacted the Cable Telecommunications Act. By recognizing the authority of local governments to grant cable-TV franchises, Congress clearly suggested it was bestowing on them a right it might choose to withdraw if the privilege it granted were abused.[17] In return for this recognition, Congress imposed a number of restrictions on the franchise and the franchising process. Although Congress allowed local authorities to continue to establish requirements for the designation and use of public, educational, and government cable channels, it also provided a process for the cable operator to terminate these locally originated programs if commercially impractical and to challenge restrictions on programming unless such programming was clearly unprotected expression under the First Amendment.

As the federal government moves to diminish its regulatory base in the field of cable communication, the FCC's efforts to reduce, if not eliminate, its regulatory control over broadcast program content create yet another area of potential conflict over the relative rights of federal and state authorities in the field of electronic mass media regulation. Although Congress has authority to reduce the requirements it now imposes on those who have been granted the privilege of a broadcast license, it does not necessarily follow that it can use that same authority to prevent state and local governments from claiming the powers that it no longer exercises over broadcasting and other electronic mass media service.

The previously mentioned *Dumont* case was decided during an era when the federal government not only claimed exclusive jurisdiction over the regulation of broadcast content, but exercised this jurisdiction as well. Although the federal courts thus far have generally recognized the federal government's continuing preemptive right to control all aspects of cable communication and broadcast operation, it is well to remember that the FCC's deregulatory program is far from complete as yet.

At the moment, the dimensions of broadcast deregulation in the United States are somewhat less impressive in scope than some of the literature in this field suggests. Virtually all of the obligations imposed on broadcasters by the Communications Act of 1934 remain in force even though the FCC, through a series of policy decisions, has become less and less diligent in enforcing compliance with these standards of conduct. Yet, even if the FCC were abolished tomorrow, many of the public policy functions it now performs would have to be continued by another federal agency; and allocation and assignment, communication common carrier supervision, and technical standards would still exert significant influences on various electronic mass media competitive practices.

In addition, the capacity of federal law to limit state or local supervision of electronic mass media operations remains in doubt and creates the distinct possibility that federal deregulation will lead to state or local reregulation of communication activities now thought to be preempted by federal authority. In arguing against this result, supporters of deregulation often cite the First Amendment, overlooking the fact that another constitutional amendment, the Tenth, expressly reserves to the states all powers not delegated to the federal government by the Constitution. Whether this or even the lenient attitude federal courts have displayed toward state *police power* in the past will have any effect on the ultimate resolution of this complex legal controversy is, of course, impossible to predict at this point. Yet, as long as this controversy remains unresolved, there is reason to question any projection of deregulatory trends that overlooks the role that states might play in this area of public policy in the future.

The most important question to answer, though, in attempting to assess the probable impact of federal deregulatory policies on future broadcast and other mass media operations is: How substantially does this new policy modify the traditional practices and processes of American broadcast regulation? In other words, to understand more precisely where we may be going, it will be helpful to know exactly where we have been.

Notes

1. "Making Life a Bit Easier; Re-regulation Gets Under Way," *Broadcasting,* 6 Nov. 1972, 19.
2. "The Laissez Faire Legacy of Charles Ferris," *Broadcasting*, 19 Jan. 1981, 37.
3. "Gleam in Fowler's Regulatory Eye," *Broadcasting*, 14 Sept. 1981, 27.
4. "Omnibus Budget Reconciliation Act of 1981," Public Law No. 97–35, 95 Stat. 357.
5. Further details about these FCC deregulatory proceedings and judicial challenges of the FCC's deregulatory powers can be found in the following legal sources: "Abolishing Ascertainment for Small Market Television," 78 FCC 2d 444 (1980) and 86 FCC 2d 798 (1981), challenged unsuccessfully in *National Black Media Coalition v. FCC*, 706 F. 2d 1224 (D.C. Cir. 1983); "Deregulation of Noncommercial Radio and Television" Notice of Proposed Rulemaking in MM Docket 83-670, 48 Fed. Reg. 27239 (17 Aug. 1983); "Deregulation of Radio," 84 FCC 2d 968 (1981), 87 FCC 2d 797, challenged unsuccessfully in *Office of Communication of the United Church of Christ v. FCC*, 707 F.2d 1413 (D.C. Cir. 1983); "Postcard Renewal," adopted by 46 Fed. Reg. 55116 (6 Nov. 1981), challenged unsuccessfully by United Church of Christ. Although the federal judiciary remains unsatisfied at present with this specific "ten-issue" approach of the FCC, it is unlikely that the commission will ever be compelled by the courts to return to the full-scale "community ascertainment" surveys of the past.
6. "12-12-12 Fait Accompli," *Broadcast*, 31 Dec. 1984, 38.
7. The FCC made explicit in the Communications Act of 1934 what it contended was already implicit in terms of balance and fairness obligations in "In the Matter of Editorializing by Broadcast Licensees," 13 FCC 1246 (1949). In 1959, Congress amended section 315 of the communications act

to add the following language to incorporate fairness within its legislative provisions. "Nothing shall be construed as relieving broadcasters from the obligations imposed under the Act to operate in the public interest and to afford reasonable opportunity for the discussion of conflicting views over issues of public importance." Some now argue that this rather limited language does not obligate the FCC to continue to enforce the fairness doctrine as broadly as the FCC itself described its own obligations in 2 RR2d 1901 (1964).

8. For an excellent description of national obligations in the ITU's operational process, see George A. Codding, Jr., and Anthony M. Rutkowski's *The International Telecommunications Union in a Changing World* (Dedham, Mass.: Artech House, 1982), particularly Chapters 2, 9, and 14.

9. See, for example, the issues summarized by the FCC in its initial proposal for the dropping of additional VHF allocations into its original television allocation plan in "Report and Order in Docket 20418," 81 FCC 2d 233 (1980).

10. Broadcasters are currently battling at the FCC to avoid a tariff increase on the carriage of full-time video service (series 7000) for broadcast interconnection; and AT&T, after divestiture, is seeking to adjust the ending of its revenue-sharing arrangements with the Bell Systems in this field. See "Memorandum Opinion and Order on CC Docket 81–351," 88 FCC 2d 1656 (1982).

11. See Robert H. Stern's *The Federal Communications Commission and Television* from the series "Dissertations in Broadcasting" (New York: Arno Press, 1979), particularly Chapter 5.

12. "Memorandum Opinion and Further Notice of Proposed Rulemaking in Docket 21313," 45 Fed. Reg. 59359 (9 Sept. 1980); "Report and Order on Docket 21313," 47 Fed. Reg. 13152 (29 Mar. 1982).

13. "Notice of Proposed Rulemaking on BC Docket 81–741," 46 Fed. Reg. 60851 (14 Dec. 1981).

14. See, for example, the arguments raised in V. Rostow's *The President's Task Force on Communication Policy*, Staff Report No. 1 (Washington, D.C. 1969).

15. See, for example, Don R. Le Duc's "Control of Cable Television: The Senseless Assault upon States' Rights," *Catholic University Law Review* 24:4 (Summer 1975): 795–813.

16. "Third Report and Order in Docket 18397," 24 RR2d 1501 (1972).

17. "Free at Last: Cable Gets Its Bill," *Broadcasting*, 15 Oct. 1984, 38.

Tracing the Patterns: Primary Sources

Decades ago Max Weber, the German legal and administrative scholar, observed that "Information forms the foundation for all bureaucratic authority" in his *On Law in Economy* and *Society* (New York: Simon & Schuster, 1954, 35). Traditionally, administrative agencies, as described in Anthony Down's *Inside Bureaucracy* (Boston: Little, Brown, 1967) and

William Boyer's *Bureaucracy on Trial: Policy Making by Government Agencies* (Indianapolis, Ind.: Bobbs Merrill, 1964), sought to extend and expand their surveillance functions as a fundamental tactic in their strategies to maintain influence over industry functions they were required by law to supervise.

In that sense, the FCC's decision to begin reducing its own capacity to monitor the activities of electronic mass media organizations under its regulatory jurisdiction not only runs counter to all historical precedent, but also diminishes the relevance of research founded on the assumption that bureaucracies, by their very nature, will seek to broaden the base of their power at all times through all means available. This new administrative mood is described in Martha Derthick and Paul J. Quick's *The Politics of Deregulation* (Washington, D.C.: Brookings Institute, 1985), but there is as yet no way of predicting how Congress will ultimately respond to a congressional agency that seeks to avoid the responsibilities delegated to it by law.

What is even more difficult to predict at the moment is how and in accordance with what legislative guidance the federal responsibilities for the allocation and use of spectrum space, the development of technical standards, and the supervision of communication common carrier functions will be discharged during an era when the FCC's primary role as a protector of public interests in electronic mass media service has ended. As the discussion in this chapter suggests, every decision relating to spectrum usage, standards adoption, or common carrier tariff approval will have profound implications in terms of communication policy and will affect both national and international communication interests. Regardless of how avidly the federal government wishes to disengage itself from the public telecommunications policy process, even the refusal to make any decision will, in itself, exert a significant influence on future patterns of communication service in this nation.

As George Codding and Anthony M. Rutkowski indicate in *The International Telecommunications Union in a Changing World* (Dedham, Mass.: Artech House, 1982), American spectrum and satellite orbital-assignment practices cannot be adopted independently in a community of nations where every decision may infringe to some extent on the sovereign rights of other countries following different policies of communication development. Even if the United States abandons the International Telecommunications Union, as some now advocate, the physical limitations of usable frequencies and available space will make some type of continuing federal control in this field absolutely essential.

Similarly, the federal government has no alternative but to continue to provide some degree of guidance, even if as mediator rather than arbiter, in the area of technical standards. In reality, as Rhoda J. Crane suggests in

The Politics of International Standards: France and the Color TV War (Norwood, N.J.: Ablex Publishing, 1979), a relatively passive role in this field may ultimately be quite damaging for American telecommunications interests and may inhibit the evalution of new services such as videotex or high-definition television while weakening the competitive position of American electronic manufacturers in a world market. As a result, it is quite possible that the same industry spokespersons who advocate total deregulation of American mass media services may soon be arguing as eloquently for the preservation of a governmental role in the adoption of uniform national technical standards.

Finally, there seems to be no way that the federal government can abandon its supervisory role in the field of communication common carriage, if only because of the need to coordinate the regulatory activities of state public utility commissions in establishing rate and service tariffs and in determining the proper amount of such charges to be allocated for interstate delivery of such services. If anything, the AT&T divestiture appears to have increased, rather than decreased, the need for federal intervention to resolve conflicting state and regional telecommunication interests; therefore, it seems highly unlikely that even the most ardent supporters of deregulation would urge that this area of federal jurisdiction over communication be abandoned.

Here again, as in the first chapter, the literature available provides a far clearer picture of the traditional regulatory environment we have known than of the mixed environment of unregulated and regulated communication service we have now entered. If it is true, however, that bureaucracy, whether public or private, shares many of the same characteristics and that international negotiations follow the same patterns of conduct in the area of telecommunications as in other areas of trade, it may well be that certain characteristics of the process already isolated by this literature may serve as a basis for at least limited projections of future trends and tendencies in these fields.

CHAPTER THREE

LICENSING AND COMPETITION

Diversity as Public Policy

The Radio Act of 1927 directed the Federal Radio Commission to distribute broadcast licenses "among the different States and communities so as to give fair, efficient, and equitable service to each of the same."[1] A year later the FRC announced its master plan to achieve this goal by drawing on a resource of 96 separate domestic broadcast channels, an impressive number even in comparison with modern broadband system capacity, in an effort to create a diverse, competitive pattern of broadcast service in the United States. The FRC apportioned these channels carefully in its first full-scale planning effort and created three distinct and complementary types of station coverage to provide American broadcast audiences with the widest array of national, regional, and local programming. Forty stations, designated as being clear channel, were each granted exclusive use of a single channel for high-powered nighttime transmission in order to offer the public national service; 35 regional channels were set aside for more than 100 stations to provide programming to specific portions of the nation; and the remaining 21 channels were to be used by a vast number of low-powered stations for local or community-oriented programming.

If the FRC had been capable of enforcing this licensing assignment plan as it was designed, a truly competitive marketplace would have emerged in American broadcasting. Audiences in each area of the nation would have had the opportunity to select regionally and locally oriented stations. However, instead of competing with one another for public attention, stations sought to affiliate as soon as possible with a national network and delegated their own distinctive roles to one of only three national network program services.

The advent of television gave the commission yet another opportunity to establish a diverse, community-oriented broadcast service in the United States. In 1952, after more than four years of deliberation, the FCC adopted a policy that assigned the more than 2000 new stations it would authorize to specific communities throughout the United States and did so without concern for each community's capacity to provide a market large enough to support network television service.[2] Although the commission's public commitment to a diverse, competitive broadcast marketplace continued to be strong, it failed once again in this instance to establish a type of competitive structure in broadcast service that the industry itself did not wish to have.

During this same era, the FCC also tried to make standard (AM) broadcasting more competitive by increasing the number of broadcast stations licensed in this service from less than 1000 to more than 4000. The FCC hoped that these new stations would be more committed than the older, established stations to seeking out and satisfying the communication needs of the communities they were licensed to serve. Instead, for the most part, this major expansion in the number of AM stations operating within the United States simply allowed a larger number of national distributors to find broadcast outlets for the music and records the distributors produced. Audiences in each radio market did gain access to a greater number of narrowly formatted music services through this FCC policy, but this music reflected and responded to national rather than local tastes, and the stations offered little or no access to musicians, performers, or composers from the areas the stations served. Even more significantly, perhaps, these stations tended to avoid coverage of issues of local or regional interest and relied instead largely on national wire services and weather reports for the public information they did provide.[3]

The situation with regard to nonaffiliated independent UHF television stations was much the same a decade later. When applications for these licenses finally began increasing during the 1960s, it was not because of any growing interest in providing the community-oriented programming that had prompted the commission to set aside these assignments in the first place. Rather, the applications increased only because of a growing inventory of older network programming that was no longer being scheduled and that could fill an independent's broadcast schedule at a reasonable cost.

Even in the era of cable TV, when the commission faced a much less formidable industry opponent, operators simply ignored the FCC's 1969 order that all large cable systems must originate their own programming as a condition for the carriage of broadcast signals. The Supreme Court finally approved this extension of agency authority but did so in such a hesitant manner that the commission refused to enforce the rule from that time onward.[4]

Another policy approach toward diversification, if not localization, of broadcast service involved both general rules against certain types of mass media holding combinations and specific preferences to be awarded in comparative license hearings to those without other media holdings. Through the years the FCC has tried a number of different tactics to make ownership of broadcast stations more diverse in the hopes that this might help to make broadcast programming more diverse as well.

The earliest of these rules prohibited any entity from owning more than one station within a single broadcast market.[5] Later, when television and FM emerged, the FCC prohibited joint ownership of television and either an AM or FM facility but "grandfathered" those who already held such broadcast properties in a single market.[6] In addition, commission rules prohibited the ownership of three broadcast stations if any two of these stations were within 100 miles of the third. In this way, the commission sought to prevent a single broadcast owner from dominating broadcast service within a given region of the nation.

The commission has also placed an absolute limit on the number of broadcast stations a single entity might own. Until recently, this number was 21, with a maximum of seven AM, seven FM, and seven TV facilities, no more than five of which could be VHF stations. The limit has been increased to 36; however, the combined audience of the television stations cannot exceed 25 percent of the total American television audience.[7]

Finally in 1975, the FCC prohibited newspaper ownership of a broadcast facility within its own main service area, grandfathering most newspaper owners but requiring 16 owners who controlled the only broadcast station in their community to divest.[8] In other actions the commission denied broadcasters or telephone companies the right to own cable systems in their own service areas and prohibited any television network from owning a cable system.[9]

In view of this nearly continuous campaign to stimulate the development of a more diverse, locally oriented, competitive broadcast service during the past half-century, it is difficult to understand how the current commission leadership can describe this regulatory record as one suppressing the natural industry tendency toward greater viewing or listening variety. At the same time, of course, it is also difficult to understand how a half-century of concerted commission policy effort achieved so little in terms of realizing its primary objectives. The answer to both these questions seems to lie in the nature of the process the FCC has been required to follow in its efforts to regulate American broadcast service.

The Limitations of the Licensing Process

The entire broadcast-regulatory structure must depend on the foundation of the licensing process, both for its constitutional support and for the mechanisms employed to enforce agency rules. Every attempt by the agency to enhance the locally oriented characteristics of American broadcast service, for example, required for its success a process capable of selecting from among broadcast license applicants for each available channel the one most likely to accept and follow the commission's policies relating to localism. Equally important, this licensing process had to provide some means of monitoring the successful applicant's performance to make certain that the applicant fulfilled the promises, relating to local service, that had led to its receiving the license in the first place. If not, full compliance with the applicant's promises could either be made a condition for renewal or the basis for refusal to renew the license. The license could then be granted instead to some other applicant that the agency judged to be more dedicated to this policy objective.

But what if no applicant were willing to accept this local-service objective as a primary programming goal? In that very common situation, the agency has had only two regulatory options, neither of which advanced its goals or objectives. The FCC could simply refuse to issue any license and thus deprive a broadcast audience of the additional service it would otherwise receive or it could select from the applicants the one most satisfactory in terms of other characteristics or qualifications. All of this, of course, presupposed that the license selection and renewal processes of the commission not only elicited the type and quality of information necessary to make such regulatory decisions but also that such information was being carefully studied and evaluated by an agency staff capable of making precisely focused, policy-oriented decisions based on this analysis. Unfortunately, in terms of agency policy objectives, neither of these suppositions was well founded.

The license-application forms documented the applicant's citizenship, character, financial qualifications, and media holdings and were supplemented by engineering studies, a community ascertainment survey, programming proposals, and, from 1969 onward, an equal employment opportunity plan. If the application were uncontested and the filings were in order, the commission was empowered to issue a license without a hearing or any further investigation.[10] If another applicant sought the same license, however, or if granting the application would materially affect the operation of another broadcast station, the commission was compelled to hold a hearing before deciding whether or not to issue a license.[11]

Broadcast licenses were granted for a period of three years. The main function served by the three-year license term was to provide, through the FCC's processing of the license-renewal application, periodic review of the licensee's performance. To facilitate the application processing, the commission divided the 50 states into 18 geographical groups. The licenses of the stations within each group expired at two-month intervals over the three-year licensing cycle. For example, the licenses of all stations located in New Jersey or New York expired in June 1975, 1978, 1981; while those in Delaware and Pennsylvania expired in August of the same year. Each licensee submitted its renewal application to the commission at least four months in advance of its license's expiration date. This application included engineering, employment, and program performance information about the preceding three years of operation, as well as the licensee's programming plans, described in quantitative terms, for the renewal period.

The 3000 renewal applications the FCC received each year were processed by the staff of the commission's Broadcast Bureau, then were forwarded for more specific review by agency attorneys, engineers, and programming specialists. In an average year, however, all of this paper shuffling resulted in virtually no corrective actions being taken by the commission. In 1976, for example, the agency processed 2995 applications, of which it designated just 23 for hearing and ultimately denied only 8.[12] In other words, 99.7 percent of the licensees who filed for renewal were granted their three-year extension; 99.2 percent were granted the extension without need of hearing, and, in at least five of the eight cases in which a renewal was denied, the decision was based primarily on evidence not in the renewal application itself.

It would be comforting to believe that this extremely low percentage of license-renewal refusals reflected an unusual degree of diligence and dedication on the part of broadcasters in meeting the public-interest obligations imposed on them by federal law and commission policy. Unfortunately, there is little evidence to support this optimistic view of broadcaster performance and much to suggest that the explanation must lie elsewhere.

Through the years virtually every short-term survey of broadcaster programming practices has revealed a substantially lower level of public service, news and information, and locally originated programming than the stations in that region had pledged to provide in their previous renewal applications. As an example, one survey of 35 television-license applications granted between 1952 and 1965 revealed that although these stations had promised to devote an average of more than 31 percent of their broadcast day to local programming, they were in fact providing, at the time the survey was conducted, an average of less than 11 percent of their daily schedule to such programming.[13]

The fundamental flaw in the renewal process was that the FCC had almost no idea of how conscientiously a station had attempted, during its current license term, to fulfill the programming promises it had made in receiving its grant. The agency did not monitor any broadcast programming except in cases where a specific complaint was made about the unlawful or obscene content of a particular program. Instead the FCC, for its evaluation of the public-interest program performance of a broadcaster, relied almost totally on the *composite week report* it instituted in 1946. This report, submitted with the renewal application, required each station within a given region to forward to the agency its program logs for seven randomly selected days during its current three-year license period. These logs, revealing little more than the title of a program, the number of commercial spots it contained, and the time it was broadcast, were used by the agency staff to estimate the proportion of a station's broadcast schedule devoted to each of the various categories of programming recognized by the commission's reporting form and to gauge its degree of commercialization. However, because this seven-day sample might not fairly represent the 156-week period it was meant to reflect, major allowances were made by the staff for deviations between the broadcaster's promises and the type of per-formance the logs revealed. As a result, it was virtually impossible for this composite log examination to disclose anything that might lead the commission to refuse renewal of a station license on the basis of inadequate programming in the public interest. The truth of this observation is suggested by the fact that a recent survey of the 142 FCC decisions made from 1934 through 1978 to refuse to issue or renew a broadcast license showed that less than 20 decisions were based on some aspect of inadequate programming, a revocation or refusal rate of less than one station every two years.[14]

Yet, even if the commission had been able to gather the type of information necessary to evaluate the quality of each renewal appli-cant's programming more effectively, it would have lacked the capacity to consider it. Only 350 of the commission's 2000-member staff were assigned to the Broadcast Bureau, and the Renewal and Transfer Division handling these applications generally consisted of no more than two dozen full-time employees.[15] Each year this group faced a workload of 3000 renewals, with each television application requiring the analysis of a 21-page form prescribed by the commission, as well as accom-panying exhibits prepared by the broadcaster to document statements in the form. To have added additional evidence to this review process and to have insisted that it be considered carefully before any contested renewal was granted would have imposed an impossible burden on the limited staff. Unfortunately, this is precisely what the much heralded *United Church of Christ* decision in 1966 did require of the commission.[16]

Until that time, only an opposing broadcaster could compel the commission to hold a hearing before awarding or renewing a broadcast license; and the broadcaster could only do so if it could demonstrate that granting the application was likely to cause the complaining party serious transmission interference or economic injury.[17] In all other instances, the FCC decided whether or not such an elaborate and time-consuming process was necessary to safeguard the public interest. Rather predictably, the agency seldom found this situation to exist.

However, the *United Church of Christ* decision held that the commission was no longer the sole protector of the public interest and that citizens within a station's area had a right to intervene to protest the quality of service being provided by the licensee. By 1970 various citizen groups and public-interest law firms had mobilized to make use of the *petition to deny* tactic the court had authorized for challenging license renewals. From 1970 to 1977, the commission received a total of 447 citizen petitions or objections involving 936 broadcast stations, almost 10 percent of all the commercial stations the commission then licensed.[18]

Well aware that the commission staff was incapable of providing the type of elaborate broadcast-service evaluation the court had ordered and the citizens' groups demanded, the agency attempted to avoid this dilemma by announcing a new comparative renewal policy in 1970. The policy allowed the agency, by finding the incumbent broadcaster's programming to have been "substantially attuned" to local interests and needs, to terminate the renewal proceeding without need of a hearing to consider any other evidence.[19] A federal court blocked this line of retreat the following year and declared that this policy virtually guaranteed renewal to the incumbent broadcaster.[20] In frustration, the agency then broadened the scope of a 1965 policy statement, which had been enacted for new broadcast licenses, to include incumbent comparative proceedings as well.[21] However, when a commission application of this 1965 policy statement seemed to reveal the same overwhelming preference for the incumbent broadcaster, the court reversed the agency's decision and remanded it with the statement that the FCC had given undue preference to the existing station's past service and too little attention to the challenger's attributes.[22] The commission professed itself to be unable to understand, much less apply, the comparative criteria that the court was directing it to employ in these situations and petitioned the court for a clarification of its new position.[23] In its clarification, the full court seemed to move closer to the original FCC position presuming that the incumbent's license should be renewed if its past programming performance was at least "substantial" in nature.

The only possible benefit gained from overburdening the capacities of the comparative licensing process might have been the encouragement of citizen-broadcaster agreements to resolve the conflicts about broadcast service at the local level. Even this benefit, however, may have been a somewhat illusory one. As the FCC observed in 1975, when it intervened to insist that it approve all such agreements before they took effect, the threat of citizen license challenge might well pressure broadcasters into improperly delegating programming authority to groups that might in no way be representative of the audiences for whom they claimed to speak.[24]

What this period of conflict and chaos seems to illustrate quite clearly is the futility of attempting to impose on a rather simple and mechanical administrative process a set of complex and sophisticated policy standards. A rule specifying the number of broadcast facilities an entity may own or one prohibiting ownership, within a single service area, of two of the same type of stations can be administered quite effectively by an agency staff. However, when a regulatory agency has the obligation to evaluate the commitment of competing license applicants toward locally oriented programming and to assess the adequacy of their performance in realizing agency policy objectives, a staff this small and a process this limited cannot possibly be successful.

In the last analysis, although the FCC steadfastly pledged, through its licensing process, its commitment to public policies of localism, diversity, and competition, it lacked an administrative process capable of imposing these characteristics on the industry it regulated. Thus, although the FCC's public record as a champion of a true broadcast marketplace is impressive, its actual record as a regulatory agency may well justify the arguments of its critics that this role should now be ended.

Patterns in the Licensing Process

The regulatory reaction of the commission to the entire license-renewal and challenge fiasco was to attempt to withdraw as rapidly as possible from all policy positions it no longer felt capable of protecting. Sections 309 (a) and 310 (d) of the communications act empower the FCC to grant an application for license transfer or renewal only if the agency first determines that the "public interest, convenience and necessity" will be served by this change. In 1974 a commission decision approving the transfer of a classical music station in Chicago to an ownership planning to program rock music was remanded to the commission with instruction to consider whether or not this action would deprive that particular broadcast market of its sole source of classical music.[25] Rather than become entangled in the process of determining which format changes tended to diversify or to limit the degree of diversity within a given market, the commission issued a policy statement declaring its intention to allow the broadcast marketplace to decide what formats were economically viable for each station.[26] The Supreme Court accepted certiorari when this policy decision was appealed, and the Court sustained the FCC's decision to refuse to become involved in format-change controversies.[27]

Successful in this effort to limit its own regulatory jurisdiction, the agency moved at the same time to reduce its administrative burdens as well. In March 1981 the commission replaced its long and involved renewal-application form with a postcard-sized document and required only that the renewal applicant state whether or not proper reports were on file with the commission and whether or not the applicant had been found guilty of any felony, anticompetitive practice, or unfair labor practice.[28] This time, aware of the Supreme Court's attitude toward the commission's deregulatory policies, the federal court of appeals refused to grant relief to a citizen group contending that the use of such a form would deny it and other groups information necessary to challenge renewal.[29]

In 1981 Congress also displayed its support for the commission's deregulatory efforts, not only by extending the stations' license periods to five years for television and seven for radio, but also by amending section 309 (i) of the communications act to allow the FCC to substitute a random selection (i.e., lottery) licensing process for the comparative hearing in competitive situations where a hearing was previously required by law.[30] Since this time the commission has used a lottery, which is adjusted to provide for minority and other preferences, only in awarding new low-power TV (LPTV) and MMDS licenses. However, the lottery may well be adopted for all future license assignments and may thus effectively end the last vestiges of influence that the federal government could exert over the nature of American broadcast service. Perhaps, as the present commission chairman suggests, this would be an unmitigated blessing. Setting the current agency annual costs for conducting comparative hearings at $300,000, the chairman points out that beyond the savings taxpayers would realize from this action, broadcasters as well could profit from the ability to invest their funds in programming rather than administrative procedures.[31]

Certainly no coldly rational cost-benefit study could justify the expenses of the FCC licensing deliberations in terms of their value in enhancing the overall quality of American broadcast service through the years. Despite the best of intentions, the agency found itself unable to do more than threaten or try to cajole broadcasters into providing the public with the programming they promised to schedule when they obtained their license privilege from the commission. Yet, inefficient as this technique may have been, it did at least offer a legal process for making broadcasters accountable to the public they served and responsive in a societal, rather than simply in an economic, sense to the concerns of those audiences whose values they shaped. To achieve this end, the process did not have to be particularly effective. If the FCC, either acting on its own accord or in response to public or congressional criticism, indicated to any station manager that certain of the station's programming policies were likely to be reviewed quite closely at time of renewal, it was highly unlikely that this concern would go unnoticed. This was true even if these criticisms were expressed to broadcast-network executives, because the five extremely valuable television stations they owned and operated were licensed by the FCC and had undoubtedly carried the network programming that had caused the commission's concern. Although the broadcast industry realized the agency almost never refused to renew a license on the basis of inferior programming, few station managers or network executives were willing to take even the small risk involved. NBC or Westinghouse Broadcasting might eventually triumph over any tactic the FCC attempted, but the question was always whether or not any risk, however small, was worth taking when the license was so rewarding financially and the programming modifications necessary to end the criticism were so simple and inexpensive to make. It must be remembered, too, that during the first stages of such negotiations, it was not the broadcast group or the network facing the FCC, but a highly paid broadcast-group or network employee whose job security depended on being able to resolve such controversies, avoid the costs of litigation, and, above all, never risk the loss of the organization's most precious, irreplaceable asset — its broadcast license.

In some instances, broadcasters who capitulated to various citizen group demands during the 1970s rather than face license challenge later described themselves as having been blackmailed into submission. Similarly, the commission itself has been charged from time to time with using the same tactics in efforts to compel broadcasters to honor their programming promises.

Under these circumstances, then, it is easy to understand why even a relatively limited and ineffectual licensing and license-renewal process has been viewed as such an ominous threat by broadcasters. Yet, although this process may have been subject to abuse, it seems fair to ask whether or not the industry, from this point onward, will likely be responsive to any public communication concerns or needs other than those reflecting substantial economic pressure or demand.

No one can claim that the FCC has been successful in achieving, through its policy strategies, the type of locally oriented, responsive, and diverse broadcast service that public law directed it to provide. At the same time, though, it must be observed that the FCC's failure has resulted from the opposition of an industry unwilling to offer the public the diverse, competitive marketplace of varied programming alternatives that public law has attempted to create.

If, as the commission's economists have been insisting for the past decade, the natural tendency of electronic mass media is to provide the American public with an ever-increasing range of programming choices, why is there nothing in this pattern of industry responses to the commission's competition-oriented policies during the past half-century that reflects this tendency? One possible answer to this question may be that although the FCC's licensing policies were framed in terms of diversity and competition, its program-content controls tended to discourage such innovation or experimentation. To determine to what degree, if any, the FCC's program-regulatory process may have inhibited the emergence of a true marketplace in electronic mass media services in the United States, it is necessary at this point to examine that process in greater detail.

Notes

1. Public 632, 69th Cong. (23 Feb. 1927) sec. 9.
2. "Sixth Report and Order," 41 FCC 148 (1952).
3. Don R. Le Duc, *Cable Television and the FCC* (Philadelphia: Temple University Press, 1973), 52–54.
4. "First Report and Order on Docket 18397," 17 RR2d 1570 (1969); challenged in *Midwest Video Corp. v. FCC*, 406 U.S. 649 (1972).
5. 47 CFR 73.35. For a full discussion of the NBC case 319 U.S. 190 (1943) that challenged the FCC's authority to establish such restrictions, see Frank J. Kahn, *Documents of American Broadcasting*, 4th ed. (Englewood Cliffs, N.J.: Prentice-Hall, 1984), 124–127.
6. CFR 73, 240, 73.636. To "grandfather" is to enforce a rule only prospectively and to allow all those currently in violation of a newly enacted rule to continue the existing practice without penalty. From an equitable standpoint, grandfathering avoids penalizing those who acted in good faith at a time when their action was not in violation of regulations. From a practical standpoint, it avoids a great deal of litigation on the part of those who otherwise would lose their existing rights. The greatest drawback of grandfathering is that it creates a crazy-quilt pattern of policies, with different rules applying to the same situation, depending solely on the date when rights vested.
7. 47 CFR 73.35 (a); 43,240 (a) 1; 73.636 (a) 1–2; 76.501.
8. "Second Report and Order," 50 FCC 2d 1046; amended 53 FCC 2d 589 (1975) reviewed in *National Citizens Committee for Broadcasting v. FCC*,

436 U.S. 775 (1981), allowing FCC to grandfather certain joint newspaper-broadcaster ownership combinations.

9. "Second Report and Order on Docket 20423," 55 FCC 2d 540 (1975).
10. Title 47, USC, sec. 309 (d) (2).
11. *Ashbacher Radio v. FCC*, 326 U.S. 327 (1945); see also *Carroll Broadcasting v. FCC*, 258 F.2d 440 (1958).
12. As cited in Barry G. Cole and Mal Oettinger, *Reluctant Regulators: The FCC and the Broadcast Audience* (Reading, Mass.: Addison-Wesley, 1978), 135.
13. Ibid., 147. This insider's view of FCC policy making is undoubtedly the most useful source for a clear sense of the realities of this process during the turbulent 1970s.
14. John Abel, Charles Cliff III, and Frederick Weiss, "Station License Revocations and Denial of Renewal 1934–1969," *Journal of Broadcasting* 14:1 (Fall 1970): 411–21; Frederic Weiss, David Ostroff, and Charles Cliff III, "Station License Revocations and Denial of Renewal 1968–1979," *Journal of Broadcasting* 24:2 (Winter 1980): 69–77.
15. FCC personnel figures vary from administration to administration and from budget to budget. These particular figures are from the FCC organizational chart of May 1977.
16. *Office of Communication of the United Church of Christ v. FCC*, 359 F.2d 994 (D.C. Cir. 1966).
17. Title 47, USC sec. 316 (b).
18. Comptroller General, Report to the Congress, "Selected FCC Regulatory Policies: Their Purposes and Consequences for Commercial Radio and Television," CED 79–62, 4 June 1979, 17.
19. "Policy Statement Concerning Comparative Hearings Involving Regular Renewal Applicants," 22 FCC 2d 424 (1970). This policy statement was also an effort to reassure broadcasters concerned about the broader implications of the refusal to renew a television license in the *Greater Boston TV* decision, 16 FCC 2d 1; as affirmed in 444 F.2d 841 (1970).
20. *Citizens Communication Center v. FCC*, 447 F.2d 1201 (1971).
21. "Policy Statement on Comparative Broadcast Hearings," 1 FCC 2d 393 (1965).
22. *Central Florida v. FCC*, 598 F.2d 37 (D.C. 1978) cert. den. 441 U.S. 957 (1979).
23. *Central Florida v. FCC*, 683 F.2d 503 (D.C. 1982).
24. Comptroller General, "Selected FCC Regulatory Policies," 18–19.
25. 38 FCC 2d 838; 40 FCC 2d 233; *Citizens Committee to Save WEFM v. FCC*, 506 F.2d 246; see also *Citizens Committee of Atlanta v. FCC*, 436 F.2d 263, (1970).
26. "Development of Policy re Changes in the Entertainment Format of Broadcast Stations," 57 FCC 2d 580 (1976); reconsideration denied 58 FCC 2d 617 (1967).
27. *FCC v. Listeners Guild*, 450 U.S. 582 (1981).
28. "Report and Order on BC Docket 80–253," 46 Fed. Reg. 26236 (11 May 1981). According to these regulations, 5 percent of the licensed stations will

receive the older, long form, on a random-selection basis, to monitor the effectiveness of the new system.

29. *Office of Communication of the United Church of Christ v. FCC*, 707 F.2d 1413 (D.C. Cir. 1983).

30. "Omnibus Reconciliation Act of 1981," 95 Stat. 736–37; as amended by Public Law 97–259, par. 115. The statute requires that the commission first determines the basic qualifications of each applicant in such a lottery selection process. For an assessment of the validity of such a process, see Harvey Zuckman and Martin J. Gaynes's *Mass Communication Law in a Nutshell*, 2d ed. (St. Paul: West Publishing, 1983) 384–387.

31. "Fowler's Regulatory Program Revealed," *Broadcasting*, 21 Sept. 1981, 104. Of course, considering the fact that the United States has about 80 million taxpayers, this $300,000 would result in a savings to each taxpayer of less than $0.01 annually.

Tracing the Patterns: Primary Sources

Disenchantment with the licensing process as a means of achieving locally owned and oriented American broadcast service was already apparent in the deliberations that led to the adoption of the Communications Act of 1934. In the report *Study of Communications by an Interdepartmental Committee* (United States Congress, Senate; Committee on Interstate Commerce [Washington, D.C.: Government Printing Office, 1934]), legislators were made aware of the fact that the ambitious goals (of diversity in control and programming) ordained by the Radio Act of 1927 had not been realized in practice through the licensing process of the FRC. Despite this forewarning, Congress did nothing to alter the basic licensing standards to be applied by the FCC and virtually guaranteed that past failures would be repeated in the future.

A quarter-century later, a similar report, titled *Regulation of Broadcasting: A Half Century of Government Regulation of Broadcasting and the Need for Further Legislative Reform* (United States Congress, House Committee on Interstate and Foreign Commerce [Washington, D.C.: Government Printing Office, 1958]), pointed out many of the same problems. It was, however, unsuccessful in stimulating any meaningful legislative reform. Reports of this type, such as the Government Accounting Office's *Select FCC Regulatory Policies: Their Purpose and Consequences for Commercial Radio and Television* (Washington, D.C.: Government Printing Office, 1979) continued to be issued with monotonous regularity through the years, but except for its ill-fated efforts to rewrite the entire Communications Act of 1934, chronicled in Chapter 9 of Erwin G. Krasnow, Lawrence D. Longley, and Herbert A. Terry's *The Politics of Broadcast Regulation*, 3d ed. (New York: St. Martin's Press, 1982), Congress seemed content to do no more than blame its regulatory agency for defects in a process Congress itself has been unwilling or unable to remedy.

Although this body refused to aid the FCC, it was the federal judiciary that actually caused the collapse of the regulatory structure by requiring of it a degree of responsiveness and perceptiveness far beyond its capacity. As writers such as Joseph H. Grundfest, *Citizen Participation in Broadcast Licensing Before the FCC* (Santa Monica, Calif.: Rand Corporation, 1976), and Donald Guimary, *Citizen Groups and Broadcasting* (New York: Praeger, 1975) have described the rights of public intervention and license challenge recognized by the courts during this era, it is obvious why the reaction of the commission was to use every strategy at its disposal to escape this massive new set of responsibilities imposed on it by the judiciary. At the same time, it is important to note that Congress made no effort during this period to augment the FCC's staff so that it might be able to comply with the courts' dictates.

In truth, then, it might be argued that many of the limitations in the broadcast-licensing process, pointed out in such works as Harvey J. Levins's *Fact and Fancy in Television Regulation: An Economic Analysis of Policy Alternatives* (New York: Sage Publications, 1980) or Stanley Besen's *Misregulating Television: Network Dominance and the FCC* (Chicago: University of Chicago Press, 1984), may not be defects inherent in a broadcast-regulatory structure, but rather only in part a reflection of congressional unwillingness to face the wrath of the powerful broadcast organizations its actions might offend.

In any case, it is interesting to observe how remarkably successful the broadcast industry was during this entire half-century in restraining the impulses some economists believe would have impelled it toward more diverse or competitive service. As writers such as Laurence Bergreen, in his *Look Now, Pay Later: The Rise of Network Broadcasting* (New York: Doubleday, 1980), and Stewart Long, in his *The Development of the Television Network Oligopoly* (New York: Arno Press, 1979), among others, clearly reveal, whatever the tendencies of such media entities might be in the long run, their short-term policies certainly seemed designed to expand their degree of control over programming sources and to exercise this control in a manner that would limit the number of competitive listening or viewing options available to American audiences.

Perhaps this type of conduct was encouraged to some extent by a regulatory environment in which such actions were seldom challenged, but it is difficult to discover in these private policy patterns any justification for believing that the natural inclination of the mass media organizations is toward an ever-broader and more diverse range of services in the future.

CHAPTER FOUR

CONTENT CONTROLS: PUBLIC AND PRIVATE

Public Content Controls

In 1929, only two years after it began regulating broadcast service in the United States, the Federal Radio Commission issued the first comprehensive description of federal broadcast program policy. Initiating a regulatory tradition that would endure until the 1980s, the agency pointed out in this first program policy statement that it would not set up a preferred list of programming categories; rather, it sought to have each station offer its audience a balanced schedule of different types of programs capable of serving the needs of every segment of the population within the station's listening area. As the FRC explained its programming objectives,

> The tastes, needs and desires of all substantial groups among the public should be met, in some fair proportion, by a well-rounded program schedule, in which entertainment...religion, education and instruction, important public events, discussions of public questions, weather, market reports, and news, and matters of interest to all members of the family find a place.[1]

In listing these program categories, the FRC emphasized that it was not attempting to "propose to erect a rigid schedule specifying the hours or minutes that may be devoted to one kind of program or another."[2] Instead the agency declared that its intention was only to indicate the general types of programming that licensees were expected to provide in order to satisfy their public-service responsibilities.

Two years later the commission refused for the first time to renew a broadcast license on the basis of the broadcaster's past programming performance not adequately serving the public interest. The broadcaster appealed the FRC action and contended that, by attempting to influence the type of program material and advertising the station presented, the agency was engaged in censorship, a practice prohibited by the First Amendment. In affirming the action of the FRC, the Court declared,

It is apparent, we think, that the business is impressed with a public interest and that, because the number of available broadcasting frequencies is limited, the Commission is necessarily called upon to consider the character and quality of the service to be rendered. In considering the application for a renewal of a license, an important consideration is the past performance of the applicant, for 'by their fruits shall ye know them' (Matt. 7:20).[3]

The FCC devoted its first decade of policy making toward efforts to reduce the degree of network domination over affiliate station programming; but in 1946 the FCC issued a report, the so-called "blue book," *Public Service Responsibilities of Broadcast Licensees*, which once again stressed the federal regulatory agency's commitment to balanced, diverse broadcast programming. To accomplish this goal, the commission urged that broadcasters give particular consideration to the scheduling of three types of programming: sustaining (that is, programming without commercial sponsorship), locally produced features, and public issues–oriented programs. The commission explained its preference for the sustaining programs as an important element of public service broadcasting by pointing out that such nonsponsored features performed a fourfold function in

> maintaining an overall program balance; providing time for programs serving particular minority tastes and interests; providing time for non-profit organizations — religious, civic, agricultural, labor, educational, etc. and providing time for unfettered artistic self-expression.[4]

However, as one broadcast scholar has observed,

> The very potency of the "Blue Book" rendered it ineffectual. Its theme of balanced programming as a necessary component of broadcast service in the public interest, coupled with its emphasis on a reasonable ratio of unsponsored programs posed too serious a threat to the profitability of commercial radio for either the industry, Congress or the FCC to want to match regulatory promise with performance.[5]

In 1960, the FCC made yet another attempt to define programming in the public interest as the scheduling of diverse, balanced features to serve all segments of the broadcast audience. In its *Report and Statement of Policy re: Commissions en Banc Programming Inquiry*, the commission declared that it intended, not to guide the licensee along the path of programming, but to help the licensee find this path "with the guidance of those whom his signal is to serve."[6] To do this the agency listed 14 types of programming traditionally considered necessary to meet the needs and desires of the community and suggested that the programming types be considered by the licensee in determining whether a balanced program schedule was being offered its audience.[7] At the same time, however, the FCC disclaimed any intention to force each licensee to offer all of these types of programming in equal measure in order to obtain a license renewal and declared,

> The elements set out above are neither all-embracing nor constant. We re-emphasize that they do not serve and have never been intended as a rigid mold or fixed formula for station operations.[8]

Instead, the FCC introduced a new licensing requirement with this order, directing each broadcaster to discover the "tastes, needs, and desires" of the public served and to demonstrate to the commission the broadcaster's intention to develop programming capable of satisfying these specific tastes, needs, and desires. In practice, unfortunately, the agency's process for realizing this policy objective asked for less than this of broadcasters and directed only that surveys of community leaders be taken in those areas they served in order to isolate what these leaders saw as being problems of greatest importance. Based on these surveys, broadcasters were then to submit to the agency a description of the programs they intended to schedule to address the problems specified.[9]

Both the FRC and the FCC faced severe legal constraints in their efforts to influence the program strategies of the stations they regulated. In each case, the major barrier of the First Amendment itself was augmented by a provision, in the legislation creating the agency, expressly prohibiting any type of censorship in the supervision of broadcaster programming decisions.[10] As a result, every attempt to broaden or diversify the programming alternatives made available to the public by broadcasters had to be limited in scope and couched in the most cautious of regulatory language.

In contrast, however, both agencies were specifically directed by law to intervene in one type of programming activity. Section 315 of the Communications Act of 1934, as section 18 of the radio act before it, declared that if a broadcast licensee permitted one person who was a legally qualified candidate for political office to use the licensee's facilities, the station was to make certain that all other legally qualified candidates for the same office were afforded equal opportunity to use these facilities under the same terms and conditions as the first candidate.[11]

In 1941, in response to a complaint filed by an unsuccessful applicant for a broadcast license, the commission cautioned the successful licensee that a "broadcaster cannot be an advocate."[12] Taken in context, the FCC's admonition simply meant that broadcasters were not to abuse their positions of public privilege as license holders to propagandize for a specific political, social, or religious cause. The industry, however, chose to understand the agency to mean that broadcasters were to avoid the presentation of any controversial issues in their news or public affairs programming.

To clarify its position, the FCC, in 1949, issued a report, *Editorializing by Broadcast Licensees*, declaring that

> one of the most vital questions of mass communication in a democracy is the development of an informed public opinion through the public dissemination of news and ideas concerning the vital public issues of the day.[13]

Elaborating on this thesis, the FCC established a twofold obligation on the part of every licensee seeking to operate in the public interest. The first obligation was for the broadcaster to devote a reasonable portion of broadcast time to the discussion of controversial issues of public importance, and the second was for the coverage to be balanced and fair in nature.

In 1969 the Supreme Court had its first opportunity to consider the constitutionality of this Fairness Doctrine, as it had come to be called. Although a narrow, personal-attack portion of the Fairness Doctrine precipitated this legal action, the consolidation of this appeal with a broader one brought by a group of television news directors allowed the court to consider the entire issue of First Amendment rights in the field of broadcasting. Justice White, writing an opinion for a unanimous court, declared,

> As far as the First Amendment is concerned, those who are licensed stand no better than those to whom licenses are refused. A license permits broadcasting, but the licensee has no constitutional right to be the one who holds the license or to monopolize a radio frequency to the exclusion of fellow citizens. There is nothing in the First Amendment which prevents the Government from requiring a licensee to share his frequencies with others and to conduct himself as a proxy or fiduciary with obligations to present those views and voices which are representative of his community and which would otherwise, by necessity, be barred from the airwaves.... There is no sanctuary in the First Amendment for unlimited private censorship operating in a medium not open to all. Freedom of the press from governmental interference under the First Amendment does not sanction repression of that freedom by private interests.[14]

Responding to this vigorous judicial affirmation of its authority in this area of broadcast-program responsibility, the FCC began an extensive inquiry in 1971 that resulted in the FCC's issuing of the *Fairness Report of 1974*.[15] In this effort to consolidate and clarify more than a quarter-century of specific agency responses to various fairness questions that had arisen since the publication of its 1949 *Report on Editorializing*, the commission concluded that broadcast licensees had only two basic responsibilities under the fairness doctrine: to devote a reasonable portion of time to the coverage of public issues and, through this coverage, to provide opportunities for the presentation of contrasting points of view relating to these issues.

Groups such as the National Citizens Committee for Broadcasting and other citizens' organizations viewed this FCC effort at clarification as an attempt to retreat from regulatory guidelines that in the past were construed as requiring broadcasters actively to seek out controversial issues and to be responsible for balancing controversial viewpoints in commercial as well as in programming materials. After the commission denied reconsideration of the report in 1976, the court of appeals, when affirming the commission's position to discontinue applying the fairness doctrine to most commercial messages, did direct the FCC to give further considerations to proposals it rejected during these deliberations.[16]

In 1979 the FCC again rejected the proposals and declared that neither a broadcast access rule requiring each station to set aside time each week for both first come, first served and representative spokespersons nor a requirement that each licensee list annually its efforts to provide coverage of the ten issues the licensee deemed most significant for its audience would achieve the results intended while infringing unnecessarily on the journalistic discretion of the broadcaster.[17]

However deeply committed a majority of the FCC commissioners may have been to the Fairness Doctrine in 1974, it was evident by the end of the 1970s that what the Supreme Court found in the *Red Lion* case to be sensible and equitable in principal was far more difficult to define, much less apply, in practice. As deregulation became the general governmental response to the abuses of regulation, the Fairness Doctrine came to typify, in the field of broadcast regulation, all that was cumbersome and ineffective about federal supervision of electronic mass media.

One reason for the broadcast industry's particularly strong hostility toward fairness rules could be traced to the citizen group efforts since 1967 to obligate broadcasters to balance controversial issues of public importance that were contained in the commercial advertising messages each station carried. Although in its *Fairness Report of 1974*, the commission was able to confine this responsibility to advertisements with clear political or social statements, the possibility of a more extensive level of obligation remained until 1978, when the Supreme Court refused to review this portion of the agency's policy declaration.

In 1967 the commission had taken the position that in accepting cigarette advertising, a station obligated itself under the Fairness Doctrine to present programming or public-service announcements balancing the advocacy of smoking with information describing the threat that cigarette smoking posed to health.[18] In establishing this precedent, the commission soon found itself under pressure from a wide range of interest groups demanding that *counteradvertising*, as it was called, be extended to include almost any product with the slightest conceivable impact on the environment.

Clearly, this type of interpretation of the Fairness Doctrine would have seriously damaged the competitive position of the broadcast industry, an industry already injured by the loss of cigarette advertising revenue. Few advertisers would be likely to choose a medium that was obligated by law to provide free airtime for those who wished to criticize the products they had paid to promote. As a result, when the Federal Trade Commission (FTC) filed a brief with the FCC in 1972 that urged the FCC to institutionalize counteradvertising as a "suitable approach to some of the present failings of advertising which are beyond the FTC's capacity," the FCC realized that it was being maneuvered into a position where a logical extension of existing Fairness Doctrine principles could have severe economic impact on the broadcast services it regulated.[19] In 1974 the FCC rejected the FTC request and issued a policy statement that effectively removed product advertising from the requirements of the Fairness Doctrine unless the advertising itself expressly raised a controversial issue of public importance.[20] The FCC's new policy position was affirmed in the courts. Coupled with an earlier Supreme Court decision holding that a broadcaster was not a *common carrier* and had the ultimate right to determine what messages it would transmit, the new policy provided the agency with the justification it needed to renounce its control over *balance* as an element of Fairness Doctrine obligation.[21]

It seems apparent that what hastened the downfall of balance as a major element in the Fairness Doctrine was the effort to extend the doctrine's purview to include commercial messages. Here, as in the earlier situation of the "blue book," the industry was willing to accommodate to certain general standards for program selection and even for the structuring of its news and public affairs features; however, the industry would not countenance any interference with its commercial advertising practices.

In similar fashion, the industry, its lobbying organization — the NAB — and the FCC all were eager to extol the virtues of programming specially designed for children; however, efforts to link this concern to a reduction in the commercialization of children's programs eroded and ultimately ended the industry's and its regulator's noble intentions. Since 1929, virtually every federal regulatory broadcast-programming policy statement listed programming oriented toward the interests and needs of children as a special responsibility of the broadcast industry. During the 1960s several congressional hearings relating to broadcast service in the United States included testimony from child psychologists, pediatricians, and educators criticizing the amount of violence that television brought into children's lives. However, it was not until 1970, when a public interest group, Action for Children's Television (ACT), began to mobilize support for specific regulatory policies, that the FCC was moved beyond expressions of concern to actual hearings on the issues involved. ACT gained the attention of Torbett McDonald, chairman of the FCC's house oversight committee; and in 1971, McDonald's committee gave ACT the opportunity to present its proposals for improving the quality of television programming for children. The FCC responded to this pressure by creating a permanent children's television unit within the FCC's Broadcast Bureau. Soon afterward, ABC and NBC announced their intention to follow an NAB recommendation to reduce the number of commercial minutes per hour of network television programming for children aged 6 to 12.

In 1974 the FCC responded officially to the proposals of ACT by rejecting the group's contention that there should be no commercials in television programming designed for children but agreeing that there should be clear separation, during such programming, between the entertainment and the advertising segments. Host-selling and other formats that might tend to blur the distinction between the story line and the commercial messages being provided were to be avoided. The commission also directed broadcasters to distribute a reasonable amount of children's programming throughout the week, including programming designed to meet the special needs of preschool children. Although observing that improvement in this special area of programming was necessary, the agency expressed the hope that the industry would respond voluntarily to this need without specific rules being enacted to require such response.[22] ACT challenged this policy statement in the court as being inadequate to protect the interests of children in this area; but the court grudgingly approved the FCC's position and noted in doing so that the commission did have the authority to impose the regulations that ACT had requested and that, in affirming the agency's decision, the court was assuming that the FCC would actively "monitor the level of actual performance by broadcasters" to ensure that this vital responsibility was in fact being discharged.[23]

At this point ACT turned to the FTC and found a more sympathetic forum. In 1978 a staff report of the Federal Trade Commission recommended that no advertising be allowed in any programming produced primarily for children under the age of 9, that all commercials for excessively sugary foods and treats be banned from children's programming, and that other foods containing sugar be advertised only if accompanied by statements disclosing nutritional information about the food as well.

Congress reacted swiftly to this FTC proposal, sending a message to the agency to stop this harassment by terminating all federal funding of the arm of the FTC that had drafted this report. The federal courts went even further. Acting on a petition of the Toy Manufacturers of America (TMA) and the American Association of Advertising Agencies (AAAA), they disqualified the FTC chairman from voting on agency actions relating to the advertising of products for children in future proceedings because of his preexisting prejudice, which, they felt, would make impartial judgment on the merits of the case impossible.[24]

In 1977 the FCC announced a second notice of inquiry to evaluate broadcaster voluntary compliance with the children's programming objectives the agency had set out in its 1974 policy statement. Even though the NAB had negotiated continual reductions in the amount of time devoted to commercials in children's programming, planning to reach the level of only 6½ minutes per hour by 1978, the commission ended its review with a report that was extremely critical of the industry's performance under the voluntary guidelines. The commission found only minimal increases in the amount of children's programming being provided by broadcasters and charged that the industry was not making a sincere effort to serve the needs of this portion of its audience.

Faced with this situation, the FCC laid out five policy alternatives it might follow; these alternatives ranged from simply rescinding its earlier statement and allowing broadcasters to deal with children's needs as they wished to establishing rules concerning the amount, scheduling, and type of children's programming each station would be required to provide and making noncompliance with this requirement grounds for failure to renew a license.[25] In 1984 the agency rather predictably chose the first policy alternative as the one it would follow and delegated to the industry itself all responsibility for the special interests of the children in its viewing or listening audience.

Once again, as policy issues ranged beyond programming to commercial practices, industry opposition increased to a point where the commission felt itself virtually powerless to act. As in the case of counter-advertising, broadcasters could claim — with justification — that they alone were being singled out to correct practices other unregulated competing media could engage in without legal constraint.

In any case, it is certainly true that a broadcast industry now liberated from the repressive requirements of government has thus far shown little inclination on its own to respond to the special needs of young viewers with programming designed to educate or even to entertain them. In fact, in reaction to a steadily diminishing share of network viewership during the traditional Saturday-morning children's-programming period, CBS, as of January 1986, cut back its schedule for children to one hour a week, a tactic the other networks are expected to follow in the near future. At the same time, of course, virtually every new independent television station is bombarding preschool children with such program-length toy commercials as "G.I. Joe," "Challenge of the GoBots," "Thundercats," and "Wuzzles" on a regular Monday-to-Friday basis.

Broadcasters are not alone in their decision to consider only the purchasing power of the young viewer, however. Nickelodeon, the child-oriented cable-TV service recently cut back on its first-run programming for the young to schedule more off-network, general-appeal series programs from the 1960s. At the same time, VCR rental outlets are featuring such shallow merchandising marvels for home viewing as the *Care Bears Battle the Freeze Machine* and *Transformers: The Ultimate Doom*. In essence, then, the underlying justification for deregulating children's television has not been to free broadcasters from any governmental restrictions on the content of children's programming but rather to allow the industry to do no more for these 50 million young viewers than the industry's competitors are compelled by law to do. In that regard, this policy seems to have been eminently successful.

Obscene or indecent broadcast programming has seldom been a regulatory problem for the commission. The federal law prohibiting such content is not within the communications act itself, but rather in the federal criminal code that prescribes penalties for such transmissions.[26] However, the commission has taken the position that, even in the absence of a conviction under the criminal code, programming in bad taste, including vulgar as well as obscene or indecent comments transmitted by a station, provides grounds for refusal to renew a license. Thus, in *Palmetto Broadcasting Co.*, 33 FCC 250 (1962), the agency held that coarseness in itself was sufficient to support a finding that renewal of a license would not be in the public interest.

In the late 1960s, the FCC began receiving complaints from the public in regard to alleged drug-oriented songs played by certain broadcast stations. In response to these complaints, the commission issued a Notice to remind broadcasters of their duty to broadcast records only after they had made a reasonable effort to determine the meaning of drug-oriented lyrics. When broadcasters began to question the agency and asked for further guidance on their responsibilities, the FCC issued a second Memorandum and Order. The Commission directive made it clear that the FCC was not *prohibiting* the playing of such drug-oriented records and that no reprisals would be taken against stations that chose to play such records but that the station management was expected to know the content of the records played and to make a judgment as to whether or not such records should be aired.

One broadcaster was not satisfied with this explanation and believed that by raising the issue of record content, the commission had imposed an unreasonable burden on broadcast free speech. Using *Smith v. California*, 361 U.S. 147 (1959), as an analogy, the appeal from the commission's notice in *Yale Broadcasting v. FCC*, 478 F.2d 594 (1973), argued that if the bookseller, Smith, could not be convicted of selling obscene books under a state statute that imposed the unreasonable burden of requiring that a bookseller read all books in advance to make certain they were not obscene before selling them, then neither could a broadcaster be held responsible for auditioning each record to be played by a station for drug-oriented lyrics before it was aired.

The Court was unimpressed with this reasoning. Pointing out that, unlike the bookseller, the broadcaster schedules only a limited number of records within any 24-hour period, the opinion stated that this was not an unreasonable burden to place on station management, because "in order for a broadcaster to determine whether it is acting in the public interest, knowledge of its own programming is required." In summary, the Court declared,

> Far from constituting any threat to freedom of expression of the licensee, we conclude that for the Commission to have been less insistent on licensees discharging their obligations would have verged on an evasion of the Commission's own responsibilities.

Similarly, the commission's actions against vulgar or sexually oriented talk shows were affirmed by the federal courts in *Illinois Citizens Committee for Broadcasting v. FCC*, 515 F.2d 397 (D.C. Cir.) and *FCC v. Pacifica Foundation*, 438 U.S. 726 (1978), without any showing of obscenity. In the *Pacifica* case, the Supreme Court expressly approved the concept that material that is "patently offensive or sexual in nature" might be punishable even if *not* obscene, particularly if broadcast during times when children could be presumed to be in the audience.

For major broadcast organizations, however, this issue has never been a significant one, because the private content controls they exercise over the programming they purchase and schedule have always been far more strict than any standards the FCC might impose on them.

Private Content Controls

The National Association of Broadcasters issued its first guide to self-regulation of broadcast practices in 1929, only two years after the FRC was created. In its initial *Code of Ethics and Standards of Commercial Practice*, the NAB warned its member stations against "the broadcasting

of any matter which would commonly be regarded as offensive," specified certain limitations on the presentation of advertising material, and
provided a private means for determining whether or not any of these
standards were violated. The NAB designated its board of directors as
the body responsible for investigating such charges and notifying the
stations involved of the board's findings.[27] The only penalty that the
NAB could impose on a member station was to deny it membership in
the NAB, but this was a more severe sanction than it seemed to be.
Both the FRC and the FCC viewed the NAB as their unofficial partner
in the effort to maintain the quality and integrity of the American
broadcast service; thus, any member station expelled by the NAB for
cause was quite likely to have its next application for license renewal
studied with particular care.

In 1937 the NAB adopted a much more detailed and elaborate code
of standards of practice, revising it extensively in 1945. In 1952 the NAB
adopted its first code for television and revised it annually until the early
1980s. Both sets of broadcast codes echoed many of the sentiments of
FCC programming policy through the years and stressed the special
responsibility of broadcasters toward children, toward the communities
their stations served, and toward the needs and interests of each segment of their potential audiences.

However, it was actually the broadcast networks that determined the
major characteristics of American broadcast service from the early
1930s onward; these organizations not only imposed strict standards of
content control on every program they distributed but also dictated
most of the terms and conditions contained in the NAB codes. During
the radio era, the networks delegated the programming of a substantial
portion of their prime-time evening schedule to advertising agencies but
retained absolute authority to censor any program material they found
to be inappropriate. In 1937 NBC aired the celebrated "Adam and Eve"
sketch featuring Charlie McCarthy, a ventriloquist's dummy, and Mae
West. It was in this sketch that the professional wicked lady of the silver
screen uttered the immortal lines

> I like a man that takes his time. Why don't you come home with me? I'll let
> you play in my woodpile. You're all wood and a yard long.

The sketch was celebrated simply because it was so unique during
this era of strict network program supervision. This single episode of
semiracy dialogue so shocked the FCC that its chairman sent NBC a
strongly worded protest criticizing the network for this "serious offense
against the proprieties of the American public."[28]

In the late 1950s, when television networks began commissioning
independent Hollywood producers to provide the bulk of their prime-

time series programming, the same type of absolute authority was exercised over every aspect of these productions. Special network departments, variously titled Program Practices, Broadcast Standards and Practices, or Broadcast Standards, were established to examine every frame of film and each sentence of dialogue for possible breaches of taste or morality. Necklines were raised, skirts were lengthened, and any possibility of a double entendre in dialogue was deleted.

During the early 1970s, a number of well-organized interest groups found this narrowly centralized private content-control process to be ideally suited for their own purposes. Using a carefully orchestrated combination of political activism, media showmanship, and economic pressure, organizations such as NOW, the Gay Media Task Force, and Moral Majority have all exerted an influence on network programming decisions during the past decade.[29]

The most extensive example of negotiation, cooperation, and accommodation among the leadership of the FCC, the NAB, and the television networks undoubtedly occurred in 1975. The FCC had issued a report in which it declared its confidence in the industry's willingness to respond voluntarily to mounting public concern about television violence, particularly as it was portrayed in network series programming scheduled during the early evening hours, when a substantial portion of the audience consisted of children. The NAB realized that the FCC needed some tangible sign of industry responsiveness in order to protect its position. Therefore, the NAB immediately adopted a family-viewing policy as an addition to its television code and declared that the early evening hours should be free of any television shows not suitable for viewing by the entire family. Thus, this family-viewing period was actually a private policy response to pressures Congress had exerted on the FCC after the commission had refused to heed congressional advice to enact regulations banning *all* violence on television.[30] The networks, instrumental in steering the NAB's policy statement through to adoption, then pointed to it as a standard they felt bound to adhere to when planning their fall 1976 programming schedules. Thus, in a brilliant series of policy maneuvers, the FCC's faith in the industry had been vindicated, those urging regulation had been made to look foolish, the NAB had adopted a responsible, responsive position toward the public, and the networks, not bowing to government pressure but simply reacting professionally to their own organization's standards, offered the remedy all had sought.

Unfortunately, one small dissident group that no one had considered while formulating this grand strategy was able, within a few short months, to discredit the entire public relations effort, even though the policy itself was not affected by their action. When the networks decided to adopt this new programming policy, it was clear to each of them that many of the series they had already contracted for in Hollywood would not be appropriate for scheduling in this family-viewing slot. As a result, some series already in production were canceled, others substantially revised, and still others newly commissioned to meet the requirements the networks just adopted. Most independent producers, docile because of their total financial dependence on the networks, complied with the new content directives; however, a few producers, joined by the Screen Actors and Screen Writers Guilds, sued not only the networks but also the FCC and the NAB. The group filing suit charged that the networks, the FCC, and the NAB worked in concert to deny creative artists their First Amendment rights in the field of television program production. Because they claimed a violation of basic First Amendment rights rather than directly challenging a commission regulation, they were able to bring this action before a federal district court judge in Los Angeles, who was likely to be far more sympathetic with film-industry problems than any court of appeals justice in Washington.

In November 1976, Judge Warren F. Ferguson issued an opinion declaring that the voluntary guidelines the networks had imposed on their own scheduling practices were unconstitutional because they were not, in fact, voluntary. Instead, Judge Ferguson found that there had been a closely coordinated process of accommodation among the parties by which the networks had improperly delegated to the NAB and the FCC judgments the networks themselves were responsible for making. The opinion stated that "censorship by government or privately created review boards cannot be tolerated."[31] Judge Ferguson admitted that his court had no authority to order the networks to abandon the family-viewing policy they had adopted, but he held that the NAB should immediately rescind the programming principles on which the network decisions were allegedly based. In 1979 the court of appeals for this Los Angeles district court reversed Judge Ferguson's decision on juris-dictional grounds and held that the court of appeals for the District of Columbia was the proper forum in which challenges of FCC actions should be heard. The case was finally dismissed in 1984, but the damage its revelations had inflicted on the historic pattern of accommodation between the FCC and the industry were irreparable.

In 1980 the NAB code came under pressure from the U.S. Justice Department, which was investigating advertiser complaints that the code's limitations on multiproduct ads in a single commercial segment denied smaller or less prosperous businesses the opportunity to adver-tise on television. The NAB position was adopted to protect against *clutter*, the practice of using a single 30- or 60-second spot for several different product messages, each only a few seconds in duration. A number of audience surveys showed that the public perceived this practice as being much more irritating and distracting than the viewing of a single commercial message during that same period of time. However, in 1982, a federal district court ruled favorably on the Justice Department complaint and held that denying an advertiser the right to use multiproduct commercials on television caused some businesses to pay more than necessary for broadcast advertising and therefore tended to increase the cost of their products to the public. At the same time, the court struck down the NAB code prohibitions of the advertising of hard liquor, contraceptives, lottery information, and program-length commercials and scheduled for trial the antitrust implications of the code limitations on the number of commercial interruptions per hour of programming and the number of minutes per hour devoted to commercial messages.[32]

Rather than struggle further against the trends of the time, the NAB simply abolished the code and dismantled the entire review process that had formed the self-regulatory structure for broadcasting during the past six decades. Yet, perhaps in making this decision, the organization was only bowing to the inevitable; even if the NAB were to deny a station membership because of violation of its standards, it was doubtful during this deregulatory era that anyone at the FCC would take particular notice of the NAB's action.

The Collapse of Consensus

From 1927 until the 1980s, the programming-control relationship between the broadcast industry and its federal regulator was a symbiotic one. Each participant performed a role on which the other depended and one that it could not perform for itself. Hemmed in by constitutional and legislative restraints, the commission's program policy initiatives had only limited capacity to shape industry programming practices. On the other hand, the industry and, most particularly, the networks had absolute dominion over broadcast programming but were vulnerable, because of this power, to political pressure.

By regulating broadcasting, the FCC brought the process within the political system, preempted other governmental bodies from asserting control, and guaranteed the industry a stable and predictable environment in which it could prosper. In return, the industry accommodated to FCC programming pronouncements whenever possible and achieved, through its private legal and policy processes, the changes in form, if not substance, that the commission proposed but lacked the ability to achieve on its own. The NAB was the crucial intermediary in this process. It transformed governmental policies into industry standards and principles so that conformance became an image-building professional responsibility rather than submission to an edict threatening to erode First Amendment rights. In addition, the NAB's influence extended far beyond the networks and major market stations to gain compliance from smaller stations that the FCC process seldom reached. This allowed for a degree of uniformity in practice no government agency could attain on its own.

In the last analysis, however, it was the network structure that made the process truly effective — by enforcing, through its private production and distribution processes, the content standards that determined the nature of American broadcasting service. The fact that there were only three major network services during the entire broadcasting era made each of them more susceptible to both political and economic pressures than if there had been a larger number of competing services in the network field. Such a triumvirate seemed particular vulnerable to the regulatory tactic of "divide and conquer." The commission would negotiate accommodation with one network whose dedication to the public it praised, while the other two visibly undedicated networks moved frantically to leave their position of isolation. In addition, as the clearly identifiable media barons of broadcasting, these three organizations were the obvious targets for every attack launched on the quality of American television. Because of their visibility and their resulting vulnerability, the networks tended to be far more responsive to public and private demands than their power and size would suggest they might be. In fact some would argue that the networks were far too accommodating to these pressures and allowed various narrow-interest groups to exert more influence over the nature of television programming than they had any right to exercise.

There were, however, obvious limits to the patterns of accommodation among the industry, the government, and the public. No amount of political or public pressure could compel the industry to modify an advertising policy it felt was essential for its economic welfare. This was particularly true if such a modification might provide a competitive advantage for media not under government supervision. The process was, after all, totally dependent on mutual benefit for its existence; and broadcasters saw no benefit in commercial-practice restrictions that could outweigh the losses they were likely to sustain in advertising revenues if these restrictions were accepted. Similarly, the mutuality of this relationship depended on the FCC's not only protecting the industry from direct political pressure but shielding it from instability and competitive challenge as well.

As the FCC began a decade ago to encourage competition in electronic mass media service, the inducement for continued industry cooperation and accommodation diminished to the same extent. At the same time, broadcasters could now argue that, as in the case of earlier advertising controls, they were being singled out and placed at a competitive disadvantage by government restrictions that did not apply to their competitors.

If this traditional relationship between government and broadcasting comes to an end, it will close the only channel that has existed for public criticism and concern to have some influence on the process that creates the mass cultural environment in which we live. We have been told, however, that this is of no concern because the newly emerging marketplace in electronic mass media services will not only provide any communication service the public may wish or need but also be so diffuse in nature that no small group of corporate entities will have the capacity to dominate its function.

Through examining how private policy processes have responded to such competitive opportunities in the past, it should be possible to evaluate more accurately just how reasonable these visions of the future may be.

Notes

1. In the matter of the application of Great Lakes Broadcasting, 3 FRC Annual Reports 32 (1929), as republished and described in Frank J. Kahn, ed., *Documents of American Broadcasting*, 4th ed. (Englewood Cliffs, N.J.: Prentice-Hall, 1984), 63–69.
2. Ibid., 64.
3. *KFKB Broadcasting v. FRC*, 47 F.2d 670 (1931).
4. Kahn, *Documents of American Broadcasting*, 148.
5. Ibid., 149.
6. 44 FCC 2303 (1960).
7. These 14 types of programming as specified by the FCC were: (1) opportunity for local self-expression, (2) development and use of local talent, (3) programs for children, (4) religious programs, (5) educational programs, (6) public-affairs programs, (7) editorializing by licensees, (8) political broadcasts, (9) agricultural programs, (10) news programs, (11) weather and market reports, (12) sports programs, (13) service to minority groups, and (14) entertainment programming.
8. 44 FCC 2303 (1960), 2310.
9. Ascertainment Primer, 27 FCC 2d 650 (1971).
10. In the Radio Act of 1927, this restriction was contained in sec. 29; in the Communications Act of 1934, in sec. 326.
11. The commission's interpretation of this section of the act tended to be rigid and mechanical. Thus, a political opponent of an incumbent mayor was authorized by the FCC to receive equal access to the facilities of any station

that had covered the official activities of the mayor during a campaign period as a part of their regular news broadcasts. Congress remedied this problem in 1959 by expressly exempting bona fide newscasts, bona fide news interviews, bona fide documentaries, and on-the-spot news events from section 315 equal-access requirements.

12. Mayflower, 8 FCC 833 (1941), as republished in Kahn, *Documents of American Broadcasting*, 120–123.
13. 13 FCC 1246 (1949); see also, "Handling of Controversial Issues of Public Importance," 29 Fed. Reg. 10415 (1964).
14. *Red Lion Broadcasting v. FCC*, 396 U.S. 367 (1969).
15. "In the Matter of Handling of Public Issues under the Fairness Doctrine," 48 FCC 2d 1 (1974).
16. 58 FCC 2d 691 (1976). In *National Citizens Committee for Broadcasting v. FCC*, 567 F.2d 1095 (D.C. Cir. 1977), the FCC's decision to limit the fairness doctrine's application to commercial advertising was upheld. NCCB appealed from this portion of the decision, but the Supreme Court denied certiorari. 436 U.S. 926 (1978). One interesting sidelight of the controversy surrounding the Fairness Report of 1974 is that, while it was being criticized as a retreat from the FCC's earlier requirement that a station actively seek out issues of public importance, the commission, in 1976, for the first time actually imposed this specific responsibility on a broadcast station. See *Rep. Patsy Mink*, 59 FCC 2d 987 (1976).
17. 74 FCC 2d 163 (1979).
18. *Banzhaf v. FCC*, 405 F.2d 1082 (1968).
19. FTC Docket 19.260 [WCBS 8 FCC 2d 381 (1971)] (6 Jan. 1972).
20. The FCC rejected the FTC request as part of its broader policy statement (see note 15).
21. *Neckritz v. FCC*, 502 F.2d 411 (D.C. Cir. 1974); *CBS v. Democratic National Committee*, 412 U.S. 94 (1973); *Public Interest Research Group v. FCC*, 522 F.2d 1060 (1st Cir. 1975).
22. "Children's Television Report Policy Statement," 50 FCC 2d 1; affirmed *ACT v. FCC*, 564 F.2d 458 (D.C. Cir. 1977).
23. Ibid., 462.
24. "Perschuk Disqualified in Children's Ad Proceedings," *Broadcasting*, 6 Nov. 1978, 34.
25. Notice Proposed Rulemaking in Docket 19142, 75 FCC 2d 138 (1977).
26. Title 18 USC sec. 1464.
27. See Kahn, *Documents of American Broadcasting*, 70, for a reprint of the earliest NAB code provisions.
28. Lawrence W. Lichty and Malachi Topping, *American Broadcasting: A Sourcebook on the History of Radio and Television* (New York: Hastings House, 1975), 530.
29. For examples of such successful private group pressure, see Richard Levine, "How the Gay Lobby Has Changed Television," *TV Guide*, 30 May 1981, 3; Edith Efron, "This Time the Indians Won," *TV Guide*, 22 Jan. 1972, 8–12; Leonard Gross, "TV under Pressure," *TV Guide*, 22 Feb. 1975, 10–14, 1 Mar. 1975, 16–20, 8 Mar. 1975, 13–16.

30. "Report on the Broadcast of Violent, Indecent and Obscene Materials," 51 FCC 2d 418.
31. *Writers Guild of America West v. FCC*, 423 F. Supp. 1064 (C.D. Cal. 1976); later vacated at *Writers Guild of America v. ABC et al.*, 609 F.2d 355 (9th Cir. 1979).
32. "NAB Lifts TV Radio Advertising Codes," *Broadcasting*, 15 Mar. 1982, 45.

Tracing the Patterns: Primary Sources

As this chapter suggests, the FCC has been much more successful in discouraging certain types of program practices than in encouraging broadcasters to produce and schedule features the industry views as being unprofitable or in some way unconventional. Thus, for example, the commission's decade-long crusade to improve the quality of children's television ended in failure, despite the documentation of abuses in this area of programming contained in such books as William Melody's *Children's Television: The Economics of Exploitation* (New Haven, Conn.: Yale University Press, 1973), and allowed the networks to set their own terms in dealing with the nation's young viewers.

In reality, of course, as studies by John A. Abel et al. ("Station License Revocations and Denials of Renewal 1934–1969," *Journal of Broadcasting*, 14 [Fall 1970]: 411–21) and Frederic Weiss et al., ("Station License Revocations and Denials of Renewal 1970–1978," *Journal of Broadcasting*, 24 [Summer 1980]: 301–10) indicate quite clearly, the FCC has been extremely reluctant to base any disciplinary action on programming practices and has preferred instead to work through the industry to achieve a consensus acceptable to those subject to its terms, a process of accommodation described in detail in James L. Baughman's *Television's Guardians: The FCC and the Politics of Programming 1958–1967* (Knoxville, Tenn.: University of Tennessee, 1985).

Similarly, in Barry Cole and Mal Oettinger's *Reluctant Regulators: The FCC and the Broadcast Audience* (Reading, Mass.: Addison-Wesley, 1978), the commission's role as a mediator or broker of conflicting media and audience interests is shown to be one that severely limits its ability to shape the nature of American broadcast programming. With these constraints in mind, a number of authors have questioned whether an agency incapable of exerting a positive influence on programming practices should be allowed to continue to exert a negative, or chilling, effect on broadcast services.

As Fred W. Friendly points out in his fascinating study of the *Red Lion* case, *The Good Guys, the Bad Guys and the First Amendment* (New York: Random House, 1976), this widely heralded access decision actually reflected the successful stifling of right-wing commentary by a well-organized political-action group. Looking at the fairness doctrine from a broader perspective, Ford Rowan in his *Broadcast Fairness: Doctrine, Practice, Prospects* (New York: Longman, 1984), comes to the conclusion that, although repealing the requirement of balance and objectivity in the broadcast coverage of controversial issues may entail certain social and political risks, they are risks worth taking in order to encourage free and robust discussion of these issues by our electronic mass media.

Despite this optimistic assessment of the degree of public commitment on the part of an industry allegedly constrained at the moment by the "chilling effect" of government control, it may be well to remember such episodes as the one involving children's programming, where the withdrawal of federal authority should have been expected from this viewpoint to have stimulated the production and scheduling of a broad array of imaginative, intellectually stimulating features for America's young viewers. Perhaps this era will arrive someday, but even a cursory glance at the listings in *TV Guide* provides little evidence that this exciting new trend in children's programming has as yet begun.

In the meantime, as books such as Todd Gitlin's *Inside Prime Time* (New York: Pantheon Books, 1983) and Richard Levinson and William Link's *Stay Tuned: An Inside Look at the Making of Prime Time Television* (New York: St. Martin's Press, 1981) and articles such as David Black's "How the Gosh-darn Networks Edit the Heck out of Movies" (*New York Times*, 26 Jan. 1975, sec. 2) indicate, broadcasters continue to exert their own private content-control rules and standards on their program suppliers, a "chilling effect" on creativity that deregulation is unlikely to abate to any degree.

CHAPTER FIVE

COMPETITIVE POLICY IN THE BROADCAST ERA

Broadcast Delivery of Mass Culture

The American broadcasting industry had already begun to develop its own private policy structure before the Radio Act of 1927 became law. In 1923 the American Society of Composers, Authors, and Publishers (ASCAP) demanded that each radio station broadcasting recorded music pay a fee to ASCAP for every composition published or composed by those the organization represented. Recorded music was the one form of professionally produced, nationally distributed mass entertainment that local radio stations could offer their audiences in the days before network service; and to lose the right to schedule this most popular portion of their programming would have left the stations in an almost impossible situation.

ASCAP stood on solid legal ground because it was authorized by the Copyright Act of 1909 to collect payments on behalf of its members for any performance of musical selections in which they had a creative or ownership interest. At the same time, most broadcast stations stood on shaky financial grounds; only a handful of them earned sufficient revenues to meet their current operating expenses.

Rather than turning to government for relief from this difficult situation, the industry formed its own group, the National Association of Broadcasters (NAB), to attempt to negotiate with ASCAP on behalf of member stations. Many smaller station owners were unhappy with the NAB for voluntarily accepting to pay a music license fee. However, the agreement that the NAB achieved with ASCAP not only guaranteed broadcasting's continued access to what was its most popular mass-entertainment programming at the time but also excluded the federal government from a private policy process the industry would soon use even more effectively.

That time came in 1937, when ASCAP demanded yet another increase in the rates broadcast stations were to pay for the use of the music ASCAP controlled. Rather than capitulate, the industry launched a competing music-licensing organization, Broadcast Music Incorporated (BMI), that undercut ASCAP's bargaining position and attracted a significant portion of ASCAP's former members. The new organization offered broadcasters a lower licensing fee than ASCAP previously had been willing to accept. Faced with a U.S. Justice Department inquiry concerning the degree of competition in the music-licensing field, ASCAP eventually capitulated in 1940 by rolling back its fee demands to a percentage roughly similar to that in effect in 1937.[1]

During the 1930s broadcasters also clashed in similar fashion with the American newspaper industry. The press, alarmed by the competitive threat of breadcast news, attempted to deny radio stations access to the wire services that broadcasters were relying on for their news broadcasts. Because these wire services were dominated by their newspaper owners or clients, the newspaper industry was able to tell broadcasters in 1934 that from then on they could receive this wire service news only through a *Press-Radio Bureau*, which imposed major limitations on the use of such information for radio news broadcasts.

Here again, the broadcast industry did not seek to invoke public law but simply waited until the newspaper coalition collapsed on its own. During this era most stations had only a minimal interest in news programming; therefore, they had the advantage of being able to wait as long as necessary for the wire service to be restored. An even greater advantage lay in the fact that a number of the most profitable broadcast stations were owned by newspapers, who were unlikely to deny their own facilities the opportunity to present broadcast news. Within the year the newspapers disbanded their Press-Radio Bureau and lifted their use restrictions. These actions once again allowed American broadcasters unlimited access to the wire services.[2]

In each of these stages, the broadcast industry achieved a solution to its problems without government intervention. Undoubtedly, the industry was aided in each case by the possibility of either the Justice Department or Congress interceding, if necessary, on its behalf; but by avoiding this necessity, broadcasting also avoided the intrusion of public policy or law into an area of private-industry practice and thus preserved the autonomy it required for other types of private policy less consistent with the standards of federal law.

One area in which industry policy was directly contrary to that of government was in the development of nationwide networks for stations licensed as locally programmed facilities. The network affiliation contract actually predated federal regulation in the field of broadcasting. In 1924 WEAF, the American Telephone and Telegraph–owned station in New York, launched a programming service on a regular basis to 20 stations in the East. In 1926 the newly formed National Broadcasting

Company (NBC) took over this networking function from WEAF; but it was not until 1929, when both NBC and CBS services spanned the nation, that networks began to become the dominant programming force in American broadcasting.

The affiliation contract was a carefully crafted private agreement binding the affiliated station to act exclusively as its network's outlet for programming in a given market. During the radio era, these contracts generally ran for a five-year period, with the network retaining the right to cancel the contract at the end of any contract year. According to contract terms, stations were required to option a large portion of their daily broadcast schedule to the network and to agree to carry whatever commercially sponsored programming that network chose to provide.

In 1940 the FCC did attempt to coerce the network-affiliated stations it licensed into reclaiming at least some portion of the national, regional, or locally oriented program production the stations seemed so eager to avoid. To encourage a greater variety of program alternatives for American audiences, the commission passed rules placing limits on the number of hours per day that each station could act only as an outlet for network programming and reduced the amount of *option time* any station could be compelled by contract to offer to its network for any features the network chose to provide.[3] The agency, however, was unable to achieve the degree of diversity it sought in broadcast programming and was forced to settle for an industry accommodation offering unique local productions only during *fringe* hours, when listenership was certain to be limited.

In 1963 the FCC prohibited any further optioning of time to the network; and in 1970 it tried yet another tactic to reduce network domination of television programming. The FCC limited network affiliates in the nation's largest makets to only three hours of network-supplied prime-time programming each evening.[4] This *Prime-Time Access Rule*, modified and amended several times to make it more effective, was designed to stimulate local-station production during a popular viewing time or, at the very least, to allow other program suppliers access to major-market television audiences.

As the FCC was attempting to limit the degree of network domination over American television station programming, the Justice Department was studying the tactics the networks used to obtain from their program producers in Hollywood ownership and syndication rights to the series the networks agreed to distribute. By 1970 the Justice Department decided that network program-procurement policies were anti-competitive, because the independent program producers had no realistic alternative but to accept almost any terms a network offered for the national distribution it provided. Without such network exposure, no television series could build the popular reputation it needed to earn its producer a profit during its later syndication. The networks, following parallel practices if not acting in concert, advanced only basic production costs for a series being developed under its specifications, thus providing the producer with a profit only through the generally more lucrative syndication-license payments the producer received from later off-network use by local stations and from foreign broadcast organizations. Thus, if an independent producer believed, however erroneously, that a network would be more likely to select a series for its fall schedule if the network had a financial interest in its success, there would be every inducement to make such an offer. To prevent such a misunderstanding from occurring, the Justice Department in 1972, commenced action against the three television networks and alleged that their dominant control over the American television market provided them with an anticompetitive advantage in dealing with television program suppliers.

Only two years before this, the FCC had acted in a manner it believed might prevent the threatened Justice Department intervention from occurring. It enacted financial interest rules that denied the networks any future right to participate in revenues earned in the distribution or exhibition of any programming that the networks themselves had not produced. The Justice Department, however, was not satisfied either by the scope of these rules or by the commission's commitment to their enforcement; therefore, the litigation and the negotiations that surrounded it continued until 1980 for CBS and ABC.[5] (NBC settled with the Justice Department in 1976.) Ultimately, the protracted process only added a few dimensions of detail to the rules the FCC enacted in 1970. In essence, then, from that time onward, networks were barred from using their position as television distributor to demand or even accept any payoff from their program suppliers in the form of sharing in any syndication revenues such programming might earn.

This victory for television program producers, however, was a costly and perhaps temporary one as well. Although the networks vehemently denied that they were attempting to benefit financially from their dominant position as television distributors, their immediate response to the restrictions was to begin reducing their program production expenses by "individually" deciding to advance less than the full production cost of each series they had commissioned. This action forced the producer to bear the remaining production costs for any series not ultimately selected for use. During the past decade, this situation became even more financially perilous for independent producers. Network scheduling strategies called for cancellation of many series before 13 episodes were produced or shown; this left the producer not only with a net loss for being "successful" in making the schedule but also with virtually no off-network or foreign syndication value to compensate for this loss.

In addition, in 1982 the FCC issued a *Notice of Proposed Rule Making* to consider repealing its prohibition on network snydication of television programming and financial interest in subsidiary uses of this programming[6] and announced, in August 1983, its intention to rescind these rules. In the meantime, the Justice Department indicated its willingness to withdraw from this controversy, so it appeared that the networks would soon be able to reclaim the interests they had lost in television programming during the 1970s. At the last moment, however, in the tradition of the Hollywood Western, the program producers rallied enough opposition in Congress, and even involved President Reagan, to strike up a campaign that led the FCC to postpone acting on this rescission.

There is little evidence in the six decades of private broadcast mass entertainment policy that suggests any tendency on the part of the industry toward offering the American public an ever-broader range of viewing or listening options. From the earliest dealings with ASCAP to the most recent negotiations with independent film producers, the broadcast strategy has always been to seek to lock in a reasonably priced, regular supply of professionally produced programming from sources in the mass-entertainment industry rather than to risk producing its own material that would lack the glamour and polish those in show business could provide. Despite broadcasting's impressive bargaining power, the basic cost of this material was so high that there was every incentive for the industry to spread the expenses as broadly as possible through nationwide distribution networks. The trend within the industry has always been toward consolidation and centralization, thus reducing rather than increasing the degree of program diversity in the United States. This is not to say that broadcasters and, in particular, broadcast networks have not produced programming of their own. Today, all news, documentaries, and sports and most daytime dramas are produced by the networks themselves, as well as "made-for-TV" movies and a growing number of miniseries generally coproduced with a major film studio. In reality, however, in its day-to-day programming efforts, broadcasting is, as it has been from the beginning, essentially a derivative rather than an originating medium. It is dependent on established film and music distributors for the attractive, appealing content that made radio and later television the most popular mass medium in the United States.

Because electronic media are outlets for, rather than originators of, mass-entertainment content, numbers of systems such as *96 channels,*

2000 assignments, or *10,000 licensed broadcast stations* tell us far less about the degree of diverse, competitive communication services available to audiences in each market than does a survey of the program suppliers on which these media rely. But an inherent limitation on the ability of a broadcast station to meet the program balance or variety that the federal government has sought is the fact that the single channel available for distributing programming and generating revenue can carry only one message at any given time. Thus, a decision to schedule children's programming or a classical-music segment may please 10 percent of an audience while depriving the remaining 90 percent of the regular station programming they enjoy. For that reason, cable television could promise greater diversity simply because of the nature of its distribution system. It could provide its audience with an entire spectrum of channels through which specialized and generalized services could be offered simultaneously allowing the viewer rather than the programmer to decide which service to select at any given time. In this way cable TV can serve as a prototype for evaluating the competitive tendencies inherent in most other new electronic mass media delivery systems. As DBS and MMDS, cable TV offers a system of channels to earn its revenues and therefore is not dependent on a single communication service for its financial survival.

The Cable-TV Challenge

No one actually "invented" cable TV. During the 1930s Bell Lab developed coaxial cable, a specially designed high-capacity conduit capable of providing a vast number of telephonic circuits within a single wire. However, even in the late 1940s, when AT&T began to use this cable for network-television interconnections, there was no thought of connecting individual homes to a television source in this manner. In truth, cable television was simply an unforeseen by-product of a regulatory experiment designed to create a system of community-oriented, locally produced broadcast television. The FCC allocation plan of 1952 provided for more than 2000 television stations to operate in approximately 1300 communities throughout the nation. The engineering staff at the commission based its coverage and service projections on just such a fully operational system. Instead, eight years later, only 530 of the stations had begun broadcasting, although nearly 85 percent of all American households were already television homes.

Initially, *community antennas*, as cable systems were originally known, were exactly that — shared master-antenna hookups that allowed a cluster of houses lying beyond the coverage area of the nearest television station to receive a minimally acceptable picture. What transformed this informal, passive pooling of reception into a privately owned *CATV industry* was a second FCC regulatory action, which, when coupled with the continuation of its television-station allocation policy, created the competitive conditions essential for cable's growth.

In 1956 nearly half of America's television homes could receive only one television signal. Located in less populous markets without sufficient households to support a second or third station, these audiences had access to only one-third of the exciting television fare about which they heard and read. During this era one enterprising CATV operator asked the commission for permission to lease a microwave system to import the two missing networks' programming to his community from the closest affiliates of each network.[7] Microwave authorizations were granted by the commission's Common Carrier, rather than Broadcast Bureau; and because communication common-carrier regulation involved only the reasonableness of the charges for service rather than the policy implications of the service itself, the application was approved in a routine manner.

Microwave opened an entirely new domain for CATV operators and allowed them for the first time to enter the somewhat larger communities where some television services were already available. Until this time only towns on the outer fringes of existing television station contours offered cable-TV opportunities. Cities within the coverage area could receive a signal without cable; but those outside the range of any television transmission could not be helped even by the highest antenna a system could erect. The capacity to enter an existing television market to offer potential subscribers the second or third network channel they could not receive over the air brought cable into its first direct conflict with the broadcast industry.

Although affiliate stations whose network programming was being exported, without permission or payment, by CATV to other markets were the first to complain about the new CATV operations, they actually sustained no economic injuries by the unauthorized use of their signals.[8] Almost none of the programming being exported by CATV operators was owned by these stations, and the wider circulation each station's advertising messages received through cable dissemination increased, rather than diminished, their potential to earn revenues through this usage.

Instead, the damage was being inflicted on those small market television stations located in areas where CATV systems were operating. Until this era, station managers had generally been pleased with the community antenna systems that sprang up on the edges of their coverage contours, for they extended a station's transmission range at no expense to the broadcaster. Now, however, CATV subscribers in small television markets were being offered competing network channels that were not previously available in that market, which diminished the local television station's share of audience and thereby reduced its base of potential advertising revenues.

What had been a symbiotic relationship between the station and community antenna became a parasitic one, for CATV preyed on the smaller market stations in the weakest financial condition. Yet, ironically, it was the marginal nature of these markets that saved CATV from immediate FCC control. Because the networks and the major stations instrumental in establishing the NAB's policies saw little need to protect their outlets in areas that cumulatively represented less than 0.5 percent of their total broadcast audience, no effort was made to convince the FCC to intervene in this situation.[9]

In 1960, at the urging of several congressmen whose local television broadcasters faced such CATV competition, a congressional committee considered legislation that would place the cable industry under FCC regulatory jurisdiction. The commission vigorously opposed this legislation and declared that it did not believe that the cable threat was severe enough to justify the heavy administrative burden its supervision would create.[10] Ultimately, the bill died in committee; and because Congress never again acted to amend the Communications Act of 1934, the FCC was forced throughout the entire period of its cable control to operate at the very edge of its jurisdictional base and was never certain when the federal courts would say that the agency had exceeded the boundaries of its congressionally granted authority.

Because the federal government did not preempt cable regulation, states were encouraged to consider common-carriage–type cable regulation, while local governments began to develop more sophisticated franchise agreements for cable-system applicants. These franchise agreements included for the first time local-origination, public-access, and educational channel services. As large corporations began buying groups of cable systems throughout the United States, a major shift in the policy position of the National Cable Television Association (NCTA), the industry's trade organization, became apparent. The new owners supported federal regulation of cable to preempt state or local control and end the crazy-quilt pattern of individualized franchise agreements that made uniform management from a corporate headquarters impossible. On the other hand, the small system operators who had launched the industry had close ties with local and state officials and were totally opposed to severing these ties in order to deal with federal bureaucrats in Washington.

Between 1962 and 1964, the NAB and the NCTA tried to draft an agreement to submit to Congress that would confer on the FCC some degree of regulatory control over cable. However, bitter factional clashes between pro- and antifederal regulation coalitions within NCTA and between broadcast groups that did and did not own cable systems became too intense to allow for any type of consensus to emerge.

The commission had been hoping that the private policy process would provide a solution to this regulatory dilemma, either through trade-group negotiation or through broadcast litigation. When the NAB and NCTA ended their discussions without an agreement and the federal courts refused to recognize a broadcaster's right to control the use of a station's transmissions, the agency felt it had no alternative but to act.[11] In early 1965 major cable-TV organizations stood poised to enter several of the "top 100," or largest 100 broadcast markets, in which 90 percent of the nation's television homes were located. The competitive threat was no longer a minor one in the eyes of the NAB's board of directors, and the commission understood quite clearly what the nation's major broadcasters expected the agency to do.

In 1963 the commission had actually begun, on a case-by-case-basis, approving or denying the use of microwave relay to import television programming to a cable system, when a federal court sustained the FCC's authority to use its communication common carrier powers in this way.[12] In 1965 the agency simply extended this authority in order to enact general rules for all cable microwave relays. At the same time, however, in a brilliant tactical move, the commission, in a companion Notice of Inquiry, declared that it would approve no more applications from cable systems to import broadcast signals into the nation's largest 100 television markets until its deliberations about the nature of the rules it would enact were completed.[13] This "temporary" freeze lasted for seven years; but because the FCC described the freeze as an interim condition it imposed only while considering these complex issues, the cable industry could obtain no legal relief. As the agency realized, the federal courts would only intervene when a ruling was final, not when a conditional rule might be modified at a later date.

Between 1965 and 1968, there seemed to be a possibility that the commission might escape its role as the guardian of broadcasting's economic interests. From the beginning, the agency understandably had favored a private law control process to limit cable TV's competitive impact, with the NAB establishing a fee system for cable importation of broadcast signals, setting conditions for usage, and perhaps creating a fund from these revenues to reimburse broadcasters damaged by a cable competition. If the necessary antitrust implications of such an arrange-ment could be worked out with the Justice Department, the FCC could then withdraw from the field and allow the broadcast industry itself to face the wrath of those who favored cable growth.

Unfortunately, the fatal flaw in this plan was one the federal courts had pointed out as early as 1961. In an unbroken line of cases, courts in various districts rejected every theory broadcasters advanced to justify restricting the use of the programming they transmitted. In each case, the courts observed that as mere outlets for the programming of others, broadcasters had no ownership interest to assert against those who sought to use the programming. Thus, the derivative nature of the affiliate station's mass media function defeated efforts to use the judicial process for protection against such competition.

In 1965, however, Congress began efforts to revise the Copyright Act of 1909; and if the NAB could convince Congress to include cable carriage as an unauthorized use of a broadcast signal, the industry's self-regulation-of-cable approach might still become a reality. Such copyright control was feasible in major markets because, unlike the smaller-market situation, the actual owner of a package of feature films was much more likely to incur the expense of copyright infringement litigation when the potential economic damage could be so substantial. For example, if a film package were licensed by a syndicator for use by a broadcaster in Twin Falls, Idaho, and carried by cable to Kalispell, Montana, the fact that the Kalispell television station would eventually insist on a lower license fee for films already viewed by the cable subscribers in its audience would hardly justify the time and expense of copyright litigation. On the other hand, if this film package were being televised in Philadelphia and delivered to Baltimore, where cable would erode its first-run value before the package could be offered to the television stations in that market, the syndicator's attitude would be entirely different.

The likelihood of damage was increased still further by the fact that no major-market cable system could attract subscribers by simply offering the three networks' program channels they could already receive over the air. Instead, the cable systems would have to augment their service with independent-television-station transmissions from neighboring markets, transmissions loaded with exactly those feature-film and off-network series programs that syndicators were most concerned with protecting from overexposure or premature release.

As 1968 ended, it was clear that the commission's hopes for an early resolution of cable's competitive challenge through private industry controls would not be realized. Congressional efforts to revise the old copyright act were still in the hearing stage; and the Supreme Court had just decided that, under the old act, not even the actual copyright owner could prevent unauthorized cable usage of copyrighted television programming after its transmission by a television station.[14] At the same time, the Court, in another opinion, affirmed the authority of the FCC to control cable-TV practices that might erode the capacity of broadcast stations to provide public interest program services.[15]

During the next four years, the agency dedicated itself to the thankless task of trying to work out some accommodation between broadcasting and cable in terms of television signal carriage and operation in major market areas. Its first effort, a rule requiring all cable systems with more than 3500 subscribers to *cablecast*, or originate its own programming on one system channel, was eventually suspended when system owners simply ignored it.[16] Learning from this experience, the agency attempted to impose no more programming requirements on cable operators until it was prepared, in 1972, to launch its full regulatory program for cable operation.

It was difficult for the commission to impose rules on cable systems, because the agency did not license cable operations. There was a serious legal question as to whether or not the FCC had the authority to license an electronic medium not requiring broadcast spectrum access in order to operate. In any case the administrative burden of adding the licensing of more than 2000 cable systems to its existing workload discouraged even considering this possibility.

Lacking the capacity to exert pressure on a cable system through the threat of a hearing or the imposition of a forfeiture, the agency's only option was to deny a cable system the right to carry broadcast signals and, if necessary, to enforce this denial through a federal court order. However, since the effect of this order would be to deny the system's subscribers any of those services for which they had paid, it was an action the commission was reluctant to take. This clearly foreshadowed the difficulty the agency would face in regulating any subscriber-supported delivery system such as MMDS or DBS in the future and has been one factor motivating the FCC to avoid such problems through deregulation.

In 1970 the commission enacted regulations prohibiting the network ownership or co-located television-station ownership of cable systems. In March 1972 the commission was finally ready to adopt the elaborate set of cable rules it had been promising to complete since 1965.[17] In essence, the major competitive effect of these rules was to allow cable systems to operate in all but the largest 50 broadcast markets in the United States. This dividing up of the spoils, achieved when the Office of Telecommunications Policy worked out this compromise between the NAB and NCTA in November 1971, protected 75 percent of all television households in the largest 50 markets from cable competition and granted cable the right to enter markets 51 to 100 to reach the 15 percent of all television homes located within these markets' boundaries.

After Congress finally managed to pass a new copyright act in 1976, the FCC reduced and eventually abolished these restrictions on major market television signal importation and was at last able to extricate itself from its role of defender of broadcast interests. Ironically, the cable industry's right to distribute feature films, series, and other syndicated programming under the Copyright Act of 1976 was not based on the freely competitive marketplace bargaining that this industry had so vigorously advocated when it was fighting FCC restraints on its use of broadcast signals in the past. Instead, the cable industry gained a *compulsory license* provision in the act. This provision required syndicators to allow cable carriage of their programs and thereby denied syndicators any right to bargain freely with cable operators in order to obtain reasonable payment for the material cable used.[18]

Equally ironic, perhaps, was the FCC's decision to determine the extent of cable-TV regulatory requirements on the basis of the particular broadcast market in which the cable system was located, after decades of defining all electronic media rights and responsibilities solely in terms of local or community-oriented service. The *broadcast market* had no political or legal dimensions. The term was simply the creation of a commercial survey organization concerned only with allocating communities among television's coverage areas for advertising purposes. As a result, each of the top 50 markets would contain literally hundreds of different urban, suburban, and even rural communities, all of which had vastly divergent types of communication needs. In establishing its uniform federal franchising standards for the first locally regulated electronic medium, however, the commission totally disregarded these local distinctions and insisted on the same access, educational, and governmental requirements for any metropolitan area or hamlet that happened to be within the same television advertising area.

The Cable TV Bureau within the FCC soon came to be as sympathetic to the needs of its constituent industry as the Broadcast Bureau had been to the television stations threatened by cable. This rivalry had become somewhat less intense through the years, as broadcast-group ownership of cable systems continued to increase. By 1972, for example, one-third of all cable subscribers were served by broadcast-group–owned systems. This situation made narrowly partisan NAB or NCTA industry positions virtually impossible to maintain.[19] Instead, the Cable-TV Bureau directed its energy toward imposing as much uniformity as possible on state and local cable regulation and edged as close to de facto preemption of that authority as it dared under its regulatory mandate.

However, discouraging local control and orientation, freeing cable from a wide range of signal-importation restraints, and even granting cable, through compulsory licensing, the absolute right to use syndicated programming materials were not enough to stimulate the growth that in 1972 had been predicted for the industry. Instead, it would be another seemingly unrelated FCC communications common carrier decision that would ultimately trigger the cable industry's explosive growth during the 1980s.[20]

Patterns of Competition and Protection

Broadcasting in the United States has always been more of a delivery system for, rather than a producer of, mass entertainment. It has turned, wherever possible, to the press, the film industry, and the music industry for its content and produced only what it has been unable to purchase at a reasonable price. The broadcast industry's experiences during the ASCAP and "press war" negotiations illustrated the value of negotiating collectively to gain maximum benefits from the industries on which it depended. The broadcast networks used these same tactics when they dealt with their affiliate stations and with their Hollywood film producers.

Public policies favoring diversity would have reduced the single advantage stations held in relation to their music suppliers and that networks held in relation to their affiliates and producers — the power to provide access to larger audiences than any other media could attract and to revenues that such exposure could produce. Stations, as local outlets, and networks, as national distributors, realized that they operated most efficiently by using their single delivery channel to schedule the most attractive programming those who specialized in its production could produce. Trying to compel a local station to risk alienating its audience by scheduling its own locally produced programming seems almost as unrealistic as asking a theater owner to devote his precious screen time to a week of home movies. Similarly, trying, through policy pronouncements, to convince a network to reduce its hold on its affiliate stations is tantamount to having asked Paramount or MGM, in the days of "Hollywood," to reduce their studio production so that their theaters could devote a month per year to feature films from their independent competitors.

Thus, it is easy to understand why public policies designed to encourage the providing of a broader range of program alternatives for broadcast audiences were not simply minor irritations. These policies were actually major challenges to the financial integrity of an industry dependent for its profits on limiting those choices both to keep programming competition from driving production costs up and to keep the massive audience base necessary to support this system from being eroded. Under these circumstances, the hostility of the broadcast industry to cable TV is easy to understand. Cable simply took the programming that broadcasting had commissioned and for which it had paid and used it without concern for the market advertising structure that broadcasting had constructed to allocate advertising revenues among the stations in each market.[21] For a decade, cable was able to exploit the NAB's insensitivity to the economic threat cable posed to smaller-market television; but in the mid-1960s, when cable moved inexorably toward the most profitable broadcast markets, that threat could no longer be tolerated.

The cable systems represented a threat, not simply to the economic vitality of the broadcast industry, but also to the carefully designed local-television allocation plan that the FCC had labored so diligently to attain. In reality, the cable systems were simply a by-product of the commission's failure to sense the level of public demand for a full range of network television programming, but through their function the cable systems diminished the audience base that the agency hoped would eventually support a local television station in many of America's smaller markets.

When broadcasting was unable, either through its private policy or its use of public law, to limit cable's usage of its programming, the commission saw no alternative but to use the same communication common carrier process that had given cable its competitive advantage to deny it that advantage. The action was one of pure protectionism, but the agency could argue that it did not diminish the degree of diversity in American electronic mass media service, because cable offered virtually no programming of its own to augment the broadcast services it delivered. It was, in fact, a far more derivative medium than broadcasting because it offered no significant local service and did not even finance the production of the programming it did carry.

Why was cable TV, as the first system or spectrum of channels, incapable of filling some of its unused channels with additional communication services that could only increase its attractiveness to potential subscribers? Even though the typical system of the 1960s had only a 6- to 12-channel capacity, both post-1965 FCC rules and basic signal-importation costs limited most facilities to only four or five channels of broadcast programming. Although the cable operator, unlike the broadcast station manager, did not have to displace a popular revenue-generating show in order to offer the public other features, why was there no significant trend toward using this unique capacity to diversify viewer options? In other words, with no financial stake in any of the channels being delivered, why weren't cable operators motivated to expand subscribership by offering the marketplace of competing features they had the technical ability to offer? Perhaps it was because most cable operators, as most broadcast station managers before them, had no intimate knowledge of mass entertainment and saw themselves, not as showmen, but simply as marketers of the others' product. In that case, then, diversity would have had no relationship to the number of channels available for delivery of programming but only to the number of different national programming sources each marketer could feasibly provide for the local audience being served.

In any case, the emergence of cable foreshadowed the difficulties the FCC would have in adapting its policies so that they would operate without the support of its licensing process. Cable TV, as the first private, nonspectrum delivery system, could be reached only through a narrow channel of broadcast related jurisdiction. From this point on, the agency would never have the ability to adopt and enforce a policy uniformly across all areas of electronic mass media services. This, perhaps, more than any other single factor, created the conditions that would lead to the deregulatory era of the 1970s.

Notes

1. For a more detailed discussion of these negotiations, see Christopher H. Sterling and John M. Kittross, *Stay Tuned: A Concise History of American Broadcasting* (Belmont, Calif.: Wadsworth, 1978), 131–32, 193–94. For a discussion of recent development in the music-licensing field, see Chapter 8.
2. For the details of this Biltmore Agreement, see Frank J. Kahn ed., *Documents of American Broadcasting*, 4th ed. (Englewood Cliffs, N.J.: Prentice-Hall, 1984), 101–5.
3. FCC rules CFR 47. 3.101–3.108.
4. 23 FCC 2d 382 (1970); modified by 44 FCC 2d 1081; further modified by FCC 2d 829.
5. The FCC rule is at 47 CFR 73.658 (j); for details of these settlements, see "NBC Breaks Ranks; Settles with Justice," *Broadcasting*, 22 Nov. 1976, 21; "CBS Settles with Justice," *Broadcasting*, 12 May 1980, 29; "It's Settled; ABC, Justice Come to Terms," *Broadcasting*, 25 Aug. 1980, 31. See also the commission's deliberations regarding network-program-procurement practices, 62 FCC 2d 548 (1977).
6. "Notice of Proposed Rulemaking in BC Docket 21409," 47 Fed. Reg. 32959 (30 June 1982).
7. FCC 54–58; In the Matter of J.E. Belnap. For a discussion of the impact of this decision on cable-TV development in the 1950s, see Don R. Le Duc's *Cable Television and the FCC* (Philadelphia: Temple University Press, 1973), 74–76.
8. For a decision to this effect, see *Intermountain Broadcasting v. Idaho Microwave*, 196 F.2d 315 (D.C. Idaho, 1961).
9. For a more complete discussion of this situation, see Le Duc, *Cable Television and the FCC*, 82–113.
10. "In the Matter of Inquiring into Impact of CATV...upon the Orderly

Development of Television Broadcasting," Docket 12443, 18 RR 1573 (1959).

11. In *CableVision v. KUTV*, 335 F.2d 348 (9th Cir. 1964), the most elaborate effort of broadcasters to formulate a right of control over their broadcast transmissions was rejected by a federal court that observed that only the copyright owner of the programming could exert such control.

12. *Carter Mt. Transmission v. FCC*, 321 F.2d 359 (D.C. Cir. 1963); cert. den. 375 U.S. 951 (1964). Cf, Le Duc, *Cable Television and the FCC*, 121–23.

13. "First Report and Order on Dockets 14895 and 15233," 4 RR2d 1677 (1965); "Proposed Rulemaking in Docket 15971," 1 FCC 2d 463 (1965) in which the "temporary" freeze was adopted.

14. *Fortnightly v. United Artists*, 392 U.S. 390 (1968).

15. *United States v. Southwestern Cable*, 392 U.S. 157 (1968).

16. "First Report and Order on Docket 18397," 17 RR2d 1570, (1969).

17. "Second Report and Order on Docket 18397," 19 RR2d 1775 (1971); "Third Report and Order on Docket 18397," 24 RR2d 1501 (1972).

18. Title 17, United States Code, "Copyright Act of 1909" was rescinded and replaced by Public Law 94–553, 94th Stat. 2541 (1976).

19. Christopher H. Sterling, *Electronic Media: A Guide to Trends in Broadcasting and the Newer Technologies 1920–1983* (New York: Praeger, 1984) 70.

20. From 1972 to 1980, the annual growth rate in the percentage of all TV homes that were cable served never increased more than 2 percent per year. From 1980 onward the increase has been at the rate of 5 percent per year.

21. Sterling, *Electronic Media*, 21. In reality the competitive damage of cable was minimized by the fact that rating services during this era assumed that every television household within a market was viewing programming from the local affiliate and ignored cable viewing in their reports to advertisers.

Tracing the Patterns: Primary Sources

To talk of broadcast programming is somewhat misleading because both radio and television content have been provided primarily by a mass-entertainment industry commissioned by the networks to provide its most popular material. As Thomas A. Delong indicates in his *The Mighty Music Box: The Golden Age of Musical Radio* (Los Angeles: Amber Crest Books, 1980), it was radio that popularized particular melodies, lyrics, and groups during the 1930s and 1940s, as it was music that provided broadcasting with its strongest audience appeal. David McFarland's *The Development of the Top 40 Radio Format* (New York: Arno Press, 1979) reveals how a more focused radio service during the era of television not only created specific audiences, but also shaped demand for particular musical selections. Carried still further, Clive Davis's *Clive: Inside the Record Business* (New York: Ballantine Books, 1976) reflects the awesome influence that making the radio-station playlist exerts on the music business's every creative element, from the selection of the works to be recorded to the most minute detail of their eventual production.

The same type of relationship began to exist between television and the film industry after the broadcast networks supplanted Hollywood as the primary vehicle for mass entertainment during the 1950s. As Fredric Stuart describes the process in his *The Effects of Television Upon the Motion Picture and Radio Industries* (New York: Arno Press, 1976), television transformed both of its competitors into more specialized mass-cultural channels and offered film, not only a secondary market for its major features, but more significantly, production revenues for television-series programming that allowed its major studies to survive. By the late 1960s, this system became a fully developed structure completely dependent on the networks for financing and distribution, as described in an Arthur D. Little report, *Television Program Production, Procurement, Distribution and Scheduling* (Cambridge, Mass.: Arthur D. Little, Inc., 1969).

However, the derivative nature of television's programming power made the medium vulnerable to the competitive challenge of other distribution systems equally capable of offering the same features to their audiences. Initially it was the individual television station that found itself without property rights to assert against CATV systems appropriating its transmissions, but as this author has indicated in *Cable Television and the FCC: A Crisis in Media Control* (Philadelphia: Temple University Press, 1973), even the networks themselves were eventually forced to turn to the FCC for protection that their own existing legal rights in such commissioned programming did not provide. In this way, then, the commission was compelled to become involved in a controversy it had sought desperately to avoid, a controversy that would ultimately destroy its bargaining position with the broadcast industry as it demolished its reputation as a protector of the public interest.

In the last analysis, however, it is quite possible that the most significant portion of this chapter remains to be written. The television industry, for so long reliant on its dominant electronic mass media distribution position in dealings with the mass-entertainment entities, must now compete for the first time for services its three networks have always counted on as being theirs alone to commission and purchase.

CHAPTER SIX

NEW MEDIA — OLD MESSAGES

The New Networks

The FCC's Common Carrier Bureau began stimulating competition in the communication field long before it became fashionable to do so throughout the federal government. In 1959 the bureau decided to authorize communication carriers other than Bell or Western Union to provide private point-to-point microwave network service.[1] In 1968 the bureau crossed another traditional threshold by ordering Bell and AT&T to allow customer-supplied equipment to be connected to their communication networks.[2] It was the third in this series of marketplace-oriented decisions, however, that would have the most important consequences for electronic mass media in the United States.

In 1962 Congress passed the Communications Satellite Act, which created a public corporation, Comsat, with exclusive rights to operate the American segment of Intelsat, the international satellite network contemplated by this legislation. In 1965 the American Broadcasting Company applied to the FCC for permission to launch and operate a domestic satellite to interconnect its 268 network affiliate stations for the relay of its network-television programming. At the time ABC was paying nearly $12 million a year to AT&T for these interconnection services and estimated that it could save $5 million a year by operating its own system.[3]

Even though the FCC eventually rejected this proposal, it caused the commission to begin considering policies for establishing a domestic-satellite service. For several years, the commission struggled with the questions of whether Comsat, because of its unique position in American satellite development, should be granted exclusive authority to operate domestic satellites or whether competition among rival domestic systems might better serve the public.

In June 1972, by a 4 to 3 vote, the commission adopted what it termed an *open skies* policy for domestic satellites. The policy permitted entry into this field by any organization meeting certain basic qualifications.[4] In doing so, the FCC tried to balance the competitive positions of the applicants by limiting AT&T usage of satellite facilities and by refusing to approve a joint Comsat-AT&T satellite proposal in part because of AT&T's ownership of almost 30 percent of Comsat stock. Rehearings and litigation delayed the launching of the domestic-satellite systems; but in April 1974, Western Union's Westar I began the domestic-satellite era in the United States. Soon afterward, RCA's Americom was launched; and pay-TV, whose "advent" had been heralded with monotonous regularity for more than a quarter-century, finally arrived.

In 1951 Zenith, the television set manufacturer, started an experimental pay-TV system in Chicago called Phonevision. An estimated 300 families were linked by telephone lines that unscrambled the transmission of feature films they ordered. Soon afterward, another pay-TV organization, Skiatron, tested its Subscriber-Vision in New York, while a third organization, Telemeter, conducted tests in California. At the request of these groups, the FCC held hearings in 1955 to consider licensing such stations on a regular basis. In 1957 the commission instead authorized further tests, then postponed this authorization in the face of congressional opposition, and finally reissued the authorization on a more limited basis in 1959.

During this era, a cable system in Bartlesville, Oklahoma, began offering pay-TV service to approximately 800 subscribers. This provided an excellent opportunity to determine the financial viability of pay-TV without need of FCC approval. Within a few months, the system was losing $10,000 a month. This loss proved to those looking for such proof that the American public would never pay to watch television when they received so much entertainment from it free of charge.

The next, and for a decade the last, episode in this continuing saga of pay-TV failures occurred in 1964, in California, where Subscription Television, a corporate entity with more than $25 million available in risk capital, built cable delivery systems in Los Angeles and San Francisco for pay-TV service. Film industry and other antipay-TV groups in California were able to pass a referendum declaring pay-TV an illegal activity; and before the California Supreme Court could declare this action unconstitutional, Subscription TV was in receivership.

When Home Box Office (HBO), a subsidiary of Time-Life, leased channel space on RCA's Americom domestic satellite for pay-TV distribution to cable systems in 1975, it changed the fortunes of that service in the United States. HBO had been in the pay-TV business since 1972 and served a number of microwave-linked cable-TV systems in the Northeast. What distinguished this new approach from all previous pay-TV efforts was simply a matter of scale of distribution. By creating a nationwide audience for a single pay-TV service, HBO was able to generate the massive amount of revenues necessary to gain rights to major motion pictures on a regular basis.

Most previous pay-TV efforts required those who intended to offer the service to allocate a substantial portion of their revenues to the construction and operation of facilities to deliver the films to each subscriber home and to bill and collect for their usage. HBO avoided much of this expense by offering cable-TV operators an opportunity to earn revenues from a vacant channel on their system to be devoted to the delivery of this service. Depending on the amount of collection work the system owner was willing to do, HBO began by offering to share pay-TV subscriber revenues with the operator on a 50-50 or 60-40 basis and to provide each operator with promotional material to launch the service.[5]

At the other end of the process, HBO leased a satellite transponder in a competitive environment, rather than using AT&T long-line networks for national distribution. Thus, HBO gained great flexibility in connecting new systems simply at the cost of a receiving dish and reduced its actual operating expenses by more than 50 percent annually.[6]

When HBO began operation in 1975, only 75 of the nation's 3500 cable systems carried pay-TV programming. By the end of 1976, this number had increased to 364 systems as subscriber homes grew from 260,000 to almost 1 million.[7] Although its first major rival, Viacom's Showtime, began operation in 1978, HBO remained the dominant entity in the pay-cable field into the 1980s and still serves about 70 percent of all cable-delivered pay-TV subscribers.

Because of its dominant position, HBO could not only obtain rights to almost any feature film it wanted for release but could also virtually dictate its terms for their release. To challenge this dominance, four major motion picture distributors — Columbia Pictures, MCA, Paramount, and Twentieth Century-Fox — with the financial backing of Getty Oil, formed Premiere, a competing cable-delivered pay-TV service. The four companies agreed to release all feature films for exclusive use to Premiere at least nine months before licensing them to any other pay-TV service. The U.S. Justice Department intervened and contended that this arrangement would constitute an illegal constraint on pay-TV competition. In December 1980 a federal court granted the Justice Department the injunction it sought, denying Premiere the right to begin operations until the anticompetitive constraint issue could be resolved through trial.[8] Soon afterward, Premiere was dissolved because the delay in beginning operation created a greater drain on its founders' investment than they were willing to accept.

In 1977 Home Box Office was also victorious in its challenge of FCC rules that restricted pay-TV programming in order to protect broadcasting from its competitive pressure. In 1968 the commission established rules for the operation of subscription television (STV) services, or over-the-air transmissions of pay-TV programming, and denied these services the right to compete with broadcasters for sporting events recently shown on free-TV or 3- to 10-year-old feature films that formed the major portion of broadcast network movie packages. The following year the FCC applied these same content restrictions to cable-delivered pay-TV programming, and it was from this action that HBO appealed to the federal courts.[9]

The court of appeals overturned the commission's cable pay-TV rules and declared that neither its efforts to diversify mass media service by creating a differently oriented pay-TV program channel nor its concern that pay-TV might siphon away free-TV's most popular features justified the FCC's imposing content limitations on a system not requiring the broadcast spectrum to deliver its programming. Even though this decision allowed the agency to continue to control STV program content, the FCC rescinded most of these regulations in 1977 and completed its release the following year.[10]

The same relatively low-cost national satellite distribution and local cable-TV channel outlet system that was put together so successfully by HBO soon became a channel for other types of program service as well. In 1976 Ted Turner, owner of a small UHF station in Atlanta, began offering his station to cable systems throughout the nation. The systems could carry his station on one of their channels and would be charged only a few cents per system subscriber per month for the satellite relay of its signal to their head ends. Turner, whose ownership of the Atlanta Braves baseball team and part ownership in the Atlanta Hawks basketball team allowed him to offer professional sports as well as the usual assortment of older syndicated material, generated his revenues through the higher advertising rate he could charge sponsors for his vastly expanded national audience in the United States. By the mid-1980s, his basic, or free, service was reaching more than 12.5 million American homes, or roughly one-sixth of all television homes.

In 1977 USA, the first advertising-supported cable-TV network, began operation. It was seeking, at least initially, to cover its costs and generate profits solely on the basis of the commercials it could place in this programming. Although cable operators received no payment from these advertising-supported channels, and in most cases now pay a monthly fee per subscriber for the privilege of carriage, the benefit the operators received from acting as local outlets for such programming was in the larger number of subscribers attracted by the exclusive non-broadcast features.

Additional satellite-linked services were being announced with monotonous regularity from 1977 to the early 1980s. Although many of them never progressed beyond their original promotional handouts, services such as Christian Broadcasting Network (CBN, 1977), Entertainment and Sports Network (ESPN, 1979), and Cable Satellite Public Affairs Network (C-SPAN, 1979) were among the basic, or nonpay, services that emerged and survived through this period.

One particular cable service launched in 1980 deserves special mention. Ted Turner offered to cable systems Cable News Network (CNN), an around-the-clock, $3-million-a-month news, features, sports, and weather channel financed initially only by advertising revenues. When Group W and ABC joined together in 1982 to offer cable systems two channels of news and headline news service, Turner countered by offering a headline service of his own, CNN-2. The Westinghouse-ABC venture lasted only a few months. When Turner took over the rival operation to leave himself without competition in the field, he suddenly instituted a cable system subscriber fee to recover the costs he had sustained during this competitive era.

In late 1979 the FCC repealed its rules requiring rigid technical specifications and a license for the operation of a satellite-antenna system. As a result, the price of such an installation immediately dropped from $100,000 to $30,000 and later dropped another 50 percent.[11] This price reduction soon increased the number of cable systems capable of receiving satellite programming and led to more than 30 different satellite-delivered services being available to cable operators by the end of 1981.[12]

Unfortunately these services needed more than a cable system equipped with an antenna dish to reach cable audiences. The few domestic satellites devoted to cable-delivered services were soon fully booked, and regular satellites would not effectively substitute for the "cable birds" because the inexpensive cable satellite antennas could not be realigned effectively to receive their transmissions. An even greater restriction, however, was imposed by the limited channel capacity of the average cable system. As late as 1981, more than 60 percent of these systems had no more than a 12-channel delivery capacity, a capacity reduced still further by franchise and FCC must-carry requirements.[13]

Although cable TV was the first to benefit from the greatly reduced costs of national satellite networking, broadcast stations themselves began to use these alternative networks to their advantage during the 1980s. At the end of 1979, only 50 stations were accessible to satellite through earth stations located on or near their premises.[14] Three years later that number had grown to 600. All three television networks are already in the process of converting fully to satellite interconnection, and NBC's Ku (high-power, high-frequency) band system is already in operation. The satellite has proven to be a mixed blessing for the networks, however. Although it will reduce their distribution costs, it has also given their affiliates more flexibility in refusing to clear network programs in order to carry special features offered by various ad hoc networks. Radio stations also began using satellite-delivered music and news-programming services after the cost of earth stations was reduced in 1979. More than 4000 of the nation's 9000 commercial AM and FM facilities now are served by satellite-delivered programming.[15]

The New Local Outlets

In 1972 the commission's *open-skies* domestic-satellite policy was formulated without any intention of stimulating the growth of electronic mass media services in this nation. In 1980 three FCC *new-technology* policies were formulated with exactly that intention. Only time will tell whether or not the commission's carefully planned strategies will be as successful as the results it has achieved by chance.

Despite the relatively rapid expansion of cable TV in certain portions of the nation, urban cable development lagged far behind earlier projections of its growth. Most major cities remained unwired, thus limiting the diffusion of the numerous programming services offered by satellite. To end this bottleneck, the FCC began deliberations in 1980 to authorize three new types of mass media delivery techniques: low-power television (LPTV); multichannel multipoint distribution services (MMDS); and direct broadcast satellite (DBS).

Initially, the commission's proposal for LPTV suggested that its role would be primarily that of a local-access channel for areas without cable service. The FCC proposed that LPTV stations, granted the right to operate on extremely low power and using an existing VHF or UHF channel in such a way as to cause no interference, would be limited to one per applicant and that preference would be given to minority and noncommercial interests.[16] By March 1982 the commission had radically revised the orientation of LPTV stations, allowing multiple ownership, and interconnection of stations in different markets and imposing no programming requirements on these facilities.[17] Changing the orientation of the 4000 new stations suddenly made them very attractive, particularly to those seeking an inexpensive means of operating an over-the-air or subscription pay-TV outlet. Unfortunately the commission could not foresee just how attractive LPTV licenses would be, and it soon faced a backlog of more than 32,000 applications. After having begun processing in September 1983, the agency is now issuing, using a lottery technique, about 250 applications per month.

For many years 32 channels in the 2500- to 2690-megahertz

microwave band were allocated by the FCC for Instructional Television Fixed Service (ITFS), a short-range relay service used by schools for educational-program interconnection. In 1980 the FCC began a real-location proceeding and proposed to divide this largely unused spectrum space among multipoint distribution and operational fixed service (OFS) users as well.[18] The OFS was to be used primarily for digital data transmission, although multipoint was already being used to a limited extent to relay pay-TV programming to reception stations in large apartment complexes. Microband of America submitted a *wireless-cable* proposal to the commission as a part of this proceeding. The proposal requested that the two channels for multipoint distribution in the nation's largest 50 markets be increased in number so that an operator could offer a full spectrum of television services, particularly in urban areas where cable systems had not yet been constructed.

Eventually the commission decided to create two four-channel multichannel multipoint distribution services (MMDS) per major market, grandfathering all existing ITFS license assignments. After receiving 16,499 applications for the new MMDS four-channel licenses, the FCC instituted a lottery process for their award. At the same time, the agency authorized ITFS licensees to lease their excess channel capacity to others for profit. As a result, a successful wireless-cable–license applicant could actually operate a system with more than four channels and could lease additional unused licensed ITFS frequency space to augment service.[19]

The cable industry has bitterly opposed this agency action, charging that MMDS will "skim the cream" from major urban areas that cable systems are planning to wire by diverting the most profitable aspect of operation, pay-TV revenues, to corporations not bound by a franchise contract to offer cable's full range of service. However, just to be on the safe side, a number of cable organizations — United Cable, Cox Cable, Warner-Amex Cable, and Daniels and Associates — have all filed their own MMDS applications. At the moment, other than the leisurely pace of the FCC's licensing process, the only factor inhibiting MMDS's growth is the relatively high cost of individual reception equipment, which is necessary if operators hope to extend their subscriber base beyond large apartment and condominium complexes.

In 1979 Satellite Television Corporation, a subsidiary of Comsat, announced its plan to launch a direct broadcast satellite (DBS) to provide three channels of pay-TV service to the eastern United States. This plan is the first segment of a long-term, six-channel system of service for the entire United States. In response to this proposal and a general concern that America lagged behind Canada, Western Europe, and Japan in the development of DBS service, the commission began a proceeding to establish regulatory policies for this new medium in October 1980.

In April 1981 the commission requested applications to provide DBS service and, in October 1981, accepted the applications of CBS, Inc.; Direct Broadcast Satellite Corporation; Graphic Scanning Corporation; RCA American Communications, Inc.; United States Satellite Broadcasting; Video Satellite Systems; Western Union Telegraph Company; and Focus Broadcast Satellite Company.[20] CBS asked the commission to consider a proposal to allocate at least a portion of the 12.2- to 12.7-gigahertz spectrum channel space for high-definition television usage (HDTV). The agency refused, however, which indicated once again that it would let the marketplace set all technical standards for the service including the choice of how the channels assigned to each applicant would be used.

As in the case of LPTV, no restrictions were placed on ownership of either channels or entire systems, no program requirements were established, and no public-access obligations were imposed on the applicants. The only expectation was that each applicant would begin construction of a satellite system within one year from issuance of a construction permit.

In this area the actual authority of the FCC to assign frequencies and orbital slots for these systems depended on the outcome of a Regional Administrative Radio Conference (RARC) in which the United States would have to negotiate with 32 other nations of Region II (North and South America) for its domestic allocations. This conference, held in June 1983, resulted in the United States receiving the eight orbital slots it had sought. However, because their positions are not the optimum ones originally requested, only five are fully usable for coverage of the continental United States. In addition, although the United States had hoped for 36 television channels per satellite allocation, the regional agreement only provided 32 channels per satellite.

For the moment, however, obtaining sufficient channel and orbital space is the least of DBS's problems. After pioneering in this field for more than five years, Comsat's STV pulled out of the DBS business in November 1984. Two other organizations not among the original applicants had already abandoned their efforts to enter the field before the cumbersome DBS award process was completed. Rupert Murdoch, the Australian media entrepreneur, planned in 1983 to begin Skyband, a five-channel service to be delivered through an existing fixed-service satellite (FSS) system; but Murdoch ended this planning six months later, citing the need for a more powerful satellite to reduce the costs of household reception devices. Another operator, United States Communications Inc., also using a lower power FSS satellite for its system, ended in receivership after operating for more than a year in the north-eastern region of the nation.

In 1986, Hubbard Broadcasting's United States Satellite Broad-casting, Direct Broadcast Satellite, and Dominion Video Satellite are the only remaining applicants from the original FCC DBS licensing process. However, in March 1984 the commission approved four new applications and established procedures for a third round of applications in 1986.

While DBS investors proceed cautiously and await the low-cost home-dish-antenna conversion equipment and the innovative pro-gramming concepts needed to recoup start-up expenses estimated to run from $150 to $200 million, others have begun to look to an estimated 1 million households that already have an antenna dish in their backyard as the most promising satellite audience to serve at this time. The FCC's decision to end its satellite-antenna licensing process in 1979 had an impact not only on broadcast stations and cable systems but also on families dissatisfied with available broadcast or cable service in their area.

Electronic-equipment manufacturers lost no time in developing this new market and pointed out to prospective purchasers that they could have the same wide selection of program sources as the commercial broadcast or cable system simply by aiming their large dish antennas at one of the low-powered domestic satellites providing these services. In passing the Cable Communications Policy Act of 1984, Congress legalized this household reception but at the same time recognized the right of these program sources to scramble or encrypt their signals in order to charge for their reception.[21]

At the beginning of 1986, HBO became the first satellite-delivered service to encrypt its transmissions. The home-satellite lobbying organi-zation, SPACE, worked effectively to make the task as difficult as pos-sible; but the results of HBO's four-year, $15-million effort to locate, purchase, and market a scrambling system that could overcome all legal and political objections blazed a trail that others (such as Showtime, the Movie Channel, the Disney Channel, ESPN, USA, MTV, Nickelodeon, CNN, and CNN Headline News and superstations WGN and WOR) all intended to follow.

Initially, the Justice Department, at the urging of SPACE, indicated that it might consider the potential anticompetitive implications of any scrambling efforts that compelled the home-satellite owner to buy a number of different unscrambling devices in order to receive signals being encrypted in different ways. After a year of negotiation, nearly all the satellite-delivered services have agreed on the M/A Com Videocipher I, a unit with a list price of approximately $400, as the single decrypter that will be capable of unscrambling all encrypted transmissions.

In addition, both Congress and the Justice Department expressed concerns about scrambling signals before the individual satellite owner has the opportunity to obtain the equipment necessary for their proper reception. For this reason, HBO delayed its move until it was certain that an adequate supply of decrypters was on the market as well as available from the local cable-TV operator, who could lease them to satellite owners in the surrounding area. HBO launched its service with a $19.95 monthly fee for the HBO-Cinemax package or $12.95 for HBO alone. The owner of the decrypting device can pay HBO directly or deal with the local cable-TV owner authorized by HBO to collect the proceeds for the pay-TV service. SPACE contends that as other services join HBO in this marketing effort, each satellite-served household may face the prospect of paying hundreds of dollars monthly for something it has already invested $700 to $2000 to receive free of charge; however, it is highly unlikely that this will occur. A far more realistic projection, based on the economies of scale in administering the system once dozens of program suppliers are involved in this operation, is that generous packages of channels will be offered for monthly rental at price not substantially higher than that now being charged by HBO. As these program suppliers have indicated, their primary concern is not to deny the individual household access to their services but to compel hotels, motels, and others who use these services without payment to compensate program suppliers for their use. In the long run, the threat that scrambled pay-TV satellite-delivered channels pose does not appear to exist for those who have invested in home-satellite reception devices; rather it exists for those who have invested in cable-TV systems or who are involved in the development of DBS systems. Cable operators have reason to fear that high-rise apartments within their franchise area might opt for direct-satellite delivery instead of cable subscribership; while DBS developers realize that every home served by a low-power satellite relay system is one less subscriber they so desperately need to underwrite their massive start-up costs.

Yet, even if the FCC were to believe that one type of delivery system should be restrained to allow another to develop more fully, its ability to do so has been seriously eroded by the emergence of the VCR, over which it has no jurisdictional control. As of mid-1985, it was estimated that 18 to 20 million American households already had VCRs and that they had a projected growth rate of 10 percent per year.[22] Under these conditions, any effort by the Commission to shape the characteristics of future delivery systems through constraints will more likely increase the demand for VCRs and their software than stimulate audience support for the system that the agency favors.

The Meanings of *Marketplace*

During the past decade, new national domestic-satellite–linked, low-cost earth station networks have stimulated a surge of new electronic mass media services. The pay-TV packagers of Hollywood feature films were soon followed by the superstations with their nationally viewed local baseball, basketball, and feature-film schedules. The superstations were followed by the specialized sports, music, and news services that eventually overburdened the capacity of the local-delivery circuits necessary to offer the services to the public. This encouraged the FCC to authorize new techniques to augment local-delivery capacity, creating opportunities for LPTV, MMDS, DBS, and quasi-DBS operators to compete with broadcast stations and cable systems in providing this service.[23] With so much activity, it is certainly true that the American television audience has a broader variety of viewing alternatives at any given hour of the day than were available in even the largest markets during the AT&T-interconnected, affiliate-station-distributed broadcast era.

Even without a VCR, the typical viewer can tune in some form of sports, music, news, or feature-film entertainment at virtually any time and is limited in choice only by the degree of access that the household's cable system or backyard antenna provides to various program-service relay satellites. Although the number of national services seems to vary from week to week, there are now at least 45 of them; and they range in orientation from religious programming to soft-core pornography.

Does this mean, then, that we have created or are in the process of creating a diverse, truly competitive electronic mass media marketplace with the capacity and the willingness to respond to every major societal communication need? Or stated another way, can we rely on the sheer number of different programming services available in themselves to guarantee the breadth, balance, and independence of the process that shapes every value our society shares?

Among these 40-some services that have emerged during the past decade are several unique ones such as C-SPAN, the Cable News Network, and, to a lesser extent, Nickelodeon and the Arts and Entertainment channel. These services have certainly augmented the limited programming choices available to viewers during the broadcast era. On the other hand, it would seem fair to describe a substantial number of these services as simply delivering the same syndicated series, game shows, or feature-film packages at different times of the day. It is only equally fair to point out, of course, that most of these services are under-capitalized, have inadequate local dissemination, and are still in the process of finding a format to survive in an area without guidelines of experience.

Yet, one trend is already discernible in this field and becomes clearer with each passing year. The great expansion in electronic mass media delivery capacity has not stimulated the production of a correspondingly greater amount of mass-entertainment material to fill the channels. Reacting to this situation, major pay-TV organizations such as HBO and Showtime have attempted to produce their own feature films and major entertainment specials but have had results as discouraging as those the broadcast networks experienced a decade ago with their own feature-film productions.[24]

Why has the mass-entertainment industry failed to respond thus far to the extensive new distribution opportunities that national electronic mass media channels have been offering them for the past decade? Such response is essential, of course, if the hope of a marketplace is ultimately to be realized. Diversity must be based on the breadth of material from which a viewer may select, not simply on the number of different channels on which the same material may be seen.

To gain a clearer understanding of whether this is only the temporary reaction of an industry uncertain of its role in this new field or an ingrained pattern of operation unlikely to be altered by time, it is important to examine in some detail the area generally overlooked by electronic mass media studies — the structures and private policies of the American mass-entertainment industry.

Notes

1. "Allocation of Frequencies in the Bands Above 890 MHz," 27 FCC 359 (1959).
2. 13 FCC 2d 4201 rehearing denied 14 FCC 2d 571 (1968).
3. As quoted in 31 FR 3507 (2 Mar. 1966).
4. "Domestic Communication Satellite Facilities," 35 FCC 2d 844 (1972); *Network Project v. FCC*, 511 F.2d 786 (D.C. Cir. 1975).
5. "After Ten Years of Satellites: The Sky's No Limit," *Broadcasting*, 9 April 1984, 123.
6. Paul Kagan and Associates, *The Pay TV Newsletter*, 15 July 1981, 1.
7. Christopher Sterling, *Electronic Media: A Guide to Trends in Broadcasting and the Newer Technologies 1920–83* (New York: Praeger, 1984), 58.
8. 1980–81 Trade Cases, 63698.
9. "Fourth Report and Order on Subscription TV," 15 FCC 2d 466 (1968), affirmed in *National Assn. of Theater Owners v. FCC*, 420 F.2d 194 (1969). These same content restraints were imposed on cable-delivered pay-TV in 20 FCC 2d 201 (1969). They were overturned as to cable in *Home Box Office v. FCC*, 434 U.S. 829 (1978). Soon afterward the FCC rescinded these rules for over-the-air pay-TV as well.
10. 41 RR2d 1491 (1979); remaining sporting events and commercial advertising activity restrictions rescinded, 42 RR2d 1207 (1978).

11. 46 RR2d 698 (1979).
12. "They're Free and Clear," *Panorama*, April 1981, 54.
13. Sydney Head, with Christopher Sterling, *Broadcasting in America*, 4th ed. (Boston: Houghton Mifflin, 1982), 296, as derived from material gathered and correlated by Christopher H. Sterling and Timothy R. Haight.
14. "After 10 Years of Satellites," *Broadcasting*, 123.
15. Ibid.
16. "Notice of Proposed Rulemaking in BC Docket 78–258," 82 FCC 2d 47 (1980).
17. "Report and Order in BC Docket 78–253," adopted 4 Mar. 1982, 17 Fed. Reg. 21468.
18. "Notice of Inquiry and Proposed Rulemaking in General Docket 80–122," adopted 19 Mar. 1980, 45 Fed Reg 29323.
19. "Further Notice of Proposed Rulemaking in General Docket 80–122," adopted 12 Oct. 1983, 48 Fed Reg 49309. This, in fact, is already occurring. American Family Theaters has entered into an agreement with George Mason University in Fairfax, Va., for the use of that school's ITFS frequencies.
20. "Notice of Proposed Policy Statement and Rulemaking in General Docket 80–603," adopted 22 Oct. 1981, 88 FCC 2d 100.
21. See 1984 amendments to USCA, Title 47, Sect. 305.
22. Bill Daniels, "Videocasette Sponsorship Seen as VCR Total Rises," *Variety*, 1 May 1985, 437.
23. In addition, of course, the FCC has also been in the process of adding to the number of regular television and broadcast stations through its drop-in proceedings in the UHF and VHF bands, as well as its expansion of low-power FM and daytime-only AM assignments.
24. See, for example, Lawrence Cohn, "Cable Lights Fire Under Made-For Pics; HBO Theatrical Pace Slowing Down," *Variety*, 29 May 1985, 129, 152; "Time Goes Above & Biondo With Ouster of HBO Chief; Paycable's Got Problems," *Variety*, 17 Oct. 1984, 118, describing some of the difficulties that America's largest pay-TV organization has encountered in attempting to produce popular feature films.

Tracing the Patterns: Primary Sources

Peter S. Magnant's *Domestic Satellites: An FCC Giant Step Towards Competitive Telecommunications Policy* (Boulder, Colo.: Westview Press, 1977) discusses the competitive impact of the commission's open-skies policy on services seeking lower cost national interconnection. A recent article, "After Ten Years of Satellites: The Sky's No Limit" (*Broadcasting*, 9 Apr. 1984, 123–30), suggests the breadth of these new satellite-linked services in the field of broadcasting and their equally broad competitive impact on traditional industry programming and marketing strategies.

The most extensive description of the evolution of pay-TV from a marginal, experimental service to a major force in cable-TV economics is contained in the Technology and Economics, Inc., report, *The Emergence of Pay Cable Television* (Washington, D.C.: National Telecommunications and Information Administration, 1980). Over-the-air pay-television was discussed at a time when its prospects seemed far brighter than they do today in Herbert H. Howard and S. L. Carroll's *Subscription Television: History, Current Status and Economic Projections* (Washington, D.C.: National Association of Broadcasters, 1980).

None of the newer local-dissemination systems such as DBS, LPTV, or MMDS have developed to a point where any extensive, book-length discussion of their attributes can be undertaken. There has been detailed trade-press coverage of licensing processes and system proposals from time to time, such as "LPTV" (*Broadcasting*, 23 Feb. 1981, 39–66); but until prospects for their expansion improve, it is doubtful that treatment of functions is likely to become any more extensive in the near future.

As *Broadcasting* magazine points out in its "Where Things Stand" report of 6 Jan. 1986, the "future of DBS is much in doubt these days as DBS forerunners have faltered badly" (p. 130), "while both LPTV and MMDS-license applications remain bogged down in the FCC licensing process" (p. 134).

At the same time, a new breed of independent television stations has emerged since 1980. They have been able, through satellite connection and cable-TV carriage, to transform what was once an unattractive UHF allocation in a small market into a profitable operation. As is noted in "Independent Television: The Good Gets Better" (*Broadcasting*, 6 Jan. 1986, 61–63), the number of independent television stations has grown from 98 in 1979 to 280 at the end of 1985 as independent stations' share of audience viewing during the past decade has expanded from 10 percent of the total television audience to 21 percent of that audience. Thus, it is possible that this modern type of television service, typically with only modest, local production facilities, more modest local-service commitment, and depending largely on nonnetwork sources for its programming and new delivery systems for its coverage, will emerge as the "new" local electronic mass media dissemination system of the 1990s.

CHAPTER SEVEN

THE MASS-ENTERTAINMENT MARKETPLACE

Creating Mass Entertainment

Mass entertainment in the United States may seem at first glance to be the product of a "cottage industry," with hundreds of record companies, film production units, and television-program packagers creating materials for thousands of music stores, motion picture theaters, and broadcast stations across the nation. In reality, however, all of this activity is actually dominated by less than a dozen corporations specializing in the financing and distribution of mass entertainment throughout the world.[1] This small group of corporations collects more than 70 percent of the revenues generated each year by feature film box office receipts, record sales, and television advertising in the United States. This degree of domination is intensified further through cross-media ventures and cross-licensing agreements that tend to keep all subsidiary rights to publishing, theatrical performance, music-video release, and pay-TV usage firmly within their control.[2]

In an attempt to counter this constant tendency toward consolidation, federal broadcast regulation policy, as we have seen, was designed to prevent any owner from gaining control over more than a specific number of radio or television stations. Although only the Justice Department had authority to intervene when mergers of film or music organizations, which resulted in fewer entities, might reduce the level of competition, the FCC, from the beginning, had used its licensing power to restrain this same impulse in broadcasting.

These limitations were so restraining that when the commission relaxed them in 1985, thereby increasing the number of radio, FM, and television stations each licensee could own from seven to 12, a massive surge of acquisitions and mergers burst forth. The result was a record-breaking year of $30 billion in station and allied media purchases.[3] Among the more than 100 separate transactions that each exceeded $10 million, the acquisition of RCA-NBC by General Electric for $6.3 billion, the purchase of ABC by Capital Cities Broadcasting for $3.5 billion, and Rupert Murdoch's takeover of Metromedia for $2 billion captured most public attention. Other, somewhat less glamorous transactions that occurred during this unique year, however, might ultimately have equal, if not greater, long-range implications for media service in the United States.

By offering to purchase MGM for $1.5 billion, for example, Turner Broadcasting obviously hopes to gain, through direct access to the major studio's film library, the type of guaranteed programming appeal Turner's own production efforts have failed to achieve. As his recent efforts to sell back to United Artists Corporation the MGM television and motion picture production-distribution operations suggest, Turner seems willing to dismember the entire MGM empire if necessary simply to obtain the feature films that can transform TBS into a major programming entity.

By the same token, although some financial analysts questioned the $690 million Viacom paid for MTV — the cable-delivered music service — and a 50-percent interest in Showtime and the Movie Channel, those who understand media operations see that this move, when coupled with Viacom's purchase of CBS's KMOX-TV in St. Louis for $107 million, is a sensible strategy to diversify and broaden its base of distribution alternatives.

Another example of strategic advantage can be seen in the Lorimar and Telepictures merger, a consolidation that is valued at $306 million and that combines the two competitors into a single television production company. This single company is now elevated, through this transaction, to the rank of a major studio such as Universal, Columbia, or Paramount in terms of hours of television programming it supplies to networks and syndicators each year.

Whatever the unique attibutes of each particular financial move, of course, both politicians and the public have seen this tidal wave of acquisition as a serious threat to the future independence of American broadcast service. In reality, however, there are a number of reasons for believing that this is not the case. In the first place, it is quite probable that 1985 was not typical of the future but reflected only a single, major adjustment that media interests made in response to changes in ownership rules. At this point, most of the long-range acquisition plans of major conglomerates in the field seem either to have been completed or thwarted. It also appears that far fewer properties are likely to come on the market now that these organizations have finished the initial buying and selling maneuvers made possible by the frantic marketing conditions of 1985. In addition, a number of these organizations now seem to have depleted their capital reserves and must remain dormant for a time until their new acquisitions replenish these reserves.

After all of this reshuffling, the basic structure of broadcasting and other American mass media seems basically unaffected by the transfers in title. Even though Westinghouse's Group W has left the cable-TV business, control of Storer Broadcasting has changed hands, Taft Broadcasting has expanded its television-station holdings, and Gannett has absorbed the Evening News Association, the general communication functions performed by each newly organized media empire remain much the same as they were under the old regime. Perhaps the greater mass of capital resouces and distribution services possessed by some of these new conglomerates will provide them with the capacity to range beyond their limited mass-cultural roles as outlets for the products of others, but there is little in the past policy patterns of these organizations to suggest that this may be the case. It may be interesting to note, in this regard, that the only potential broadcast purchaser to discuss the program-content implications of an offer in any detail was Ted Turner, who was acquiring, not electronic mass media properties but one of the existing major feature-film distributors.

In essence, then, although the government's broadcast-ownership restrictions may not have encouraged competition, as they were designed to do, the FCC's new policy liberalizing these numerical restraints seems no more likely to increase the quantity of programming or the number of programming alternatives available to the American public. Unfortunately no government policy seems capable of increasing the degree of competition in this field, because this concentration of control is not the result of any concerted effort to limit entry into the field of mass-entertainment production and distribution but simply the natural result of marketplace forces. Producing a feature film, a record album, or a television series is an extremely high-cost, high-risk venture. The average major motion picture now requires a production budget of $14 million; the typical 13-week, 30-minute television series costs between $6.5 and $7 million to produce; and a major record album costs at least $500,000 to release; and yet 80 percent of the films, television programs, and records distributed each year fail to return their production costs much less earn a profit for the organization producing them.

Tactics that may seem designed to discourage outside competition are actually only efforts to minimize risk, whenever possible, through combining established creative talent with proven organizational marketing skills. Each major film and record distributor is constantly seeking the blockbuster film or platinum album that will not only recoup its losses but also provide the profits needed to justify its continued operation. Although an occasional "small" film or unknown performer achieves this type of success, the industry's professionals realize that famous stars, large budgets, and heavy promotion all aid in realizing this objective.

A recent study of the five-year financial performance of 22 major communication organizations revealed that entertainment programming and distribution had yielded the lowest rate of return of the 10 different types of communication functions performed by these organizations. Yet there is always the hope that the next film produced will be another *Grease*, returning to Paramount $90 million in film rentals on a $6-million investment; *Jaws*, returning to Universal a $121-million profit on a $12-million production budget; or *Star Wars*, returning to Twentieth Century-Fox $162 million on its domestic film rentals alone.[4] In addition, an extremely strong domestic performance will also tend to increase substantially the typical 30 percent of film rentals coming from foreign distribution and the license fees paid by pay-TV and network-TV outlets for use of the film. On the other hand, there is always the fear of another *Heaven's Gate*, returning less than $500,000 in film rental on a production budget of $36 million, or *Sheena*, a $26-million, 1984 production that resulted in a $23-million loss.

In the film industry, a $4-billion annual domestic box office business will be dominated by only 15 of the 140 films released by the majors each year — these 15 films will earn one-third of the $4 billion. In contrast, the music industry relies on many more releases at a far lower production cost to achieve the same general $4-billion gross receipts.[5] In 1984, for example, the music industry released 2170 new LP titles, 2400 cassette titles, 1980 seven-inch singles, and 535 LP reissues.[6] During this period, 131 LPs achieved the Record Industry Association of America's gold-album certification, which reflects verified sales of 500,000 copies. Fifty-nine LPs also received platinum awards for the sale of 1 million units.[7] With major-album production costs now at $500,000, a platinum album will earn a music distributor a net profit of approximately $4 million; a gold album will return about half this amount in profit. Of course it is important to realize that 94 percent of the albums released each year fail to achieve this 500,000-sale level; and some 80 percent fail even to return their production costs.

The music industry, like the film industry, has a structure that clearly reflects its gradual, grudging accommodation to technological change. The music publisher, a broad title that can include many of the functions of the agent and producer, was simply a publisher and promoter of sheet music until the phonograph, and later the radio station, began to reduce the demand for music to be performed in the home. At the turn of the century, the sheet-music market, which began to expand significantly after the Civil War, produced its first million seller, "After the Ball." This composition, which was written and published by Charles K. Harris, ultimately sold 10 million copies. As the phonograph began to replace the piano as the primary source of family music in the early

1900s, publishers and the composers they represented gained compensation, through the Copyright Act of 1909, for the use of their works by recording artists. This act required that a small percentage of a record's sales revenues be allocated as royalties to the song's creator and promoter. As radio stations began to use these records for their broadcast programming during the 1920s, publishers and composers, through ASCAP, were eventually able to obtain compensation by obtaining payments of a percentage of advertising revenues from each station. These payments were allocated among ASCAP members on the basis of the amount of airtime each recorded composition received.[8]

Unlike the practice in most Western nations, in the United States performers receive no payment for broadcast use because it is theorized that broadcast exposure increases record sales and thus the recording artist's earnings. Major performers generally receive 5 percent of the retail price of a record or 6 to 8 percent for an album. Similarly, the record industry has received no payment from broadcast stations for use of their recordings and often provides the records free of charge in order to encourage their use by the stations.[9]

The music industry has gone through several eras during which new, independent labels have emerged in response to shifting music tastes that major distributors have not perceived. The new labels have eventually been absorbed by these majors to broaden their marketing base. Thus, between 1955 and 1960, independents such as Atlantic, Chess, Modern, Imperial, Sun, Alladin, Savoy, and King were the first to capitalize on the rock-and-roll craze and were then absorbed by larger distributors offering the financing, distribution system, and marketing expertise to exploit the demand these labels had created. Again, in the mid-1960s, a wave of youth-oriented ballads and folk songs spawned literally hundreds of new labels that have now all but disappeared, either having been merged into the more efficient operations of a major organization or having slipped into insolvency because of the lack of effective merchandising.[10]

The producer is generally the most influential person in the process of making a recording, selecting the compositions, choosing the musicians, supervising the artistic and technical arrangements, and ultimately deciding when a master is ready to be reproduced. The producer can work in-house, as an executive for a major distribution company, or can be an independent and offer a major company a package deal consisting of the producer's own artistic judgment and a performer or group he has under contract.

Performer contracts, whether with a producer or a major company, are generally for a period of five years. The producer or company has the option at the end of each year to continue or terminate the agreement. The typical contract guarantees the artist or group between $50,000 and $75,000 per album completed plus 6 to 8 percent of its retail sales. The most popular recording groups, however, can demand as much as $600,000 per album plus full artistic control over material, arrangements, and approval of the master, as well as the right to limit *coupling*, the recording company's reissuing of portions of the artist's or group's albums as the "greatest hits of . . ." or "the best of. . . ."

In theory, each major record organization establishes marketing strategies annually in which it allocates production budgets among the producers in its various divisions and reserves funds for independent pickups. The marketing strategies are developed in terms of projected, seasonal release dates that will provide the best promotional opportunities for every type of album the organization intends to produce during the year. In fact, these tactics change constantly, partly because of unforeseen shifts in public taste, but more often because of equally unpredictable behavior on the part of one or more of the organization's top recording stars or groups.

Successful music-industry executives realize that it is the star performer who is most likely to provide the coveted gold and platinum certificates that testify to managerial skill. As a result, star performers and groups are often able to demand more financial or scheduling concessions from major record companies than any cost accountant can justify solely on the basis of a profit-and-loss statement.[11] Unfortunately, these concessions generally are at the expense of a company's new or less-celebrated talent, whose promotional budgets are therefore reduced and whose release dates are shifted to conform to a major star's needs. This, in turn, often leads to a self-fulfilling prophecy of haphazard release and lackluster promotion, both of which virtually guarantee that a newcomer's album will not reach the minimum 100,000-sale level necessary to recover the album's expenses.

Because many of the newcomers are talented composers as well as performers, this policy of favoring the established artist not only limits the degree of diversity in musical styling but also diminishes the public's opportunity to hear a wider variety of creative work. Ironically, new technology thus far has only increased this disparity between the known and the unknown performers and groups. The $100,000 to $200,000 necessary to produce a music-video clip most likely will not be invested in promoting any but the most marketable artists an organization has under contract.[12]

If anything, the tactic of relying on proven talent to guarantee a successful return on investment has been even more pronounced in today's film industry, where the production budget for a major feature is about 30 times that of the typical record album. Until the 1950s each major studio could draw on its "stable" of actors and actresses under contract for the films it made, or it could negotiate with other studios for the proven box office stars necessary to guarantee its success. With the collapse of this system and the financial stability it afforded, the "star" is now virtually the only asset a producer can use to obtain the production funding necessary to produce a major feature film. To attract the star, the producer generally must begin by obtaining rights to a particular property in which the star is known to be interested. The producer often attempts to make the package even more enticing by including in the offer an option on the services of the star's favorite director. These packages are held together by *option contracts*, the fragile filament of law that is designed to keep all elements of a motion picture deal connected long enough for a producer to find the financing necessary for its production. Taking an option on a screenplay, novel, or story requires a much more modest investment than buying the property outright, something few producers have the ready cash to do. Typically, purchasing the option to a work requires paying only between 10 and 15 percent of its asking price. The producer then gains through this agreement the exclusive right to complete the purchase by paying the remaining amount due within a specified period of time, generally six months to a year later. If the producer is successful in finding the production financing within that time, the option is exercised. Otherwise, all rights revert to the writer at the end of the option period; and the writer retains the option payment as compensation for having kept the work off the market during the term of the option.

Talent agencies are actively engaged in this property-acquisition process for both film and television. They seek promising stories on which to purchase an option in order to offer them to prospective producers with major roles assigned to the stars the agency represents. The agencies' incentive for such efforts is not only the 10 to 15 percent they collect from each of their actors or actresses cast in the film or series, but also a substantial finder's fee paid for putting the deal together.[13]

In some cases, it is the star who begins this process, working through a personal production company to acquire rights to screenplays and, in some cases, even to advance a portion of the production expenses necessary to produce the films. Each packaging effort differs to some extent from all others, and it is often said that the most creative element of a Hollywood film today is the maneuvering that led to its production.

The traditional source of feature-film financing has been the major film company, which agrees to advance production costs in return for the film's distribution rights. However, other organizations such as HBO, Showtime/The Movie Channel, CBS, or ABC Motion Pictures now offer at least partial production support on the condition that they receive the film's exclusive licensing rights for pay-TV or network-television usage after the film's theatrical run has been completed. Banks and other lending organizations also provide production loans; and as production costs rise, it is often necessary for a producer to seek support from a number of sources, selling future rights at a reduced price simply to meet current production costs.

Recently, major film studios have begun to take a more active part in developing film projects for themselves, hoping in this way to keep a tighter rein on production expenses and the presale of profitable ancillary film rights. Even though these major film distributors are in a far stronger and more stable financial condition than are the producers, agencies, or independent production companies dealing in film properties, however, the distributors' success rate in converting options into feature films is not noticeably more impressive than the industrywide 5- to 7-percent ratio.[14] In large part, this is because studio executives are as uncertain as independent producers about which 15 of the 140 major films released yearly will dominate the field and generate the revenues essential to underwrite the $15-million budgets of the films that fail to return their production and promotional costs.[15] As a result, the studios are also eager to use the creative works they option simply to lure bankable box office names such as Clint Eastwood, Sylvester Stallone, Robert Redford, or Paul Newman to their films, and they discard properties that fail to achieve that purpose.[16]

Ironically, rather than reducing financial pressures through broader marketing opportunities, new media have actually increased them because the licensing fees for domestic and foreign broadcast, pay-TV, and videocassette usage are based primarily on the degree of success the film has achieved in American theaters.[17] As a result, the handful of hit films distributed yearly now has a far more impressive earning potential than the hits of only a decade ago and the remaining films lack the capacity to benefit substantially from additional exposure.

Another factor limiting the ability of new media to provide additional funding for feature-film projects is that all those whose creative talents have contributed to a film's success insist on sharing in its *residuals*, revenues produced from all ancillary (nontheatrical) exhibition. Learning from the bitter experiences of the early 1950s, when film studios refused to share television revenues with the writers, directors, and performers involved in a production, major guilds now demand a percentage of all nontheatrical income that a feature film generates. Top-billed performers also may insist on *points*, an additional proportion of these revenues, as an inducement to appear in the film.

Both engineers and economists have projected that feature-film production costs will decrease in the near future because of technological innovations in video cameras and editing equipment. However, they have overlooked the fact that these advances challenge the solidly entrenched Hollywood trade unions and the guild system, both of whose jurisdictional definitions, based on traditional practices, require the hiring of nearly as many union employees for electronically processed films as were necessary in the golden days of the studio era.[18] Film producers have little choice but to satisfy union demands, because most major exhibition chains in the United States employ unionized projectionists, members of the International Alliance of Theatrical Stage Employees (IATSE), who will refuse to show any feature film not certified as being trade-union made.

Although television stations are not as fully unionized as the nation's theater chains, many of the same production problems exist simply because of the close association between the television networks and the major Hollywood studios as primary suppliers of broadcast prime-time programming. During an average year, the film studios provide at least half of the series programs scheduled by the networks and rent studio space to many independent producers with network contracts.[19]

Typically, independent producers and studio representatives responsible for television program development present various concepts and packages to network-programming executives in an attempt to obtain series-development funding. Until the early 1970s, the development usually led to the production of a *pilot*, an introductory episode of a series, but rising production costs have curtailed the use of this approach. Instead, through a series of *step deals*, a network commits specific payments at each stage of a series' development, deciding as the producer progresses from story treatments to scripts to casting whether or not the next production phase shall be approved. Each network generally has as many as 50 different series concepts at some point in this process and drops or adds new productions as the network's long-term scheduling strategies change. Eventually, certain series are chosen for what is usually a 13-episode commitment, with the network underwriting about 85 to 90 percent of the total production costs in return for the exclusive right to two or three network broadcasts. After observing the new series' performance, the network decides whether or not to pick up the option for another 13 episodes. In some cases, the network makes this decision without even exercising its right to broadcast segments it has already commissioned. Here, too, as in the feature-film process, there are as many variations on this basic theme as there are producers. "Regulars," well-known producers with years of successful network productions, often receive more than a 13-week commitment, while others receive less generous treatment.[20] Every aspect of this process has been designed to control production costs, but nothing the networks have devised thus far has been particularly successful in achieving this objective.[21]

One significant loophole in this cost-control process has been the *pass-through clause*, which allows the network to make additional payments, not charged to the producer, to satisfy the demands of program stars unwilling to perform for the amount specified in their contract. After dealing rather leniently with such talent for a number of years, the networks have recently adopted a much tougher policy; but precedents have increased production costs and have encouraged highly publicized talent to pressure for continued upward adjustment of their performer fees.[22]

During the past few years, network usage of feature films has decreased substantially because bidding for rights to films with suitable broadcast content, even with extensive editing, has raised the license fee to more than $2 million per feature. At the same time, an ever-increasing portion of the audience has had access to the uncut version of the film two to three years before the film's network scheduling.[23] Also at the same time, most major studios have all but abandoned the made-for-TV movie format, because they are unwilling to accept the network's deficit production financing for features with almost no theatrical exhibition or syndication value.[24] As a result, the networks have been forced either to produce in-house films or to commission films from smaller independent producers such as Lorimar, Orion, or Viacom. The problem with this small-picture approach, of course, is that with a budget of only $3 million, one-fifth of today's typical feature-film budget, the "Lee Horsley, James Franciscus, Heather Locklear" special on child abuse, drunk driving, incest, or bed-wetting is designed primarily to fill two hours of network time inexpensively, with no serious commitment to artistic quality.

On the basis of this brief survey, it is difficult to discover any attribute of the mass-entertainment creative process that seems likely in itself to respond to a greater number of delivery channels by increasing either the quantity or the quality of its musical or film productions. The preoccupation with shaping all content to conform to the star performer's interest and talent not only tends to diminish the importance of the composition or story itself but also seems to inhibit the creative process generally.[25] Only a limited number of performers can be promoted at any given time because there are only a finite number of mass-appeal magazine covers, television talk shows, and newswire items that each distributor can command. Therefore, once the property (performance) needs of these stars have been met, there is little incentive to encourage further creativity. However, the emphasis on marketing the performer rather than the content of the work largely reflects the approach major music and film distributors have taken toward mass-entertainment merchandising in the past. With new mass-entertainment distribution channels only now beginning to operate at full capacity, is there any reason to believe that this traditional emphasis will be altered to some extent in the future?

Marketing Mass Entertainment

Although the mass-entertainment production process is certainly no model of efficiency, the distribution process is even less so because it diverts from the creative process more than half of the proceeds earned by record sales and ticket sales each year. Thus, for example, if the purchase price of a record album is $9.00, $4.50 of that amount is retained by the album's wholesaler and retailer. The typical recording artist receives $1.00 from the sale; the record company, $1.20; and the composer and publisher, $0.30. Of the remainder, $1.60 covers the record's production costs and another $0.80 is allocated to advertising and promotional expenses.[26] This 45-percent return to the production side is, however, far more generous than in film, where a distributor begins with only 40 to 50 percent of the domestic box office revenues before the film's distribution fee of 30 percent diminishes the amount returned to its producer still further.[27] Under these circumstances it would seem that any technological improvements in the delivery of mass entertainment to the public might be of great value in furnishing the material's creators and producers with a more generous portion of the revenue spent on their efforts.

Until the mid-1950s, the record business in the United States was stable in structure but stagnant in growth. Between 1939 and 1954, the number of records being sold annually actually dropped from 350 to 228 million as the population increased.[28] During this period, there were three basic patterns of record distribution: major record company through its own distributor to local outlet; small record company through independent distributor to local outlet; and, in the RCA record chain, major company to franchised dealers.

Technology altered this structure radically during the 1950s. CBS's 45-rpm and 33-rpm records not only ended the dominance of the old 78s in a single decade but also ushered in an era of lower-priced, rock-and-roll, teenage-oriented music produced and promoted by newly formed, small, independent record companies and labels. Coupled with the emergence of discount department stores in the 1960s, these new low-cost, continually changing Top 40 records led to the development of a very specialized form of music distribution, the *rack jobber*. Rack jobbers rented space in these locally owned, reduced-markup, high-volume stores to set up what in effect was an independent record shop within the larger store, marketing the same type of reduced-markup, high-volume music.

Initially, it was the independent music distributor that suffered the greatest economic damage from this change in the music marketing structure. Many small variety stores, drugstores, and foodmarkets that had sold more than 80 percent of the nation's records in the mid-1960s shifted, during this era, from selling the records the distributor provided to a less-demanding rack jobber relationship. This allowed the stores to collect rent and share, to some extent, in record sales without committing funds or personnel.[29]

However, a decade later, it was the rack jobbers whose market base was diminishing, as the discount department store's share of the record business rose spectacularly from 11 to 72 percent, while the record sales of the smaller stores, which the rack jobbers serviced, dropped from 80 percent to less than 15 percent.[30] Rack jobbers were generally local businesses, and national discount houses preferred to deal on a uniform basis with a single record supplier rather than negotiate separate agreements in each locality in which they operated. Major record distributors offered the discount department store this type of uniform sales policy; and during the 1960s, the distributors began to gain control of the smaller record companies whose popular artists generated the massive sales that discount houses expected from each department they operated.[31]

Smaller record companies were vulnerable to major distributor takeover, because they lacked not only the capital essential for effective distribution and promotion but also the breadth in popular recording artists essential for surviving a sudden shift in the fickle tastes of the predominantly teenage audience they served. Even if this did not occur, the performer in the one- or two-star company might leave the organization at the end of the contract period, realizing that the company did not have a merchandising and promotional structure capable of advancing a major recording artist's career.

The primary benefit expected to be realized through consolidation of control by a few major distributors was a much more efficient marketing process, stimulating sales through low prices while returning a greater portion of record sales revenue to the production process. After a decade of major-distributor dominance, album prices continue to rise faster than the rate of inflation, while marketing costs remain at more than 50 percent of the total sales price.

As this degree of dominance becomes even greater, the major distributors may ultimately be in a position to eliminate or at least reduce one major drain on industry revenues — the traditional practice of allowing record retailers to return unsold records for credit. This custom results in more than 20 percent of the total shipped yearly to retailers being sent back without payment. However, as audiocassettes continue to increase their share of recorded-music sales — they already account for $2.3 billion of the annual $4-billion industry sales mark — private taping expands at the same rate and is now estimated to cost the industry between $500 and $600 million per year.[32]

At the moment, then, all that can be said with any confidence about the effects on the American music industry of the revolution in record-making and the outpouring of low-cost 45- and 33-rpm records is that they have not stimulated the renaissance in new compositions and artists seen during the 1950s and 1960s as being about to emerge from the independent label trends of the times. Instead, the rise of the major distributor has discouraged such diversification and has caused a focusing more and more on the exact center of American popular-music tastes. Contemporary, Country and Western, and middle-of-the-road records now account for more than 80 percent of all records, albums, and cassettes produced and sold in the United States each year.[33]

It is too soon to tell what impact video music will ultimately have on long-term industry production and marketing strategies. For example, a radical change in traditional record-industry promotional tactics could soon have a profound effect on a number of cable services and syndicated broadcast programs. Until recently, record companies, in order to promote record and cassette sales, provided music-video clips of their newest albums to cable and television free of charge. This practice, following the custom of providing stations with free audio albums and airplay, led to the launching of Music TV (MTV) and countless other cable-delivered and broadcast services. Now, CBS Records has begun a campaign to charge for the use of its clips, distinguishing between the free audio and free video usage on the basis that record and album usage cost the record company nothing but specially edited video clips require an additional production budget of between $50,000 and $200,000.[34] If other record suppliers follow CBS's lead in demanding a license fee of $1000 to $2000 per month for programming the company's video clips, this fee, which could easily amount to $100,000 to $200,000 a year, will diminish the number of services or programs able to afford to continue this type of format.

The main reason record companies now are willing to place limits on cable and broadcast usage of their clips is that the music-video age seems to have arrived in the United States and requires no more expensive promotional effect for its growth. As the number of videocassette homes expands beyond the 25-percent mark, video music accounts for almost that same percentage of all videocassette sales.[35] Rapidly escalating production budgets, which in some cases have exceeded the $500,000 necessary for the most sophisticated audio album, still limit vides exposure to only the biggest name artists and groups. As the 10 annual releases per major distributor become 25 or 50 in response to a growing audience, it is likely that video opportunities will be available to a broader range of recording artists. However, as long as the video counterpart of the album more than doubles production costs, it is also likely that nothing released will venture far from that secure midpoint of American pop culture.

In film, as in music, there was once a belief that it was an all-powerful studio system, dictating every aspect of feature-film content, that was inhibiting creativity and diversity. Until the late 1940s, Paramount, RKO, Twentieth Century-Fox, Warner Brothers, and MGM owned more than 3000 first-run motion picture theaters in the United States. They dominated industry production, distribution, and exhibition both by offering their own theaters all their major releases and by employing a policy of trade-off and cross-preference with other studio-owned theaters to deny about 15,000 independently owned theaters access to these features until their box office appeal had been diminished.

In 1948 Justice Department antitrust litigation compelled these studios to enter into a consent decree and agree to divest themselves of either their theaters or their distribution functions in order to end this type of vertical integration.[36] Predictably, the studios sold their domestic theater holdings, realizing that it was in the field of distribution that the greatest potential for future growth lay. Soon television began to erode the popularity of film viewing. Between 1948 and 1958, weekly American film attendance dropped from 90 million to 40 million and the number of traditional motion picture theaters diminished from 17,300 to 11,300, eventually reaching a low of 9250 in 1963.[37] Independent and foreign filmmakers gained access to American film audiences for the first time, but it was a diminishing audience, and one dominated more completely each year by the tastes of those under 19, who constituted almost half of the nation's filmgoers by the 1970s.[38] Whether correctly or not, producers perceived this group as being uninterested in serious film themes; thus, the disaster, horror, and puberty-rite genres became the dominant ones of this era.

Now, more than three decades after the breakup of the Hollywood film system, the major distributors of the past still shape the industry's policies and use their superior financial position, their experience, and their nationwide and worldwide promotional structure to market a film more effectively than any of their less-prosperous or less-experienced competitors. Independent distributors may offer a producer more favorable terms for a picture's release, but they lack those attributes that year after year allow the majors to collect over 80 percent of all film rentals from the less than 50 percent of those films they agree to handle.[39]

Major distributors generally release between 15 and 30 feature films each year. Half of these films are in-house productions and the remainder are pickups of films already produced.[40] In-house productions are packages that are offered by a producer or independent film company and that a distributor finds attractive enough to finance either partially or fully in return for a share of the producer's eventual revenues from the film. In either case, the distributor's fee for its services is from 30 to 35 percent of *film rental* — that share of box office receipts that theaters must pay for exhibiting the film — plus print production, distribution, advertising, and other promotional expenses. In addition the distributor usually demands 40 to 45 percent of foreign film rental, and 25 percent of television licensing, pay-TV, VCR, and other new media uses. If the distributor has financed the in-house production, it will also have contracted for between 50 and 80 percent of the *producer's net* — film rental money after the distribution fee and all expenses have been deducted.

For theatrical release, major distributors generally launch a massive promotional campaign designed to make major exhibition chains in the United States eager to bid for the film. Typically, an advertising budget in excess of $2 million is coordinated with a full-scale mass media–public relations effort, using every connection the organization has developed through the years to gain booking for the film's stars on television talk shows, coverage of the film in magazine and syndicated newspaper columns, and access to mass-circulation magazine and newspaper covers.

The usual successful first-run bid offers the distributor 70 percent of the first week's box office receipts minus the *house nut*, the basic operating costs of the theater. An exhibition chain particularly eager to show the film may offer 80 or even 90 percent of first-week revenues, believing the audience it will attract will be an especially promising one in terms of concession stand revenues, which are retained by the exhibitor. Generally, by the sixth week of the first run, box office sales are being split on a 50-50 basis, a percentage likely to continue until diminishing revenues convince a distributor to withdraw the film. A film opens simultaneously across the nation at as many as 1000 first-run or flagship theaters. The distributor moves the film into suburban or smaller community theaters a few weeks later as it begins to lose its appeal. The distributor finally withdraws the film from circulation about five months after its release.

Customarily, foreign release of an American motion picture is scheduled a month or two after domestic release. This schedule allows any special box office strength and media attention to aid in the foreign marketing effort. Foreign film rental provides almost 30 percent of a major motion picture's theatrical earnings, and five nations (Japan, West Germany, France, Italy, and Great Britain) account for more than half of this amount.[41] It is in marketing for foreign release that major distributors excel, dealing with foreign exhibition organizations to gain the most advantageous terms for the distributors' features.

Only a decade ago, all that remained after this theatrical distribution was the licensing of the film as part of a television-network package for use three years later, syndication of the package to local television stations after network use, and possible rerelease of the film to second-run theaters a year or two after its initial theatrical run had been completed.

The three-year "window" of exclusivity protecting theaters from television competition began to close with the emergence of HBO and other cable-delivered pay-TV services, These services sought to benefit from the promotional campaign that launched the film, and they needed enough advance time on television release to justify their charging for a feature that would someday be offered free of charge. Until 1980, all films were withheld from pay-TV services until their major-market run was completed; therefore, pay-TV competition affected only smaller rerelease theaters, a source of revenues too insignificant for distributors to protect.

To encourage the sale of film videocassettes, Twentieth Century-Fox announced in 1980 that it would release certain films on cassette simultaneously with their theatrical release, hoping in this way to capitalize immediately on the films' promotional campaigns. Faced with the possibility that major exhibition chains might refuse to handle these films, Fox immediately revised its policy and promised at least a three-month "window" between theatrical and videocassette release, a practice most distributors now follow.

In 1985 film videocassette sales and rental revenues were expected to reach \$3.3 billion, or more than 75 percent of the box office receipts earned through domestic exhibition of feature films.[42] Within the next two years, the videocassette market is virtually certain to exceed the motion picture theater as the largest single source of film revenue, a situation that both pleases and frustrates the major distributors.

Although the industry is obviously encouraged by the rapid growth of this new market, it is concerned by the fact that cassette rentals now account for twice the revenues of cassette sales. In rentals the distributor's participation is limited by the "first-sale" provision of the Copyright Act of 1976, which denies a distributor the right to control the use of a cassette by a purchaser. Thus, once a retail store has purchased a film cassette, it can rent it to customers and keep all the proceeds of the rental transactions for itself. Being able to rent a cassette obviously reduces a customer's incentive to purchase it; this denies the film industry an estimated 65 percent of the revenues these cassettes actually generate each year. Some of the largest rental chains are proposing to share these rentals with distributors in return for release dates either simultaneous with or closely following a film's release to the theaters, but the constant pressure to reduce or end theatrical lead time is beginning to meet with exhibitor resistance.

Recently, for example, National Video entered into an agreement with several major film distributors to test a marketing arrangement called *pay-per-transaction*, by which National would receive its film cassettes at a price of only $6 a tape rather than the wholesale price of $50 to $60 per cassette, which video rental stores currently pay.[43] In return, National would share its rental receipts with the film company providing the tapes. National expected that an expanded volume of business based on their being able to stock more of each tape plus a higher rental price that they would charge for these premium films would make this relationship more profitable for all parties concerned. In the last analysis, of course, the success of this marketing experiment will depend on the quality of the premium films the distributors are willing to release in this fashion. This situation will once again pit the economic interests of the video rental stores against those of the theatrical exhibitors.

New *pay-per-view* (PPV) film delivery system owners have been making similar demands. They have pointed out that the ability of these systems to collect $5 to $7 from viewers who have selected a particular film to be delivered to their television screen will depend on the drawing power of the features the distributors provide. Although the majors are eager to undercut the competitive position of regular pay-TV services that now offer only 20 percent of the revenues collected as film rental, there is growing concern about how deeply the competitive advantage of early theatrical exhibition can be undercut without diminishing the level of box office popularity, which still determines its asking price for all other forms of distribution.

Perhaps DBS, MMDS, and various other pay-TV feature-film channels will make this box office measure of film success as quaint and dated as a sheet music measure of a composition's popularity. For the moment, however, the larger-than-life dimensions of theatrical-film attendance still shape all judgments relating to future marketability.

Another tradition of film marketing that, unfortunately, also lingers is the custom of allocating a disproportionately large share of box office receipts to the distribution and exhibition aspects of the business. This custom limits the return of funding to the film's creators. With almost 50 cents out of every dollar spent by film audiences remaining in the theater and another 20 to 25 cents being taken out for distribution fees and promotional expenses, it is certainly not a process designed to reward those who produce films.[44]

When the Justice Department dismantled the Hollywood film system in 1948, it was with the hope that divestment would stimulate competition and dilute the degree of domination then exercised by the industry's major organizations. Television has drastically reduced the size of the film audience and has changed its nature as well, but neither this nor public policy has had any significant effect on the film industry's structure. Paramount, Warner Brothers, Twentieth Century-Fox, Columbia, and Universal still stand astride the nation's film production and distribution channels; but they now release far less than half the number of films they did during an era when there were no new media and the population was over 100 million less than it is today.[45]

Even if all the nationally distributed independent films and made-for-TV movies were added to this total, the number of films available to a much larger American audience through all forms of media delivery is not significantly larger than it was during the studio era of the past. In reality, pay-TV and VCR seem to be narrowing, rather than increasing, film diversity for they are inducing major distributors to concentrate on only the five or six feature films each year that have the best prospects for becoming megahits, the new essential requirement for tapping the wealth of that ancillary market. These are the films assigned the choice release dates within the 17-week period in which almost half of the year's film attendance occurs, the ones that receive the full orchestrated media campaigns and that are showcased at all foreign film markets. In essence, then, the dimensions of the competitive marketplace in American film currently are substantially the same as they were when the Justice Department successfully ended the vertical integration of production, distribution, and exhibition almost four decades ago in order to free the market from these anticompetitive practices.

Why should this be the case? What has prevented either the music or the film industries from expanding their record and motion picture production in response to a growing, more affluent population and an ever-increasing number of competing music and feature-film delivery systems?

Supply and Demand:
The Economics of Mass Entertainment

In reality, what has constantly constrained the volume of music, film, and television productions through the years has not been a lack of delivery channels but rather a lack of sufficient capital to produce this additional material. After all, few investors are likely to be attracted to industries in which four out of five ventures actually completed fail to return even their original investment.[46]

The option contract is certainly not a legal instrument of choice for any producer; rather, it is one of necessity. The use of this private law device simply reflects the chronic lack of funding for mass-entertainment production and offers the only means available for holding rights together long enough for financing to be found. The so-called independent producer exists in film and television, as small record companies do in music, primarily because major distributors are reluctant to commit more than the necessary revenue to this most perilous portion of the mass-entertainment process. In reality, then, the vision of the independent producer or the small record company seeking only a nationwide channel to launch a new and competitive mass-cultural service is a rather romantic one; it overlooks the fact that what limits these efforts most severely is not simply a lack of access to the public but lack of access to the financial support that investors are willing to offer to only the largest and most stable organizations in an extremely unstable area of business.

The primary reason for this relative degree of stability is the substantial financial commitment that distributors make to the maintenance of their competitive positions. Major film distributors, for example, invest between $20 and $25 million a year simply to operate their worldwide marketing and promoting offices; each television network allocates between $6 and $8 million annually just for the development of program series; and major record distributors commit at least an equal amount to payment on exclusive artist agreements then in force with their most popular performers.

It is about as unlikely that another major mass-entertainment distributor will emerge in the near future as it is that another major auto manufacturer will emerge to challenge General Motors, Ford, and Chrysler, and for similar reasons. Large, uniquely trained staffs; close, long-term industry connections and associations; and promising projects under development all give established firms such an advantage that outside entry would be virtually impossible. In fact the present trend in this field seems to be in the opposite direction: Several distributors are considering mergers that may improve their cross-media competitive positions.[47]

Facing no serious competitive threat from independent producers who may have the skill but lack the financing or from major corporations that have the financing but lack the skill, mass-entertainment distributors have no incentive to finance or release any larger number of feature films, videos, or records than they are already doing. As long as

70 to 80 percent of the entertainment properties now in circulation fail to return their investment, the far wiser course of action to take in order to recoup losses and to improve the current financial success ratio of already-released product is to hold the production rate constant and draw on the additional revenue being offered by the new delivery systems. Unfortunately for the major distributors, this is not a classic situation of increasing demand for a scarce resource operating to increase the earnings of those who control that resource. Production costs for film and television have more than doubled during the past 10 years and have driven exhibitor and broadcast usage fees up to the same extent; but only a small portion of this additional revenue returns to the distributor, and even less returns to the producer.[48] Instead, an increasing proportion of that revenue is being absorbed by the residual rights claimed by each of the creative guilds involved in the production process and, to an even greater extent, by the box office and recording stars that the majors rely on now more than ever to reach a sales level that will guarantee the highest possible return from ancillary markets.

In the last analysis, then, what is scarce here is not so much mass-entertainment properties as it is the stars capable of motivating the public to purchase or view these properties. Although talent may not be in short supply in this nation, stars are simply because the process of creating, nurturing, and marketing this celebrity status demands such a massive investment of effort that only a few such public personalities can be developed or maintained by a distributor at any given time.

What all of this suggests and what the mass-entertainment industry's performance has demonstrated conclusively during the past decade is that there is virtually no correlation between the number of outlets available for dissemination of film or music and the amount of such material actually produced. Thus, for example, cable-delivered pay-TV furnished a vast new nationwide network for film distribution without having any appreciable effect on the number of new films produced each year.[49] Instead, distributors used pay-TV competition to justify raising the network-television licensing price for existing films, a practice that is causing networks to reduce the number of films scheduled.

This high-risk, high-expense industry, with only a few unchallenged distributors and a handful of acknowledged stars, has almost an infinite capacity to absorb additional funding without expanding production. New media outlets competing with one another for this relatively constant quantity of mass-entertainment material will simply continue to inflate production costs to a point where many outlets will be forced to withdraw from competition because they lack television's fortunate situation of having other types of programming service, such as news and sports, to substitute for those it can no longer afford.

Thus, in mass-cultural terms, whether or not MMDS, cable TV, DBS, LPTV, or STV survive as delivery systems of the future is about as relevant to the type of content furnished the American public as whether the daily newspaper is delivered by carrier or by mail. In any case the films and the music these films feature will continue to flow from the same few sources and will have the same familiar stars.

In this context, then, diversity means only the opportunity to view or hear the same things at different times on different channels. Whatever else this may be, it is certainly not the competitive marketplace of ideas that was expected to emerge one day to offer the American public broad-ranging freedom of choice in the selection of its mass-cultural messages.

Notes

1. Six major film distributors collect between 75 percent and 80 percent of all revenues generated by the exhibition of American feature films each year. In 1985 Warner Brothers earned the largest share of this nearly $4 billion of gross box office revenues; but Universal, Paramount, Twentieth Century-Fox, Columbia Pictures, and MGM/UA each earned at least 10 percent of these proceeds. Tri-Star, the short-lived combination of Columbia Pictures, Time-Life, and CBS, made a strong showing as well in 1985; but with CBS and Time-Life withdrawing from this operation, 1986 should see these majors back at the 80 percent level once again.

   The five major record distributors in the United States are CBS and Warner Communication's WCI (collecting, between themselves, more than one-third of all domestic-music record-sale proceeds), RCA, MCA, and EMI. RCA has recently merged with Ariola, a German-based competitor; and Polygram, another foreign distributor, has been seeking an American merger partner since its negotiations with WCI collapsed in 1984.

   The three television-network organizations are, of course, CapCities-ABC, GE-NBC, and CBS. Although this may seem at first glance to add up to more than a dozen companies, the fact is that CBS Television and CBS Records are under the same corporate ownership, as are NBC and RCA Records, Warner Communications and WCI Records, and MCA Records and Universal, making a total of only nine separate entities in this field. If anything, further mergers and acquisitions, as typified by Turner Broadcasting's recent purchase of MGM, are likely to decrease rather than increase the number of separate entities in these fields.

2. Although the Premiere venture of Paramount, Universal, Twentieth Century-Fox, and Columbia was blocked by the Justice Department, other joint ventures such as Tri-Star, linking Columbia Pictures with CBS and HBO for the production of feature films; Paramount's exclusive film-distribution deal with Warner Communications' Movie Channel and Showtime; as well as the joint foreign-marketing organization, United International Pictures,

which handles only releases by the majors Paramount, Universal, and MGM/UA are just some examples of the type of close coordination between the major organizations that leave independents outside, looking in.

3. "Fifth Estate's $30 Billion-plus Year," *Broadcasting*, 30 Dec. 1985, 35–41.

4. Veronis, Shuhler & Associates, "5 Year Financial Performance of 22 Selected Communication Industry Companies 1978–1983," as reported in Richard Gold, "Mounting Costs Zap Distributor Profits," *Variety*, 12 Dec. 1984, 3.

5. Lawrence Cohn, "Majors Trim Budgets for 85 Pix," *Variety*, 26 Dec. 1984, 71.

6. "Revised Figures on Music Releases Are Submitted by RIAA," *Variety*, 8 May 1985, 71.

7. "More Gold, Platinum LPs in 1984 Augur Well for Year's Net," *Variety*, 9 Jan. 1985, 1.

8. For a description of these negotiations, see Chapter 5.

9. In reality record distributors have often done more than this to encourage broadcast use of their music. The payola situation of the late 1950s, as reported in H. Rep. No. 1800, 86th Cong., 2d sess. (1960), provides many examples that ultimately led to an amendment to the Communications Act of 1934, sec. 317, which made the practice grounds for revocation of a broadcast license.

10. To illustrate the limited importance of independent labels in the record business today, a spot check by the author of three separate Billboard Top 200 LP- and record-chart lists during mid-1984 revealed only five independents listed on two of the charts and four on the third.

11. For numerous examples of this type of behavior on the part of those in the music business, see the account of former CBS executive Clive Davis in *Clive: Inside the Record Business* (New York: Ballantine, 1976).

12. "CBS Records First to Charge for Music Videos," *Broadcasting*, 1 July 1985, 32.

13. For a time agents attempted to produce or at least to accept a producer's fee for putting together packages for the talent they represented. However, the practice created a clear conflict of interest on the part of the agent-producer because as an agent there was a responsibility to gain the best possible financial arrangement for each performer the agency represented; as a producer there was a responsibility to keep production costs to a minimum by offering the lowest possible payment to talent. The finder's fee was the solution to this ethical problem.

14. Lawrence Cohn, "Majors Step on In-House Production Pedal," *Variety*, 13 Jan. 1984, 5.

15. Lawrence Cohn, "Half of Megabuck Pictures Win Maxi B.O.," *Variety*, 16 Jan. 1985, 7.

16. Will Tusher, "Valenti Sez Majors Neg Cost Up 21%," *Variety*, 20 Feb. 1985, 3. On the other hand, on occasion major studios have worked in conjuction with publishers either to cross-promote a well-known novelist's work as a feature film or in some cases to commission a novel, based on a

screenplay, in order to cross-market the property. See, for example, Richard Gold, "Novel on the Rise as Source Material," *Variety*, 17 Oct. 1984, 3 and "Dune, 2010 Pub Pushes Stir Source Novel Sales," *Variety*, 22 Jan. 1985, 22.

17. Generally this is true only indirectly because film distributors traditionally have marketed their features in packages and have offered one attractive film as an inducement to purchase other ordinary films included in that package. However, box office hits are essential for the package approach to be successful. During the past decade, this package approach has been challenged by successful film producers who have argued that distributors understated the price obtained for their film and overstated the prices of less successful films in a package in order to offset losses sustained on those films and to avoid paying proceeds to the successful film's profit participants. See, "Graduate TV Sale Case Wins Turman 999Gs," *Variety*, 23 Apr. 1980, 2; "Authors Win 400G From Film Audit," *Variety*, 24 Oct. 1979, 1; and Ray Loynd, "Fox to Return to 'Verdict' 300G purposely credited to B.O. Flop," *Variety*, 27 Feb. 1985, 3.

18. The most recent agreement of this type, with the Writers' Guild of America, pledged 1.5 percent of producers' gross for the first $1 million in revenue for all videocassette rentals or sales and an increase to 1.8 percent for rental or sale income in excess of $1 million. Even without this videocassette revenue, the Writers' Guild collected nearly $43 million in members' residual payments in 1984. This is the same agreement now in effect between producers and the Directors' Guild of America. This was the final area of ancillary payments not covered by previous Guild agreements. A *point* is 1 percent of whatever source of revenue is described in the contract. A *gross distributor's point* is the most valuable because it is taken directly from a portion of box office receipts, or ancillary rights payment. *Net*, or *producers', points* are less valuable because if a feature film fails to generate any profit, as is true in 80 percent of the cases, no payment results in such profit participation.

19. For examples of these jurisdictional disputes, see "Make-up Union Gets $10,000 in Damages Over 'Thing' Credit," *Variety*, 30 June 1982, 4. For illustrations of union hostility toward new technology, see "Control Over Videotape Union," *Variety*, 30 Mar. 1983, 96, and David Robb, "Speed Search on the Cassette Residuals," *Variety*, 29 Aug. 1984, 3.

20. For example, the fall 1985–86 schedule had 13 series from Universal, 6 from Paramount, 5 from Columbia; 4 from Twentieth Century-Fox, and 3 from Warner Brothers, more than 60 percent of the entire prime-time schedule. Independents, such as Aaron Spelling, Lorimar, Stephen J. Cannell, and Embassy, each had three or four; but many of these series will also rent major-studio space for their productions. In fact one of the more serious complaints of a number of independent producers has been that the studios, who often participate in the financing of this series programming, demand in return that producers use their studios and pay excessively high rental fees for use of production facilities.

21. See, for example, figures cited in Jack Loftus, "Pierce's Diet Keeping ABC

Trim," *Variety*, 15 May 1985, 1, citing annual increases in the network's series-production costs of 20 percent per year during the 1970s and "slowing" to 16 percent per year in the 1980s.

22. As an example of this recent "get tough" policy, see the description of the breach-of-contract suit a series producer brought against performers unwilling to work for the amount specified in their contract in "Warner TV Puts Up Its Dukes, Sues Hazzard Duo for $90 Mil," *Variety*, 30 June 1982, 42.

23. For a more complete discussion of this new network policy, see "Made-Fors Fill CBS Movie Nights As Webs Stop Buying Theatricals," *Variety*, 22 May 1985, 47.

24. John Dempsey, "Majors Pass Up Telepics & Minis," *Variety*, 17 Oct. 1984, 1.

25. This is one reason (financial reward being another) why so many composers seek to perform their own compositions. It gives them an opportunity to interpret their own works as they feel they should be performed. The attitude that most film studios have toward the authors of the works they purchase for production is suggested by the standard clause, in such purchase agreements, that compels the author to waive all artistic rights to the property at time of purchase.

26. Dean Johnson, "Where the Record-Buyer's Dollar Goes: People Who Profit From," *Chicago Tribune*, 17 July 1983, sec. 12.

27. A. D. Murphy, "Distributors' Share of BO Dips Below 40%," *Variety*, 22 Aug. 1984, 3.

28. U.S. Census of Manufacturers, as quoted in James N. Dertouzos and Steven S. Wildman, "A Study of Economic Issues in the Music Recording Industry," (memo) Stanford University, Department of Economics, Studies in Industry Economics, No. 106.

29. Christopher H. Sterling and Timothy Haight, eds., *The Mass Media: Aspen Institute Guide to Communication Industry Trends* (New York: Praeger, 1978), 41.

30. Ibid.

31. Many discount houses continued to operate on a rack jobber basis, but through organizations dealing primarily with major record distributors, rather than through smaller record labels, as in the past. Today, some 20 percent of all record sales are through rack jobber outlets.

32. "Disk Industry Volume Up 15% for 1984; Cassettes Are The Key," *Variety*, 19 Apr. 1985, 87.

33. Ibid.

34. "CBS First to Charge for Music Videos," *Broadcasting*, 1 July 1985, 32.

35. James Melanson, "Homevid Suppliers Start Looking Seriously at Music Programs; Rising Percentage of Market," *Variety*, 27 March 1985, 86.

36. *United States v. Paramount Pictures et al.* 334 U.S. 131 (1948).

37. Sterling and Haight, *The Mass Media*, 34–35, 352.

38. Ibid. 353.

39. As Thomas Guback points out in "Theatrical Film" in Benjamin M. Compaine, ed., *Anatomy of the Communications Industry* (White Plains,

N.Y.: Knowledge Industry, 1982), 254–55, this 50 percent of the majors' released films earning between 75 percent and 85 percent of all screen revenues was relatively constant throughout the 1970s and has remained so through the 1980s.

40. Lawrence Cohn, "Half of Majors' Output from Outside," *Variety*, 4 May 1983, 5.

41. A.D. Murphy, "Global Pic Rentals Tumble 8% in 1984," *Variety*, 12 June 1985, 3.

42. Tom Bierbaum, "Fairfield Group Says Homevid to Generate $3.3 Billion in 1985," *Variety*, 10 July 1985, 77.

43. James Melanson, "Majors to Share Video Rentals," *Variety*, 8 Jan. 1986, 1.

44. This brief discussion of the film distribution process is meant only to provide the basic information necessary to understand its operation in the broader context of mass-entertainment policy and law. For example, this one-dollar breakdown of film proceeds omits, for purposes of simplification, ancillary rights on one hand and ownership participation on the other and includes points in either gross or net proceeds offered as inducement to those involved in its production. Each major film is custom created and differs to some extent from all others in its structuring. For a more complete understanding of this process, see the Guback chapter cited at footnote 39 of this chapter or a basic film text such as Jason Squire, ed., *The Movie Business Book* (Englewood Cliffs, N.J.: Prentice-Hall, 1983).

45. Op. cit., footnote 39, 246. From 1940 to 1949, the major distributors were releasing an average of 421 full-length motion pictures each year. In 1980 they released 138 major pictures, a release rate that has remained relatively constant since that time.

46. One exception to this general rule is the tax-sheltered investment in film production, where the prospect of avoiding immediate taxation on earnings by being able to deduct losses from a film in production has in the past lured some capital into this field. Hollywood labored to retain this tax-deferment provision in order to encourage film investment, but recent amendments to the federal tax code have limited its value in this regard.

47. At the moment Ted Turner has acquired MGM; WCI was blocked by the FTC from acquiring Polygram, but CBS may make a similar move; RCA has acquired the recording interests of the West German media conglomerate Bertelsmann; and another merger is said to be in the process of negotiation between two major film distributors. See Richard Gold, "Major Merger Mania," *Variety*, 17 July 1985, 6.

48. Between 1976 and 1985, the average budget of a major, feature-length motion picture increased from $5.1 to $14.6 million, more than twice the actual rise in the rate of inflation during these years. The cost of a one-hour television-series episode increased from $200,000 to $800,000.

49. In fact, to the extent any cause-and-effect relationship exists between pay-TV and feature-film production, it could be argued that it operated to diminish the number produced each year. In 1970, before the pay-TV era began, major distributors released 207 films; by 1980 that number was down to 138 and increased to 140 in 1984 according to *Variety*, 3 Apr. 1985, 3.

Tracing the Patterns: Primary Sources

The American mass-entertainment industry is undoubtedly the most powerful, pervasive, and popular mass-cultural force in the world today. Robert Stanley's *The Celluloid Empire* (New York: Hastings House, 1978) is one of many books that recount the Hollywood film industry's rise to world dominance through marketing and distribution structures described in works such as Jason Squire's (ed.) *The Movie Business Book* (Englewood Cliffs, NJ: Prentice-Hall, 1983) or discussed with less admiration in Janet Wasko's *Movies and Money* (Norwood, N.J.: Ablex Press, 1982). While Geoffrey Stokes, in *Starmaking Machinery* (New York: Vintage Books, 1976), details the merchandising device that made the United States film industry famous, Thomas H. Guback, in *The International Film Industry* (Bloomington, Ind.: Indiana University Press, 1969) and in his "Theatrical Film" in Benjamin M. Compaine's *Anatomy of the Communications Industry: Who Owns the Media?* ([White Plains, N.Y.: Knowledge Industry, 1982], 199–298), describes how a combination of capital, experience, and shrewd bargaining, undergirded by carefully drafted agreements and government support, have all helped to maintain the economy of this mass-cultural empire.

The literature of the American music industry is far less copious. Other than personalized accounts, such as Clive Davis's *Clive: Inside the Record Business* (New York: Ballantine Books, 1976), or "how to do it" works, such as Paula Branov's *Inside the Music Publishing Industry* (White Plains, N.Y.: Knowledge Industry, 1980), Walter Hurst's *How to Be a Music Publisher* (Beverly Hills, Calif.: Seven Arts Press, 1980), or Dick Weisman's *The Music Business* (New York: Crown Press, 1978), only Serge Denisoff's *Solid Gold: The Popular Record Industry* (New Brunswick, N.J.: Transaction Books, 1976) and the more recent work of James N. Dertouzos and Steven S. Wildman, in "A Study of Economic Issues in the Music Recording Industry" (Palo Alto, Calif.: Stanford University, Studies in Industry Economics, No. 106, 1984), provide any sense of clear trends, issues, and economic concerns of those producing and distributing this nation's music.

The assumption that an increase in the number of mass-cultural distribution channels will, in itself, operate to dilute the degree of concentration of control over American mass culture by stimulating a larger and more diverse range of film and musical productions from an ever-increasing number of producers was a popular one during this era. It allowed policy makers to rely on telecommunications technology alone to solve all troublesome problems that might otherwise demand legislative or administrative solution. This hope was expressed during the 1960s in the Presidential Task Force on Communication Policy's *Final Report*

(Washington, D.C.: Government Printing Office, 1968), but it had become a matter of faith by the mid-1970s, as reflected in the Research and Policy Committee of the Committee for Economic Development report, *Broadcasting and Cable Television: Policies for Diversity and Change* (New York: Committee for Economic Development, 1975), as it was becoming the cornerstone for economically oriented structural rather than content control in works such as Bruce M. Owen's *Economics and Freedom of Expression: Media Structure and the First Amendment* (Cambridge, Mass.: Ballinger, 1975) and "Structural Approaches to the Problem of Television Network Dominance" (Durham, N.C.: Duke University Graduate School of Business Administration, Paper 27, 1976).

Now, during the 1980s, this optimistic view of the corrective powers of unbridled competition in the field of electronic mass media is being questioned more and more rigorously; and as the course handbook *Antitrust, the Media and New Technology* (New York: Practicing Law Institute Handbook 137, 1981) suggests, the new distribution systems may, in fact, have complicated rather than simplified the task of employing public policy to encourage the establishment of a vigorously competitive mass media marketplace in the United States.

CHAPTER EIGHT

ELECTRONIC MEDIA
AND THE MARKETPLACE

Cable TV and the Programming Marketplace

Although media lobbying organizations have been advocating a market-place solution for the problems of regulated media service since the early 1970s, it is interesting to note that their support for free enterprise in this field has tended to be somewhat selective. That is, while the NAB, the NCTA, and other trade groups support the abolition of all federal controls over media service to the public, none of them favor the rescission of the specific federal laws that protect them from market-place forces threatening their own competitive position.

Thus, for example, during the 1970s the cable-TV lobbying organization, NCTA, worked diligently for its own deregulatory freedom from broadcast carriage rules and just as diligently for the compulsory licensing provisions of the Copyright Act of 1976. This act not only forced television-program syndicators to allow cable-TV carriage of their programs when broadcast but also denied these program suppliers the right to have the marketplace establish the price for cable-TV usage of the programs.[1] In other words, while the NCTA sought freedom from federal controls over its carriage of broadcast signals, it was perfectly willing to accept federal intervention to dictate the amount cable operators would be required to pay program suppliers, who had no choice but to allow this usage.

The act described cable carriage as *secondary* transmission of a copyrighted work and created a body known as the Copyright Royalty Tribunal to develop a scale of payments cable operators would make for the use of such transmissions.[2] The money collected in this manner would then be paid by the Copyright Royalty Tribunal to various groups of program suppliers who filed claims with the tribunal for compensation. This compulsory licensing arrangement was a clear legislative victory for the NCTA because the broadcaster's NAB, the film distributor's Motion Picture Association of America, and various sports organizations all sought to make cable systems bargain for program rights in the marketplace. However, the NCTA was able to convince Congress that a single cable operator could not possibly negotiate with hundreds of program suppliers for rights to cable carriage. In addition, the cable industry pointed out that, in the absence of such a compulsory system, broadcasters and their program suppliers might attempt to use their superior bargaining position to deny cable access to these features.[3]

During the first few years of the Copyright Royalty Tribunal's operation, the cable industry had reason to be pleased with its lobbying efforts in this field. Until 1983 each cable operator was required to pay into the pool established to compensate program suppliers only 0.625 percent of the system's gross basic subscriber revenues in order to import the first nonlocal television signal and an additional 0.425 percent for each of the next three distant signals — a total of less than 2 percent of these revenues for four distant program channels. From the $15 million generated by these payments in 1978, the tribunal allocated about 75 percent of the fund to compensate program syndicators and movie distributors, 12 percent to compensate sports organizations, and only 3.5 percent to compensate braodcasters, dividing the remaining 10 percent among public television and various music-rights organizations. The NAB challenged this apportionment decision, but the Court of Appeals for the District of Columbia sustained the tribunal's determination that syndicators, film distributors, and sports organizations suffered far greater damage from cable importation practices than did television stations.[4]

However, after the FCC rescinded its restrictions on the number of distant television broadcast signals that a cable system could carry and abolished its requirement that cable systems black out programs on imported signals for which local television stations had exclusive market rights in 1982, the Copyright Royalty Tribunal instituted new proceedings to adjust cable license fees and its distribution formula to reflect these changes.[5] After lengthy deliberations, the tribunal decided to increase substantially the percentage of gross basic subscriber revenues that cable systems would have to pay for the privilege of carrying distant broadcast signals after January 1, 1983. The new rates ranged from 8 to 16 times higher than the tribunal's original fees. Thus, for example, any cable system that had taken advantage of the FCC's distant signal rule rescission to add the programming of additional independent television stations not in its broadcast market would now be subject to a new license fee of 3.75 percent of its annual subscriber revenues for each signal of this type that it wished to carry. At this point it was the cable industry that felt the tribunal's actions to be unjust and challenged this massive increase in the federal courts. Again, however, the tribunal's decisions were sustained by the court.[6]

Because of this general rate increase, as well as other upward adjustments based on the rate of inflation, the pool available for compensation of various programming groups had increased to more than $80 million by 1984. However, disputes over the tribunal's allocation of these funds among rival claimants has continually delayed disbursements. According to the provisions of the 1976 act, if the tribunal believes such a valid dispute exists, it must "withhold from distribution an amount sufficient to satisfy all claims with respect to which a controversy exists."[7] In addition to denying program owners use of this money while it remained impounded in the U.S. Treasury, these clashes have also diverted to legal fees a substantial amount of funding that was intended as compensation for losses incurred.[8]

By 1981 the process had become so difficult to administer that the first chairman of the Copyright Royalty Tribunal, Clarence James, Jr., recommended to Congress that the entire cable compulsory license system be abolished and that the marketplace be allowed to establish the fair price for cable usage of broadcast programming.[9] Yet, despite its discontent with the higher importation fees now in effect, the cable industry has shown no inclination to urge the abolition of this licensing system in order to negotiate for program rights in the same marketplace it advocates with such conviction for all other areas of media service.

Broadcasting and the Marketplace

The broadcast industry has also been somewhat inconsistent in its support of the marketplace in areas where freedom of choice might threaten its own economic interests. Rather than allow cable systems freely to choose the television programming they deliver to their subscribers, the NAB has favored continuation of the FCC's must-carry rules and has compelled any cable system located within a broadcast market to provide access on its channels for each local or substantially viewed television station in that area.[10]

Turner Broadcasting petitioned the FCC to rescind these rules in 1980, contending that its broadcast protection policy prevented many 12-channel cable systems from offering their subscibers Turner's WTBS superstation, its Cable News Network, or other specialized cable services.[11] During the same year, Quincy Cable TV, a system located between Spokane and Seattle, Washington, provided the perfect factual example of the Turner Broadcasting argument in a proceeding being reviewed by the FCC's Cable Television Bureau. According to the agency's rules, Quincy was required to devote 3 of its 12 basic service channels to the carriage of the local network affiliates in Spokane, Washington, despite the fact that a system survey indicated that its subscribers preferred to view the programming from Seattle network affiliates approximately the same distance from the cable community. The cable operator argued that being forced to carry the three less popular network affiliate services as well as the three the cable's subscribers demanded denied it the capacity to offer ESPN, superstation WOR, and other similar satellite-delivered program channels its viewers also had a right to receive. When the commission's cable bureau refused to issue a waiver exempting Quincy from the rule's requirements, the system simply deleted the unwanted Spokane signals on its own, ignoring coninued FCC directives to comply with the rule until the full commission imposed a $5000 forfeiture on the system in 1982 and ordered immediate compliance.[12]

Instead of complying, Quincy filed a petition for review in the United States Court of Appeals for the District of Columbia, arguing that the FCC's mandatory carriage rules violated the free-speech rights of both the cable operator and the cable subscriber. Sensing the magnitude of this threat to broadcasting, the NAB, the Association of Independent Television Stations, and the Public Broadcast Service all joined the Spokane television stations in intervening on behalf of the FCC in this proceeding. On the other side, only the town of Quincy, in which the system was located, joined the cable operator in its petition.

In July 1985 a three-judge panel decided that the rule, as drafted, was clearly an unconstitutional infringement on freedom of expression and that it constrained communication alternatives far more severely than any regulatory concern for local-service broadcasting could justify.[13] As Judge J. Skelly Wright observed in his opinion, in attempting to protect local broadcasters from competitive injury, the FCC adopted regulatory provisions so broad that they "protect each and every broadcaster, from the struggling UHF educational station to the most profitable VHF network affiliate — no matter how profitable, no matter how invulnerable to significant cable induced revenue losses."[14] At the same time, however, the court was unwilling to declare that no effort to impose television carriage requirements on cable systems would be acceptable; instead, the court limited its holding solely to the specific set of rules challenged by Quincy. Although not encouraging the effort, Judge Wright noted that should "the Commission wish to redraft the rules in a manner more sensitive to the First Amendment concerns we outline today, it is, of course, free to do so."[15]

Rather than appeal this decision, FCC Chairman Mark Fowler indicated his support for its holding, a sentiment shared by a majority of his fellow commissioners. However, only a few weeks later, Fowler, under pressure from the NAB and several key committee heads in Congress, agreed to issue a notice of inquiry and proposed rulemaking to consider proposals that included "a set of carefully crafted mandatory carriage rules and clear justification for the policy aims and constitutionality of such rules."[16]

Unwilling to rely completely on the commission under these circumstances, broadcast industry lobbyists sought help in Congress, where two bills designed to avoid the constitutional issues of the Quincy case were introduced as the FCC began its deliberations.[17] These NAB-sponsored bills would make the continuation of cable TV's compulsory program-license system dependent on the cable industry's willingness to continue to carry local broadcast signals. In essence, an industry constantly declaring its dedication to the marketplace seemed in this case to be using the marketplace as a threat and to be willing to trade off the future bargaining rights of program suppliers in return for the cable industry's waiver of its freedom of choice in the selection of its program sources.

Under these circumstances, however, logical consistency was the least important consideration involved in such political maneuvering by the NAB. With cable TV already serving more than 45 percent of all American television households, a decision to delete a particular local station from the cable channels of a major system in most markets would obviously have extremely severe economic consequences. Many of the 280 new independent television stations that began operations during the 1980s were uniquely vulnerable to this threat of deletion, because they were so dependent on the cable system extension of their coverage that had led to their construction in the first place and yet offered viewers no programming the system could not duplicate from other sources already on its channels. Stories began to circulate of cable systems asking as much as $20,000 a month to continue carrying the signals of the local independent stations that operators now had the right to delete; thus, the NAB was called into action to protect these stations from the rigors of the marketplace.[18]

In March 1986, the NAB was successful in wresting significant television signal carriage concessions from the NCTA. By August of this same year, the FCC, under increasing pressure from Congress, enacted a new set of must-carry requirements for cable TV that closely paralleled the terms of the NAB-NCTA agreement.[19] These interim rules, effective for the following five years, require all cable-TV systems with more than 20 channels to devote at least 7 of those channels to the carriage of local television stations. Systems with more than 26 channels must dedicate 25 percent of their channel capacity to must-carry stations. In addition, every cable system must provide at least one public broadcast station signal, no cable operator may demand payment from a broadcaster for such required carriage, and the system must provide these channels to subscribers as part of their basic service, without additional charge.

In reality, the most ingenious aspect of these new regulations is the approach the commission has used to protect them from being overturned by the same federal court that earlier rejected mandatory carriage requirements in the *Quincy Cable* decision. To accomplish this, the FCC made these new cable carriage rules temporary rather than permanent and justified their short-term imposition by stating that they provided a transitional period during which a new electronic device might restore the competitive balance between cable-TV and local television stations.

This device, known as the "A/B switch," allows a cable-TV subscriber to change easily and almost instantaneously from cable-TV to over-the-air reception. According to the FCC's reasoning, once such an A/B switch has been purchased and installed in a substantial number of cable-TV households, the viewer rather than the cable operator will be determining which locally available television signal to select. At that point, then, a truly competitive cable-TV viewing environment will have been established in which no further federal protection of local television viewership will be necessary.

Unfortunately, however, the commission seems to stand alone in its optimism about the future of the A/B switch. Experts testifying before the agency have been almost unanimous in their appraisal of the device as one whose time will never come, because only a small percentage of American cable-TV households own or are interested in purchasing the type of antenna essential for the over-the-air viewing that the A/B switch will permit. In the absence of public desire to return to the era of the mast antenna, these experts see no logical basis for the commission's faith in the eventual popularity of this device.

What they fail to realize is that whatever its future prospects, the A/B switch has already proven its value to the FCC as a legal device to shelter the agency's new must-carry rules from judicial review. As the commission knows from past experience, the federal judiciary will almost certainly defer to the agency's judgment within its special area of competence. The judiciary will refuse to overturn any experimental policy, no matter how repressive, if it involves technological issues the agency is presumed to have the unique capacity to resolve.

As the commission was guaranteeing the television industry a five-year reprieve from the rigors of the cable-TV signal carriage marketplace, it also put the cable-TV industry on notice of other industry marketplace advantages that might be in jeopardy. The FCC announced its intention to reevaluate its earlier decisions to allow cable TV unlimited authority to import syndicated and network programming; the FCC realized that it may not have fully considered the competitive advantages the compulsory license gave cable TV in its dealings with broadcasters.

At this point, then, the broadcast industry has won at least a short-term advantage in its continuing efforts to avoid the need to compete for cable-TV carriage in a marketplace environment. Yet to the extent that the FCC has exaggerated the impact of the A/B switch on television viewing behavior, the agency has merely postponed the choice it must ultimately make between protectionism and the competitive environment favored by the federal courts.

Aware of the FCC's vulnerability, the NAB continues to pressure Congress for long-term legislative relief from this competitive challenge. At the same time, the television industry has also turned to Congress to ask for federal legislation to aid stations in their long-term struggle to avoid ASCAP and BMI blanket music performance licenses. Most radio stations seemed reasonably satisfied with licensing arrangements that allowed them full use of music from ASCAP and BMI's composers and publishers in return for payment of less than 1 percent of their annual advertising revenues. For television, however, with its much larger advertising revenues and far less extensive use of music, neither the blanket license nor the per-use alternative offered by ASCAP and BMI seemed reasonably related to the actual value a station owner received in return.

Beginning in 1950, the All-Industry Television Station Music License Committee, negotiating on behalf of its member stations, sought some other type of arrangement with ASCAP and BMI that would reflect more accurately the minimal benefits the blanket licenses granted. Although each new round of negotiations resulted in a reduction in the percentage of advertising revenues charged during the subsequent license period, neither ASCAP nor BMI was willing to alter a licensing structure that, by 1970, provided an estimated 20 to 25 percent of their annual music-performing-rights revenue.[20]

Failing to renegotiate the terms for usage with the performing-rights societies, CBS television began an antitrust action against ASCAP and BMI in 1970. CBS alleged that ASCAP and BMI had acted in concert to prevent those they represented from dealing directly with the television network or its producers who sought to purchase broadcast performance rights directly from the parties who held title to them.[21] The court ultimately decided against the television network and was convinced that CBS had sufficient bargaining power with its program producers to compel them to seek and obtain the musical clearances that the music licensing organizations contended they or their members were willing to provide.

This decision encouraged each of the three television networks to begin planning for an era in which they would require every program producer to obtain clearance for all musical broadcast performing rights before offering a production to the network for inclusion in its schedule.

NBC is currently pursuing this policy most vigorously, operating under interim blanket licenses with ASCAP and BMI as it attempts to establish a source licensing arrangement through its independent producers. If successful, NBC could save the estimated $18 million it now pays annually for its blanket licenses, obtaining rights to incidental music outside these productions either by direct purchase from the composer or by payment on a per-use basis.

In 1978 a group of local television stations began their own antitrust action against ASCAP and BMI, alleging the same type of anticompetitive practices CBS had described in 1970. Unlike CBS, however, these local stations were successful in convincing the federal trial court judge that blanket music-licensing agreements were anticompetitive in nature, because ASCAP and BMI were using them to obtain payment from the stations for the broadcast use of music.[22] According to the lower court opinion, what made the conduct of ASCAP and BMI anticompetitive was their concerted effort to discourage program producers from obtaining, through a single transaction, complete clearance for all broadcast station usage of the music included in their programs. Although such source licensing would have been more efficient and competitive in nature, the court held that the licensing had been inhibited by ASCAP and BMI simply because preclearance of musical rights to 90 percent of the nonnetwork programming that each television station carried might persuade stations to abandon the blanket license for the far less lucrative per-use agreement.

ASCAP and BMI appealed this decision, and a higher federal court reversed the trial court's holding, finding that the musical licensing organizations had done nothing in constraint of trade.[23] In the view of the appeals court, if local stations found source musical licensing to be a more attractive alternative than a blanket license, they had every opportunity to insist, as the networks did, that syndicators offer them only precleared features for broadcast use. In essence, the court refused to draw a distinction between the economic position of the network and that of the local station in dealing with a program syndicator, applying the precedent of the earlier CBS case to resolve this controversy between the broadcast industry and its music suppliers.

When the United States Supreme Court refused to review this appellate court decision, broadcasting turned immediately to Congress to regain through legislation what it seemed to have lost in litigation. In October 1985 an NAB-sponsored bill, HR 3521, was introduced in the House of Representatives, which required as a matter of federal law that every television-program syndicator acquire full musical broadcast performance rights before being allowed to offer any production to a television station.[24] Two months later an identical bill, S 1980, was introduced in the Senate with Judiciary Committee Chairman Strom Thurmond as one of the bill's principal sponsors.

If the NAB legislative campaign to establish source musical licensing by federal edict is successful, it will indeed free virtually all television stations from the need for a blanket music license. The All-Industry Television Station Music License Committee has already begun discussion with the American Association of Advertising Agencies to obtain advance clearance of all music used in broadcast commercials, and several music libraries now offer background music for local production with all broadcast rights included. Because network program music has been precleared for affiliate station usage, closing the only remaining gap in the television music performance prelicensing system through public law obviously appears quite attractive to broadcasters who resent sharing any percentage of their advertising revenues with music-performing-rights societies.

Although the economic justification for seeking government control over what had been a system of privately negotiated agreements is apparent, it is interesting to note nonetheless how quickly a broadcaster's philosophical objections to federal regulation can be discarded when such an abstract sentiment would have an adverse effect on station revenues.

The Marketplace Mirage

In this way, the broadcast industry is no different from cable, program suppliers, or any other segment of the business community in that it can always distinguish between the general principle and its particular application in order to decide when a theoretical commitment must be abandoned to achieve a practical goal. Thus, to media leaders, marketplace, deregulation, and freedom of choice are not sacred ends in themselves but are simply means to justify certain industry policies; therefore, they are valid only to the extent that they aid in realizing the objectives of those policies.

In reality, there is nothing unreasonable or even improper in a largely deregulated cable-TV industry supporting continued regulation of the supply and price of its programming. Similarly, no one can criticize a broadcast industry that is philosophically committed to the marketplace while seeking to invoke federal law to compel cable carriage of its programming and musical rights to be included in the programming it purchases. It is only sensible for broadcasters, cable-TV operators, and others in the media business to be reluctant to rely totally on the marketplace for providing access to the scarce commodity of popular-appeal programming, the music such programming requires, or those channels necessary for its delivery. What these political tactics do reveal is not a lack of principle, but only a lack of confidence in marketplace solutions by those most knowledgeable about media operation. Media industry leaders realize that the marketplace is not and never has been *the* answer to the media problems regulation has been unable to solve during the past half-century, but only one possible solution to certain problems in particular situations.

For a marketplace to work effectively, there must be a wide range of both suppliers and purchasers, with spirited competition among the members of each group, and relative parity in the bargaining positions of buyer and seller. Such a condition does not currently exist in the mass media programming marketplace, with each rival media-delivery service heavily dependent on the same small band of major mass-entertainment suppliers capable of providing the proven stars, popular properties, and marketing skills essential for attracting mass audiences. Because of this, it is in that very programming marketplace where the public seeks the broadest range of competitive diversity that media interests work most diligently to protect themselves through regulatory intervention.

Perhaps, then, what all of this suggests most clearly is that if media industries are reluctant to rely on the vagaries of a marketplace in areas most significant for the media's economic survival, it may be equally unwise for the American public to rely too heavily on this same marketplace to determine the qualities of anything as significant as that mass-cultural environment these services create.

Media leaders are fully aware of the fact that simply increasing the number of delivery channels has little or no effect on the competitiveness of the programming marketplace. It would seem as though the time might have come for the public and its political leaders to arrive at the same realization.

Notes

1. Title 17, United States Code was amended in its entirety by Public Law 94–553, 94th Stat. 2541 (1976). The compulsory-licensing provisions for "secondary transmission by cable systems" are set out in par. 111, sec. D of this act.
2. The structure and functions of this Copyright Royalty Tribunal are described in secs. 801–810 of the above act.
3. A summary of these arguments and their effect on the ultimate form of the provisions of Public Law 94–553 can be found in House of Representatives Report 94–1476 (1976).
4. *National Association of Broadcasters v. Copyright Royalty Tribunal*, 675 F.2d 367 (1982).

5. *CRT 1982 Distribution Proceeding and Partial Distribution of Fees.* 48 Fed. Reg. 46412 (12 Oct. 1983).
6. *National Cable Television Assn. v. Copyright Royalty Tribunal,* 689 F.2d 1077 (1982).
7. USC 17, par. 111 (d)(4)(C).
8. At this point all of the 1978, 85 percent of the 1979, and 80 percent of the 1980 royalties have been paid out by the Treasury, as well as 90 percent of the royalties for 1981 and 1982. Legal fees are estimated to have absorbed between 25 and 30 percent of the total proceeds. See Paul Harris, "Copyright Tribunal vs. Showbiz," *Variety,* 30 Apr. 1983, 1.
9. See "Copyright Tribunal Topper Tells Stunned Congress: Scuttle the Whole Thing," *Variety,* 11 Mar. 1981, 44.
10. These mandatory carriage rules were enacted as 47 C.F.R. Parts 76.55, 76.57, 76.59, 76.61, and 76.63.
11. *Turner Broadcasting v. FCC,* No. 83–2050 (D.C. Cir. 1983), later consolidated for hearing with *Quincy Cable TV v. FCC,* 768 F.2d 1434 (1985).
12. Quincy Cable TV, 89 FCC 2d 1128 (1982), rehearing denied 53 RR2d 201 (1983).
13. *Quincy Cable TV v. FCC,* 768 F.2d 1434 (1985).
14. Ibid. 1462.
15. Ibid. 1463.
16. "FCC Decides against Must-Carry Appeal," *Broadcasting,* 15 Aug. 1985, 28 and "Must Carry: Coming to a Boil at the FCC," *Broadcasting,* 23 Sept. 1985, 23.
17. See "Going to War over Must Carry," *Broadcasting,* 29 July 1985, 23; "Must-Carry Week: The Beat Goes On," *Broadcasting,* 6 Aug. 1985, 27; and "Moral Support from Hill on Must Carry," *Broadcasting,* 13 Jan. 1986, 156. During the latter part of 1985, bills introduced by Representative John Byrant and Senators Slade Gordon and Paul Trible conditioned cable's compulsory license on a system's carriage of local broadcast signals. Another bill by Representative Barney Frank was later redrafted to delete the local carriage requirement.
18. See, for example, "Must-Carry Damage Case Study," *Broadcasting,* 16 Sept. 1985, 35 and Ron Merrell, "Long Ago and Far Away," *Television Broadcast Communications,* Oct. 1985, 8.
19. For a detailed account of the terms of the new cable-TV must-carry rules, see, "Must Carry Denouement: Enough Bad News to Go Around," *Broadcasting,* 11 Aug. 1986, 37–38. For a general description of the events leading up to the commission's action, see "The FCC and Must Carry: Converging on Consensus," *Broadcasting,* 4 Aug. 1986, 39–40, and "Cable Coming In for Cool Reassessment at FCC," *Broadcasting,* 28 July 1986, 31–32.
20. "Broadcasters Press On against ASCAP, BMI; Lotsa Bucks Hang in the Balance," *Variety,* 8 Jan. 1986, 209.
21. *CBS v. ASCAP,* 620 F.2d 930 (2d Cir. 1980).
22. *Buffalo Broadcasting Co. v. ASCAP,* 546 F. Supp. 274 (S.D.N.Y. 1982).
23. *Buffalo Broadcasting v. ASCAP,* 744 F.2d 917 (2d Cir. 1984).
24. *CBS v. ASCAP.*

Tracing the Patterns: Primary Sources

This chapter has provided only three brief descriptions of recent efforts by the broadcast and cable-TV industries to escape the rigors of the marketplace through protectionist legislation or regulation. Rather than provide a detailed listing of sources describing these specific efforts, it seems more useful to offer at least an overview of that extensive body of literature that places such maneuvering in its broader political and regulatory context.

Some classic works reflecting the skill of various industries in using public law institutions to reduce, rather than increase, the degree of competition in their fields include Marver H. Bernstein's *Regulating Business by Independent Commission* (Princeton, N.J.: Princeton University Press, 1955), Robert E. Cushman's *The Independent Regulatory Commissions* (New York: Oxford University Press, 1941), and Samuel P. Huntington's "The Marasmus of the Interstate Commerce Commission: The Commission, the Railroads and the Public Interest," (*Yale Law Journal* 61 [April 1952]: 467–509). More recent works of a similar nature include Clair Wilcox and William G. Shepard's *Public Policies Towards Business*, 5th ed. (Homewood, Ill.: Irwin, 1975), Alfred Kahn's *The Economics of Regulation: Principles and Institutions* (New York: Wiley, 1971), and the particularly insightful Bruce M. Owen and Ronald Braeutigam's *The Regulation Game: Strategic Use of Administrative Process* (Cambridge, Mass.: Ballinger, 1978).

Similar works concentrating on the field of broadcasting or electronic mass media regulation are Glen O. Robinson's "The Federal Communications Commission: An Essay on Regulatory Watchdogs" (*Virginia Law Review* 64 [March 1978]: 169–262); Bernard Schwartz's *The Professor and the Commissions* (New York: Knopf, 1959); and Roger G. Noll, Morton J. Peck, and John J. McGowan's *Economic Aspects of Television Regulation* (Washington, D.C.: Brookings Institute, 1973).

Two recent studies of particular interest relating to the issue of the compulsory license in the area of cable-TV programming are Stanley Besen, et al., "Copyright Liability for Cable Television: Compulsory License and the Coase Theorem" (*Journal of Law and Economics* 21 [Spring 1978]: 67–100) and Stuart N. Brotman's discussion of alternatives to compulsory licensing in "Cable Television and Copyright: Legislation and the Marketplace Model" (*Comm/ent Law Journal* 2 [Spring 1980]: 477–87).

CHAPTER NINE

THE LIMITATION
OF LAISSEZ FAIRE

Deregulation and Diversity

Will diminishing the degree of federal regulatory authority over American electronic mass media really stimulate the development of a more diverse, vigorously competitive programming marketplace in the United States? Although the FCC has recently seemed eager to accept the blame for inhibiting the competitive tendencies of broadcasting and other media in the past, its regulatory record does not fully substantiate this newfound sense of guilt. Looking back over nearly six decades of federal policy pronouncements in the broadcasting field, it is difficult to find any statement by either the FRC or the FCC that intended to discourage such diversity or competitiveness.

It is true, of course, that the actions of these commissions were not always consistent with the noble sentiments expressed in their declarations of policy. Thus, for example, an FCC constantly declaring dedication to the concept of the broadest possible diversity in audience viewing alternatives could at the same time suppress the growth of the cable-TV systems capable of providing this diversity. Yet, it might be argued that in doing so, the agency was simply showing its greater dedication to the principle of local service, which cable growth tended to undermine. Whether or not this was the sole motivation for the commission's broadcast-signal-carriage restrictions is certainly subject to question, but it is unquestionably true that once it assumed regulatory jurisdiction over cable TV, the FCC acted rapidly to require local cable-TV programming and later expanded this requirement to include the provision of other community-oriented service channels as well.[1]

The agency's early television and FM broadcast policies may have been less justifiable in terms of public interest, but it is only fair to note that both the FCC's reluctance to authorize full-scale television service during the 1930s and its damaging shift of the FM frequency band after World War II were positions favored, advocated, and supported by the most influential members of the broadcast industry itself.[2] This certainly does not excuse these anticompetitive policies, but it does suggest that industry leadership was no more eager to encourage such competition than was the commission.

As far as regulation of broadcast practices is concerned, the commission's licensing policies were designed to encourage both local ownership and diversified, balanced programming. In addition, the agency attempted to limit network domination of broadcast service and to restrict various combinations of broadcast and cross-media ownership.

Constitutional and legislative constraints prevented the agency from exerting a consistent, constructive influence on national broadcast programming practices. Its cumbersome process and narrow jurisdictional base allowed the networks to maneuver around FCC policy positions virtually at will.

The only strategy the FCC could employ to influence the nature of broadcast service was to create a consensus within the industry that supported the action or the position the FCC intended to take. Obviously, this severely limited the agency to policies where either the benefits from the industry's acting or the consequences of the industry's not acting were capable of motivating broadcasters out of self-interest; but the consensus strategy represented at least one channel, however narrow, for public sentiment and concern to affect national broadcast programming decisions.

During an era when conventional wisdom sees regulation as constraining competition, it may be useful to recall that at no time during this entire period of broadcast regulation did any segment of the industry seek to provide the public with a broader range of communication services than the federal government required the industry to provide.[3] Rather, during each policy conflict, it was the FRC or the FCC urging stations to provide more diverse, locally oriented service; schedules balanced with a greater variety of program categories; and more extensive use of independently produced features. These were all policy efforts that the industry steadfastly opposed.

As we have seen, it was the industry rather than the government that transformed each new allocation of frequencies into outlets of centralized national programming and fought every effort to make it more responsive to public interests through processes such as the fairness doctrine, counteradvertising, and public participation format change. Now, however, some argue that such processes or channels are no longer necessary because telecommunications technology stands poised to present us with such a vast variety of DBS-, MMDS-, LPTV-, and VCR-delivered entertainment and information options that all segments of our society will be adequately served without the need for public policy intervention. Unfortunately, this argument is flawed by its failure to distinguish between mere expansion in the number of communication channels and an increase in the volume and variety of the mass-cultural material these channels will deliver.

Once again we are being asked to place our faith in new delivery systems rather than in new sources of mass-cultural content. Perfectly rational economists who would never think of predicting that simply doubling the number of telephone circuits into the sales office of a widget company would automatically double its volume of business are making equally naive projections about the impact of additional channels on the quality and diversity of mass-entertainment content.

Deregulation may be justifiable simply on the basis that it is neither equitable nor sensible to continue to supervise the performance of one class of electronic mass media services while all others are free of government control. Even though spectrum allocation, communication common carrier, and technical standards policies will still exert a significant influence on future media activities, that influence will be a generalized one and will affect all in the same circumstances to the same degree rather than be directed at only one service, as is presently the case. It is one thing, however, to deregulate broadcasting only to end the discriminatory legal burden it alone must bear and quite another to abolish all processes for the supervision of electronic mass media service with the expectation that this abolishment in itself will create a competitive environment in which a broad, diverse marketplace of electronic mass media service will flourish.

Reducing the scope of broadcast regulatory requirements can be merely a strategic withdrawal from a policy position that the federal government seems unable to defend and that, by its nature, is limited so as to preserve a right of reentry should conditions change radically. Unfortunately, the FCC has chosen instead to rely on its philosophical commitment to the marketplace to justify its full retreat from regulatory responsibilities in the field of broadcasting, destroying as it pulls back every procedure or process that might allow some future administration to reenter the field.

At the moment, only Congress stands between the commission and the full realization of its broadcast deregulatory objectives, while local franchises, in some cases augmented by state regulation, continue to impose public-service responsibilities on cable-TV systems. As long as the Communications Act of 1934 remains in force, the public will retain the legal interests in broadcast service created by the act's provisions, rights that will be recognized by the courts in actions brought by citizen groups if the FCC refuses to act.

However, in the Cable Communications Policy Act of 1984, the tone of the legislative language clearly implies that Congress has reserved the right to preempt any state or local regulation it considers to be in conflict with federal mass communication policy.[4] By deregulating basic cable subscription fee controls and establishing a nationally uniform procedure for franchise renewal, the federal government seems intent on expanding its jurisdictional base in order to free the cable industry from as many franchise requirements as it can at this point. To do this, the federal government is using an incremental process that will ultimately deprive state and local governments of any meaningful supervisory role in this field.

As the same time, it is quite possible that Congress will eventually abandon the communications act or at least slash away all but the most routine spectrum, allocation, and assignment functions described in the act. Each session of Congress brings forth a new group of bills to rescind most of its major provisions. Debate at this point centers primarily on the price the industry will pay for the rescission, either in terms of spectrum fees or other concessions that individual congressional committees seek in return for their willingness to support such legislative relief.[5]

Thus, as we move rapidly toward the point of no return in the deregulation of American electronic mass media, what do private mass entertainment policy patterns from the past suggest about the nature of future services in a field that may soon be free of any substantial public policy guidance.

The Shape of Things to Come

It is often said that each new mass-entertainment service in the United States simply imitates the most successful formats of its predecessors. In terms of broadcasting, for example, network radio turned to vaudeville for comedy, turned to the dance hall for popular music, and adapted the Victorian serial novel approach to the needs of daytime drama. However, the situation comedy, the quiz show, and eventually the call-in program were certainly refined, if not invented, by radio.

Television, on the other hand, was far more derivative in its development. It borrowed virtually every program form directly from radio and later supplemented its schedule with feature films directly from Hollywood. In that sense, modern pay-TV, in each of its various forms, has been the least innovative of all, relying almost exclusively upon feature film to build its subscriber base, with networklike situation comedies and specials being scheduled primarily to reduce its overall programming costs.

What this seems to suggest quite clearly is the severe limitations that the costs of polished, professional, visual mass entertainment production impose on innovative programming. At our current rate of exchange, the 30-minute situation comedy produced for network radio in 1940 would cost between $4000 and $6000 per episode today, while the same half-hour of television situation comedy now costs $300,000 to $400,000 per episode to produce. Yet, even this televised production budget is comparatively modest when compared with the average major motion picture price of $15 million for the typical 150 minutes of screen time. In other words, the $200 per minute of network radio comedy becomes $10,000 per minute in the transition to television, and $100,000 per minute as a major film. With each moment of television 50 times more expensive and each moment of feature film 500 times more expensive than the old network radio shows, it is easy to understand why visual media do not encourage a particularly venturesome approach toward new entertainment concepts or formats.

Yet in their efforts to avoid risk by seeking only established formats and proven performers to build their essential audience bases, new media will only succeed in driving these prices still higher, as each rival seeks the earliest possible release date for popular feature films or the most attractive stars for its own special programming. As we have seen, the mass entertainment industry is ideally structured to absorb an almost infinite amount of additional funding without increasing its output of features, making this type of competition far more likely to reduce the field of successful delivery systems rather than to increase either the volume or the variety of programming distributed.

Structural reform has been suggested as one possible approach to creating a more vigorously competitive environment in the field of mass communications. Those who favor such a strategy for attempting to create a true marketplace in communication services urge strict enforcement of existing antitrust laws in all situations involving mass media conglomerates. They also argue for special ownership restrictions to be imposed on those engaged primarily in the production or distribution of media content.[6] Thus, for example, they would urge the Justice Department to examine the competitive implications of recent merger negotiations in the music, broadcast, and cable industries far more carefully than those occurring in other areas of commerce. In addition, they would propose certain constraints on the market or service area of any media organization, such as the maximum 25 percent of the population that can now be served by any single combination of group-owned television stations. As they point out, a major advantage of public policy focusing on the economic rather than the communication service implications of media concentration is that such legal tactics raise no First Amendment issues to constrain government action.[7]

Yet, however appealing this approach may appear to be, its fundamental weakness is that structural reform has the capacity to achieve meaningful change only if those evils it would remedy currently exist. In other words, this reform movement rests upon the assumption that the limited amount of competitive diversity in mass-entertainment content is the result of artificial constraints imposed by the industry on its production and distribution. As we have seen, there is little evidence of any such conspiracies in this field; the industry has gravitated naturally toward the degree of concentration of capital and skill that is essential for efficient operation. Thus, public policy's attempting to transform the industry into small production and distribution entities is about as futile as was the effort to break up the film system of the 1940s to achieve this same result.

Recently the FCC appears to have been following this structural approach to media competition in its efforts to encourage, or at least to not discourage, Rupert Murdoch from launching a fourth major television network in the United States. When Murdoch sought to acquire the Metromedia broadcast properties after purchasing Twentieth Century-Fox early in 1985, the one regulatory barrier standing in the path of the sale was the cross-ownership rule. Murdoch already owned newspapers in New York and Chicago, so he would have been forced by the rule to sell either the newspapers or the Metromedia stations he was acquiring in those cities. Instead, the commission granted him a two-year waiver on enforcement of the rule with the clear possibility that either this waiver would be extended or that the rule itself rescinded prior to the end of the two-year period.[8]

No one seems better situated than Murdoch to establish this new national television network. His holdings already include a television network in Australia; a satellite system in Europe; and more than 80 major newspapers and magazines in North America, Europe, and Australia. His three-continent media empire grosses more than $1 billion each year.[9] The purchase of the six major-market Metromedia television stations and the creation of the Fox Network to serve the nation's 280 independent television stations offer his conglomerate immediate access to the new feature films and television series that his Fox studios produce. Also available are the rights to the Fox library, which includes such holdings as the *Star Wars* pictures and popular television series such as "MASH" and "The Fall Guy."

This combined ownership of programming and network facilities is, of course, in direct conflict with the FCC's current network ownership and syndication rules. It is quite possible, however, that, if necessary, this regulatory barrier also will be lowered by the commission in the interests of structural reform. Although the agency prohibits network distribution of more than three hours of network-owned programming per week and denies a network the right to syndicate its own programming, terms in these rules such as "interconnection on a regular basis" and "affiliated licensees," seem vague enough to allow an interpretation that exempts Murdoch's distribution practices from regulation and yet continues to apply these same rules to existing network operations.[10]

Despite all these obvious advantages, it is highly unlikely that Murdoch will attempt to launch a full-time national television network within the foreseeable future. The major barriers even this ideally situated media conglomerate faces are not ones that the federal government can waive or rescind. Rather, they are barriers of private law and basic economics — barriers even a $1-billion-a-year media conglomerate finds too formidable to challenge.

In itself, ownership of a major film studio does not provide the elaborate structure and sophisticated process capable of commissioning, assembling, and distributing the 12- to 18-hour schedule of sports, news, daytime drama, and other general entertainment features that each network furnishes daily to its affiliates. However, even if some media conglomerate were willing to make the massive investment necessary to develop such a structure, it would still face the equally formidable task of trying to compete, at parity, with the established networks, each capable of serving a much larger television audience than the conglomerate's stations could reach. At this point, for example, if the Fox Network could somehow convince every independent television station in the United States to join the six Metromedia stations in the distribution of its programming, it would be able to serve only about 70 percent of all American television households as opposed to the 99 percent reached by each of its network competitors.[11]

Thus, the private law affiliation agreements of each network, coupled with its skilled program-acquisition practices, seem capable of withstanding any direct assault made on the network's position in the name of competition, no matter how powerful its challenger and regardless of how sympathetic the federal government might be to the challenge. In addition, as the network share of total television-viewing time diminishes, there exists a distinct possibility that available advertising revenues, although sufficient to support three competing services, may not be substantial enough to sustain a fourth. For all of these reasons, it seems far more likely that Murdoch's conglomerate will continue to develop a modest, ad hoc, limited program service for those independent stations willing to carry selected Fox Network features, rather than to seek full-time affiliation contracts with every available independent station in the nation.

As this situation illustrates, those who view the intervention of public law as capable of creating a more competitive media marketplace seem to be as overly optimistic about its capability as are those who once believed that regulation, in itself, could provide the public with a truly diverse, locally oriented broadcast service.

Another tactic that has been recommended to expand the number of viewing alternatives available to the American public is the production subsidy to provide financing for innovative programs or films unable to attract conventional support. This approach has often been coupled with a recommendation for structural reform to reduce the power of established mass-entertainment organizations while encouraging and supporting the efforts of new producers.[12]

The most extensive example of such subsidized production at present in the United States is, of course, the programming of public broadcasting. However, during the past half-century, its use has been far more widespread in Western Europe. There, subsidies have supported major broadcast organizations such as the BBC and its counterparts in Norway, Sweden, and Belgium and have provided a substantial portion of the revenue for nearly all other national broadcast services.[13] Until this decade, there were still those in the United States who believed that, in time, public broadcasting might achieve the popular acceptance it had gained in Europe during its far longer period of operation. Now, however, as European public-service broadcast audiences are being eroded by the VCR and by popular cable-TV programming, it seems far more likely that what has distinguished the European experience from that of the United States has simply been the absence of the mass-appeal competition that American public broadcasting has had to face since its inception.[14]

It can be argued that even if subsidized programming serves the needs of only one small segment of the American audience, its production and distribution are justified because they fulfill communication obligations ignored by the existing marketplace. On the other hand, there are those who argue that the taxpayer has no obligation to underwrite narrowly oriented cultural, intellectual, or other elitist fare simply to satisfy the tastes of those who can afford to rent films or VCR tapes of such material for their own amusement if they wish.[15]

The underlying problem with production subsidy is that, as in commercial financing, the selection criteria shape the content to conform to the objectives of the funding organization; thus, these criteria bias creativity in one way as clearly as commercial values do in another. In addition, if a portion of the subsidy is government provided, there also exists the problems of potential political influence and of almost continual public indignation of taxpayers who disagree with any position such public-financed programming adopts.

In the last analysis, however, the greatest flaw in the subsidy approach to stimulating mass media competition is that the programming it produces is never truly competitive. For example, public broadcasting, by offering an alternative to the popular, attractive programming of commercial television networks, foredooms itself to the modest 1 or 2 percent of the television audience sharing its aversion to commercial network productions. To an even greater extent, the cable's public-access channels seem to be approached by the public less as a viewing alternative than as an "experience," as one would watch an apartment building's lobby TV monitor in the hope of seeing a neighbor do something foolish in an unguarded moment.

Even without structural reform or subsidy, there has been an impressive expansion in the number of viewing options available to American audiences during the past decade. *TV Guide*, that index of America's video channels in each market, offers ample evidence of this expansion. It revised its format twice during the past half-decade in an effort to find space for all those new services available to homes with cable or TVRO reception capacity.

All-news, all-sports, all-music, all-religious, and even all-congressional channels have emerged to compete for viewer attention with less specialized satellite-delivered networks; and a growing number of VCR-equipped homes have yet another viewing choice beyond pay-TV and the conventional broadcast networks. It is likely that at least five or six of these specialized services will survive, functioning much as modern radio to deliver a very narrowly defined audience to a particular group of advertisers whose products are likely to be most attractive to this special group of viewers.

Patterns of consolidation that we have seen in the past will ultimately merge competing cable and MMDS systems into a single, broadband delivery service in each major market as LPTV operations go dark and DBS devotes an increasing portion of its transponder capacity to non-entertainment transmissions. The major television networks will continue to survive as the dominant, nationwide distribution system for national advertising and series programming, even though their share of the total television audience each evening may drop to the level of 50 percent of all viewership and dissemination may eventually be direct to each home, rather than though a local affiliated station.

Through all of this, the mass entertainment industry itself will remain virtually unchanged. It will continue supplying the film, music, and programming for all of these services except those extremely specialized sports, news, or religious channels and will continue furnishing the content for their VCR competition as well. In essence, then, despite the vast increase in the number of channels available to each American household, the less than one dozen major distributors of film, music, and television will continue to provide that content that will continue to attract between 80 and 90 percent of the total viewing and listening time.

During the past few years, viewing behavior in households with access to the various specialized cable-delivered channels has reflected only a very limited interest in these new programming alternatives. For instance, a mid-1985 Nielsen survey, limited to homes capable of receiving these channels, revealed that the top four services — Cable News Network (CNN), the sports service (ESPN), the music channel (MTV), and USA, a general programming network — attracted only 1 percent of all potential viewers, while Christian Broadcasting (CBN), Nickelodeon, and the Nashville Network each drew less than 1 percent of this viewership.[16]

Superstations, such as WTBS, fare slightly better with 2.5 percent viewership in households where it was available, and as did HBO, with a 9.3-percent share of viewing in its subscriber homes. However, except for WTBS's high-rated baseball and wrestling features, most of these services' programs and films are produced by the mass-entertainment industry's major distributors, rather than being original materials produced by the services themselves.

What all of this suggests quite clearly, then, is that increasing the number of electronic mass media viewing alternatives does virtually nothing to dilute the degree of dominance that major distributors in the field of mass entertainment exert over American mass culture. Ironically, in terms of hopes for an electronic mass media marketplace, the American mass-entertainment industry seems to be a victim of its own success.

Societal Interests in Mass Culture

A truly competitive electronic mass media environment requires far more than a handful of specialized communication services for those seeking for a time to escape the mass-appeal features of the dominant entertainment channels. To talk of freedom of expression or choice in this context is analogous to describing the Russian people as having freedom of religion because a few churches and synagogues remain open for attendance. This analogy is neither as exaggerated nor unfair as it may seem at first to be. In the Soviet Union, secular party doctrine dominates official expression and thought. A citizen may attend religious services, but the time devoted to religion tends to isolate an individual and furnishes no socially useful information while weakening those cultural ties that provide a sense of belonging within that society.

In much the same way, although Americans may glance at specialized all-news or all-sports channels for a few minutes each day, they rely upon the massively popular feature films and prime-time television series they share for the sense of community that has long since vanished from our society. Denied the comforting ties of the old-fashioned neighborhood, we gossip with our acquaintances about the exploits of the television characters we all know so intimately.[17]

It is reassuring to realize that as we travel across this nation, the one familiar sight in each strange city we visit will be our favorite TV characters, waiting to perform for us wherever we are and at exactly the same time each week. With as many as 50 million other Americans joining us in viewing a particular show, it is not surprising that this single bond uniting us is broader and more extensive than any other political, religious, or social connection we might also happen to share.

As legends of old, these modern mass-cultural sagas shape public attitude and belief and color the characteristics of every societal value they present in dramatic form. Yet, although traditional folklore is a simple, immutable reflection of our cultural heritage, these media epics are instead carefully crafted and continuously refined storylines and themes that are designed to exploit every new social issue or trend in taste capable of capturing public attention.[18]

Unlike the novel or newspaper, electronic mass media are not contained within individual usage. Rather, they permeate our environment and affect each of us significantly whether or not we choose to view or listen. As with the nonsmoker in a smoke-filled room, an atmosphere created by others intrudes upon our private preferences, denying them validity. From the magazine covers at the local grocery's checkout counter to the billboards of the countryside, and the boomboxes on the street corner, the images and sounds of our media idols surround us everywhere.

To suggest that personal consumer choice can alter the nature of this marketplace seems as ridiculous as believing that an individual can protect the physical environment simply by refusing to buy the products of those who pollute our air or water. Recognizing the futility of attempting to curb pollution through consumer pressure alone, the federal government ultimately adopted standards to protect public interests in a clean and healthy environment and established at the same time a process for evaluating industry performance in terms of those standards.

Currently, however, the federal government is following exactly the opposite pattern of policy behavior in the field of electronic mass media. It is relying on those marketplace forces it realized were incapable of shaping industry pollution practices to protect the quality of our mass cultural environment. Unfortunately, the marketplace demand that exists in this field is unlikely to stimulate the production of a greater number of features for children, older Americans, or minorities. Rather, it stimulates an increasingly explicit collection of violent and ribald programming for affluent Americans seeking greater titillation than most generalized electronic mass media services now provide. As we have seen, what inhibits the emergence of diversity in this field is the amount of money needed to produce a show. Electronic mass media producers cannot afford the luxury of considering any audience that does not have both a strong desire and a proven capacity to pay for the projects the producers plan. As early VCR tape sales and rentals have established, the hard-core market for sex and violence is strong and apparently insatiable, while the demand for other, less basic cultural features tends to be somewhat less pronounced.

As each mass-entertainment organization moves cautiously to locate its own marketing areas for future development, the trend is virtually certain to be away from the bland, generalized programming of the past and toward the more visually exciting, explicit features of the most venturesome of these entities. As feature-film release strategies of the 1950s and 1960s suggest, competitive pressure for a larger audience will almost inevitably cause productions to gravitate toward the sensational and the controversial, as audiences become increasingly difficult to shock or surprise.[19]

Unlike any earlier era, however, this next round of competition to capture public attention with the most daring, provocative features will take place not in some distant theater but in the home itself. At that time, the lockbox on the television set is likely to be as effective as was the chastity belt of yesteryear, and children will continue to display their talent for locating the one neighborhood household that is not a part of the coalition to protect them.

Also of significance is the fact that these pervasive and persuasive services for the first time will be free of any societal obligation to be sensitive to the impact their programming may have on the fragile commitments to religious, racial, and sexual equality that we are still striving to honor. Designed not to enlighten our minds but to play on our emotions, the industry's mass-entertainment offerings will eagerly exploit every discrepancy discovered between what we aspire to become and what we actually are and will sense that nothing is as marketable as a convincing justification for retaining the comfortable biases we already hold and share.

Abolishing federal supervision of electronic mass media content will not end censorship; it will only end the public aspect of a process that will continue to operate as it always has functioned on the private level. The mass-entertainmnt industry will remain a prime target for well-organized pressure groups, because it is ideally structured to shape the awesome power of its creativity to conform to any compromise it negotiates. Realizing this, private groups capable of translating their displeasure about certain thematic treatments into effective consumer boycotts will still be able to protect their own narrowly defined interests quite effectively.

From the beginning of the broadcast era in the United States, criticism of electronic mass media content has been channeled through the federal regulatory agency responsible for the industry's supervision. However imperfect this supervision may have been in practice, the channel itself gave each individual with a grievance a process for expressing this dissatisfaction and requesting some change in program policy. Once this channel has been closed, the public will no longer have any formal means available for lodging such protests or seeking such relief. In the absence of such a regularizing process, it is entirely possible that those in the electronic media industry themselves may wish at some point for the return of the "good old days" of regulation.

Lacking any formal outlet for their frustration about the exploitative quality of these mass-cultural services, isolated individuals will begin combining into media vigilante groups, threatening various types of economic reprisal to win from media organizations the programming concessions they are powerless to achieve in any other way. It would be a cruel irony if the policy of deregulation, designed with the intention of launching a freely competitive mass media marketplace in the United States, results instead in the creation of numerous, narrowly oriented pressure groups collectively capable of imposing a far more repressive set of content controls on the media than those the FCC rescinded.

The public seems far too dependent on its mass media and far too fearful of their influence to allow programming perceived as threatening basic social values to be disseminated without vigorous counteraction. Considering only the vehemence of recent opposition to the inclusion of the Playboy pay-TV channel in various cable-TV services across the nation, there is little reason to doubt that such clashes between public and media will be a constant characteristic of future media operation in this nation.[20]

To avoid this type of continuous guerrilla warfare, it seems essential to find some method of mediation that allows the concerns of citizens about the quality of their mass-cultural environment to be weighed against the freedom-of-expression interests guaranteed to the media by the Constitution. Unless public law has the capacity either to create such a process or at least to establish some legal guidelines capable of aiding in the resolution of such controversies, there will be every incentive for interest groups to seek to achieve their objectives through private duress. This process is likely to be far more damaging to the media's freedom of expression than any standards of social responsibility that may be imposed on it by law.

Notes

1. The first major rule the FCC issued after asserting its jurisdiction over all cable systems in 1966 was one that made local origination mandatory for all systems serving more than 3500 subscribers, "First Report and Order on Docket 18397," 17 RR2d 1570 (1969). Three years later the FCC's top 100–market cable regulations required that each system in these markets set aside channels for local access, educational, governmental, and leased services. As the deadline for compliance drew near in 1976, the agency reviewed these standards and in its "Report and Order on Docket 20363," 54 FCC 2d 207 (1975) extended these general local-service requirements to all cable systems serving 3500 or more subscribers. When the FCC formally adopted these rules in its "Report and Order on Docket 20508," 59 FCC 2d 296 (1976), its authority to compel such services was challenged and over-turned by the Supreme Court on the basis that Congress had not clearly delegated such extensive cable jurisdiction to the agency in *Federal Communications Commission v. Midwest Video*, 440 U.S. 689 (1979). However, while the commission's efforts to create a local-service regulatory obligation on the part of cable-TV systems collapsed because of the lack of a proper legislative foundation for such a policy, it is clear that the FCC did seek to add this responsibility to cable in order to counterbalance its damaging impact on the local-service capacity of television broadcasters.
2. The most detailed account of these constraints on television is provided by Robert H. Stern's *The Federal Communications Commission and Television* (New York: Arno Press, 1979), particularly Chapters 3 and 4. For FM, the most interesting, if somewhat one-sided, account of the barriers the FCC placed in the path of its develpment is contained in the biography of FM's inventor and pioneer, Lawrence Lessing's *Man of High Fidelity: Edwin Howard Armstrong* (New York: Lippincott, 1956).
3. Some might argue that the FCC's suppression of cable-TV growth in major television markets from 1965 to 1972 was precisely such a situation. However, in reality, cable during this era offered no "broader range of communication services" of its own to the American public, but only those program services of another medium it appropriated without permission or compensation and offered nothing but reception of existing television service by those unable to receive these signals over the air.
4. "Cable Communications Policy Act of 1984," Pub. Law No. 98–549, 1984. A factor that could be significant here is that while Article One, Section 8, of the Constitution prohibits a state from passing a law impairing an existing contract obligation, neither the Constitution nor the Bill of Rights imposes a similar restriction on the federal government. Thus, while a franchise is a contract, nothing at law prohibits the federal government from unilaterally altering the terms of that franchise contract through federal regulation.
5. For an excellent overview of the various legislative proposals for relief from broadcast regulation introduced during the past few years, see "Legislation," *Broadcasting*, 31 Dec. 1984, 90.
6. See, for example, the recommendations contained in the "Proceedings of

the Symposium on Media Concentration," Bureau of Competition, Federal Trade Commission (Washington: Government Printing Office, 1978).

7. As *Associated Press et al. v. United States*, 326 U.S. 1 (1945) declared, "Freedom of the press from governmental interference does not sanction repression of that freedom by private interests."

8. The FCC's current broadcast-newspaper cross-ownership rules were adopted in *Multiple Ownership of Standard, FM and Television Broadcast Stations*, 32 RR2d 954 (1975) and are stated at CFR 47, secs. 73.35, 73.240, 73.636, and 76.501. These particular negotiations were described in "Charting the Future: The Prospects for a Fourth Network," *Broadcasting*, 10 Feb. 1986, 36. In July 1986, Murdoch sold his Chicago paper, the *Sun Times*.

9. Neil Hickey, "ABC, CBS, NBC: Warily They're Eyeing Rupert Murdoch," *TV Guide*, 8 Feb. 1986, 16.

10. The FCC's network-ownership and syndication rules are contained in 47 CFR 73.658. These rules currently define *network* as an interconnected-program service operating on a regular basis for 15 or more hours per week to at least 25 affiliated licensees in 10 or more states. How regular a regular basis must be and what constitutes affiliation are just two of the areas where a carefully worded definition may distinguish the operations of a new network from those of an existing one. In any case, this problem may be solved in 1991, when the current FCC requirements expire, unless they are extended before that time.

11. "Fox Has a Mini TV Web in the Making," *Variety*, 22 Jan. 1986, 39. Fox recently negotiated agreements with several network affiliates to expand the dimensions of this coverage, but these agreements provide for carriage of Fox network programs during nonprime-time hours only.

12. This position is described very effectively by David L. Bazelon in Daniel L. Brenner and William Rivers, ed., *Free but Regulated: Conflicting Traditions in Media Law* (Ames, Iowa: Iowa State University Press, 1982) in the article, "The First Amendment and the New Media — New Directions in Regulating Telecommunication," 52–64.

13. One major exception to this general rule is the British Independent Broad-casting Authority's advertising-supported radio and television stations. These public-service broadcast organizations are now under ever-increasing competitive pressure from new cable-delivered advertising-supported services.

14. See this author's "The Plight of 'Public Interest': A Principle Lost in the Process," *Journal of Media Law and Practice* 4:2 (Sept. 1983): 130–42.

15. For examples of some of this vehement criticism of public broadcasting for its cultural elitism, see "Public Broadcasting," Hearings before the Sub-committee on Communications of the Committee on Commerce, United States Senate 93:1 Serial No. 93–10 (28–30 Mar. 1973).

16. Nielsen HomeVideo Index (NHI), July 1985, A.C. Nielsen Media Research, Northbrook, Ill.

17. In Joshua Meyrowitz's *No Sense of Place* (New York: Oxford University Press, 1984), 349, n. 37, the author cites a number of videorecorder-usage

studies reflecting the desire of individuals to stay abreast of the plot lines of the most popular prime-time series by taping broadcasts while they are away from home. If, however, they are unable to view the tapes immediately, they generally reuse the tapes without viewing them, because they no longer serve the purpose of providing the relevant information needed in conversations with friends and acquaintances.

18. As Joseph Turow, *The Media Industries: The Production of News and Entertainment* (New York: Longman, 1984), 5, points out, Scottish nationalist Andrew Fletcher declared in 1703, "Give me the making of the songs of a nation and I care not who makes the laws." If a simple ballad could have such an effect on the culture of eighteenth-century Scotland, to what extent does television shape attitudes during the more than seven hours a day it is being viewed in the average American household? For a fascinating assessment of influences television exerts on American viewers, see Meyrowitz, *No Sense of Place*, particularly in terms of his case studies of the impact television has had on children, the women's movement, and presidential politics.

19. For a more detailed discussion of this trend, see Robert Stanley, *The Celluloid Empire* (New York: Hastings House, 1978), 208–17.

20. Public success in this first crusade will undoubtedly encourage further efforts of this type. Although federal courts were not sympathetic to local franchise efforts to bar the Playboy channel, several cable-TV–group owners decided not to carry the service to avoid public controversy. Ultimately, because this private-industry policy denied it the subscribers it needed to survive, Playboy decided to drastically reduce the erotic content of its service and revised its approach to one of life-style consumerism instead. See "Brandman Unfolds Playboy Plans," *Broadcasting*, 5 Nov. 1984, 10.

Tracing the Patterns: Primary Sources

Year by year, decade by decade, as the Roper Organization, Inc., *Trends in Attitudes towards Television and Other Media* (New York: Television Information Office) reveals, American television usage increases as the degree of public reliance on its messages increases. As the massive collection of studies in George Comstock's (ed.) *Television and Human Behavior* (New York: Columbia University Press, 1978) indicates, television pervades every aspect of our lives. An even larger compilation, *Television and Behavior: Ten Years of Scientific Progress and Implications for the Eighties* (Washington, D.C.: Government Printing Office, 1982), substantiates this rather obvious fact; but it is scholars such as Joshua Meyrowitz in *No Sense of Place* (New York: Oxford University Press, 1984) and George Gerbner in "Communications and Social Environment" (*Scientific American* [Sept. 1972]: 153–60) who put this literature in perspective and suggest how the cumulative effect of the electronic mass media—delivered messages dictate the dimensions of our shared mass-cultural society.

Researchers such as Jay G. Blumler and Elihu Katz in *The Uses of Mass Communication: Current Perspectives on Gratification Research* (Beverly Hills, Calif.: Sage Publications, 1975) and Ronald E. Frank and Marshall E. Greenberg in *The Public's Use of Television* (Beverly Hills, Calif.: Sage Publications, 1980) explore the interactive relationship between viewer and medium that makes audience an active participant in the viewing experience. They seek, among other things, what Hal Himmelstein describes as the *Television Myth and the American Mind* (New York: Praeger, 1985). But as George Gerbner et al., suggests in "The 'Mainstreaming' of American Violence" (*Journal of Communication 30* [Summer 1980]: 10–29) and H.J. Eyesenck describes in *Sex, Violence and the Media* (New York: Harper & Row, 1978), such sharing can lead to a distorted view of societal values and a perverted vision of others, as Randall M. Miller (ed.) illustrates in *Ethnic Images in America Film and Television* (Philadelphia: The Balch Institute, 1978) or as Gaye Tuchman, Arlene Kaplan, and James Benet (eds.) point out in *Hearth and Home: Images of Women in the Mass Media* (New York: Oxford Universtity Press, 1978).

Sensing this power, the television industry has sought on its own to censor the programming it commissions, as Geoffrey Cowan details in *See No Evil: The Backstage Battle Over Sex and Violence on Television* (New York: Simon & Schuster, 1979). However, as Les Brown contends in *Keeping Your Eye on Television* (New York: Pilgrim Press, 1979), various citizens' groups may not be content to allow broadcast interests sole power to determine what is or is not suitable content for the public to view. Instead, as Kathyrn Montgomery points out in "Gay Activists and the Networks"(*Journal of Communication* 31 [Summer 1981]: 49–57) or Edith Efron in "This Time The Indians Won" (*TV Guide*, 22 Jan. 1972, 42–46), private pressure groups are often successful in forcing their way into this corporate content-control process and adding yet another set of standards to be applied privately in producing and scheduling programming. At one time it was hoped that public television might relieve this type of private pressure by offering a more balanced and sensitive portrait of American society to a substantial portion of the public reached by the commercial networks. Despite the careful planning reflected both in the Carnegie Commission on Educational Television's *Public Television: A Program for Action* (New York: Harper & Row, 1967) and the Carnegie Commission on the Future of Public Broadcasting's *A Public Trust* (New York: Bantam Books, 1979), however, this alternative service has never attracted either the funding or the audience necessary to serve American society effectively in this manner.

Although firmly dedicated to media free speech rights, Richard S. Randall, in his *Censorship in the Movies: The Social and Political Control of a Mass Medium* (Madison, Wis.: University of Wisconsin Press, 1967), two decades ago recognized a need for some type of public law complaint system for film to prevent narrowly defined interest groups from constantly pressuring the film industry for specific changes in film content.

CHAPTER TEN

PATTERNS IN MODERN AMERICAN MEDIA LAW

Patterns in Promises Unfulfilled

It was never quite as simple as it once seemed to be. The relationships of broadcast policy and law have always extended far beyond the provisions of the Radio Act of 1927 or the Communications Act of 1934 to encompass numerous practices and customs more crucial and more complex than those described by this legislation. It is true that the FRC and the FCC each assigned broadcast licenses to individual applicants on the basis of certain criteria established by Congress and defined more precisely by agency rules. It is true that these licenses were reviewed periodically and could be revoked or refused renewal for cause. It is true that broadcasters were obligated to conform to specific engineering standards in the operation of these stations and eventually to conform to certain standards in hiring practices as well. Yet it was never true that these narrowly oriented public law obligations exerted a significant influence on the general nature of broadcast or other electronic mass media service in the United States.

Thus, for example, the license renewal proceeding, with its elaborately detailed categories for evaluating a licensee's performance, was for the most part a ritualistic ceremony held to impress the courts and Congress rather than a method of providing an accurate assessment of the applicant's record.[1] On those rare occasions when a renewal was to be denied, the agency was almost always aware in advance of the station's flagrant violations and used the proceeding simply to document the reasons for the denial.[2]

Broadcasting was already in the process of evolving into the most efficient, cost-effective system of mass entertainment and national advertising distribution when the Radio Act of 1927 became law. Lacking congressional authority, constitutional justification, or even public support for any direct policy campaign against the broadcast networks, the FRC and more particularly the FCC became quite adept at using the regulatory process as a tactical device to gain concessions from the networks that the agencies did not possess the legal capacity to compel.

Sensing the futility of trying to achieve the congressional objectives of locally oriented or diverse broadcast service through its regulatory control over the individual station, the FCC began handling the standard application for renewal in a rather perfunctory manner, concentrating its energies instead on using the licensing process more selectively to realize somewhat less ambitious network-programming regulatory goals. The two most vulnerable elements of the broadcast network empire were the prosperous major-market stations it owned and those stations affiliated with it to carry its programming. Taking advantage of this situation, the commission could mobilize rather effective lobbying from the network's own station managers and the management of its affiliate stations for conformance with any specific program policy standards that the agency announced it would consider with particular interest at the time of each station's license renewal.[3]

In reality, of course, this federal influence on network broadcast practices was only a limited and negative one. It attained a small degree of responsiveness to public criticism but lacked the ability either to compel or to induce the broadcast industry to become more competitive in terms of the range of different communication services offered to the public. Neither the original radio broadcast nor the later television allocation and assignment policies of the federal government were successful in diminishing the economic power of the broadcast network triumvirate that dominated industry programming.

However, in this regard broadcasting was simply following the natural pattern already established by the film industry of consolidating all production activities in one place and financing polished, professional, highly publicized features through simultaneous nationwide distribution. Federal rules compelling each station to provide its own local programming were seen by broadcasters as being as illogical and as contrary to sensible economic policy as was requiring every motion picture theater owner to provide patrons with a series of feature films by local artists or home movies in order to balance the national orientation of its Hollywood film.

Furthermore, there was the strong economic incentive to carry national broadcast programming provided by advertisers who were seeking to launch nationwide marketing campaigns through commercials contained in network shows. And regional and local advertisers were also eager to buy station time during the periods when the station's popular network schedule was attracting the largest audience. In essence, then, the accommodation made in this regulatory relationship between government and the broadcast industry was that in the absence of either significant local service or diversity in national programming alternatives, the NAB and the national networks would accept a degree of public accountability and responsibility consistent with their dominant economic and cultural position in this field as long as FCC policies relating to these responsibilities did not have any seriously adverse effect on industry revenues.

At the same time, broadcast networks were developing their own centers of mass-entertainment program supply. During the radio era, they delegated this high-risk function to advertising agencies; after the film industry lost its massive audience to television in the 1950s, they delegated the function to Hollywood. A decade later when network domination over the Hollywood independent film producer became too great, both the Justice Department and the FCC intervened to protect the competitive position of these program suppliers. However, as long as only three organizations determined what productions would be delivered to more than 98 percent of the American public through television channels, no governmental decree seemed capable of allowing independent producers to bargain with the broadcast networks at parity.

This domination was diminished to some extent when pay-TV organizations began competing with the broadcast networks for rights to feature films to be delivered through their satellite-linked cable-TV channels, but the networks remained the primary market for regular series television programming. Even competition for feature films was less intense than the major film distributors had originally hoped it would be. A single firm dominated the pay-TV service, and the networks were generally willing to accept a later release date rather than bid directly against their pay-TV rivals.

Each new form of television distribution has disappointed the mass-entertainment industry in similar fashion. Ad-supported cable-TV services, subscription TV, and ad hoc independent programming networks have all sought to control costs by recycling existing features or commissioning their own low-budget films rather than underwriting the production of new major feature films or even competing in spirited fashion for television rights to major films already in production.

As MMDS, LPTV, and DBS systems attempt to enter this marketplace for mass-entertainment productions, this trend is likely to become even more pronounced. Each system will be competing for an even-smaller segment of the total American television audience; therefore, each system must be even more cautious than its predecessors in commiting the limited revenues that its audience base can generate to the high-risk environment of major feature-film production. At the same time, of course, VCR rentals are providing the public with an increasingly popular alternative to such pay-TV services and are eroding still further the demand for electronic delivery of high-cost, first-run feature films.

Nothing in these competitive patterns suggests that the quantity of major mass entertainment will increase significantly during the years ahead. Even if the revenues available for such productions grow through unexpectedly vigorous competition for exclusive rights to new feature films, television series, and music-video productions, this additional funding will in all probability, simply drive up the asking prices for the limited number of performers and, to a lesser extent, for those few producers, directors, and writers whose talents seem to offer the best guarantee of recouping the staggering production costs.

Ironically, then, instead of ushering in the long-awaited era of broad consumer choice, the new electronic mass media systems may simply succeed in undercutting the only constitutional justification provided for enforcing some degree of public responsibility in a noncompetitive mass-cultural environment. If this is the case, then we will have "progressed" from more than a half-century of indirect public influence over the three media conglomerates that dominate our mass-cultural universe to an era when that domination will continue but the public's ability to influence these conglomerates' judgments and values will have ended.

If 60 to 70 million Americans continue to depend each evening on one of three national television networks for the mass-cultural messages they share in common, isn't it possible to argue that such dominance over American thought imposes a "trusteeship" status on those networks to protect against the abuse of that unique power over our society? This is a question neither the FCC nor Congress can answer, for only the federal judiciary can ultimately determine what justifications for media content control are consistent with the restrictions placed on governmental actions contained in the First and Fourteenth Amendments.

Electronic Mass Media and the First Amendment

Most recent studies of broadcast deregulation view those procedural reforms instituted during the late 1970s by Commission Chairman Charles Ferris as the pivotal actions that began to undercut the agency's authority as a regulator of American mass media service. There is, however, some justification for tracing the origins of this trend back to 1943, when Justice Frankfurter, speaking for a unanimous court, provided the classic contitutional rationale for federal regulation of broadcast program content. In recognizing the FCC's right to establish and enforce basic broadcast programming standards, the court stated,

The plight into which radio fell prior to 1927 was attributable to certain basic facts about radio as a means of communication — its facilities are limited; they are not available to all who may wish to use them; the radio spectrum simply is not large enough to accommodate everybody. There is a fixed limitation upon the number of stations that can operate without interfering with one another. Regulation of radio was therefore as vital to its development as traffic control was vital to its development of the automobile.... But the Act does not restrict the Commission merely to the supervision of traffic. It puts upon the Commission the burden of determining the composition of that traffic.... Methods must be devised for choosing from among the many who apply. And since Congress itself could not do this, it committed the task to the Commission.[4]

In essence, the court held that in accepting the privilege of using the scarce public resource of spectrum space, each licensee also assumed the obligation to exercise this privilege in the public interest, an agreement that the FCC could enforce on behalf of the public. Following the sensible judicial practice of narrowly phrased exceptions to general legal principles, the federal regulatory role in this field was justified in the most limited terms possible. Some logical distinction had to be drawn between broadcasting and all other forms of mass communication to prevent a federal government granted this power in derogation of the First Amendment from extending that authority beyond its intended range.

Nothing, however, has prevented the court from revising that jurisdictional definition through the years to include nonspectrum media systems such as cable TV while still excluding the press, film, and other media traditionally protected from federal content controls. For example, the Supreme Court could have based the right of government regulation upon the characteristic of choice and could have authorized such control only for media requiring that some governmental process designate a particular broadcast license or cable franchise applicant as the one qualified to operate on a specific band of frequencies or within a given locality.[5] Such a distinction might also have been drawn on the basis of media access to children in the home. The Court itself stressed this when it upheld in the *Pacifica* case that an FCC penalty for indecent programming was constitutionally valid.[6]

By failing to expand this jurisdictional base, the Court placed the FCC in an extremely difficult position in dealing with cable TV. Lacking the spectrum licensing power or the process it provided for controlling programming practices, the agency was restricted by its derivative authority to a policy of broadcast protectionism.[7] Denied the ability to impose uniform standards of conduct on all competing electronic mass media, the FCC had only one equitable course of action — to reduce and eventually attempt to eliminate the regulatory burden imposed on broadcasting alone.

Pursuing this policy of deregulation, however, is beginning to involve the lower federal courts in electronic mass media controversies to an unprecedented degree. For the last six decades the federal judiciary has managed to stand aloof from the day-to-day regulation of broadcasting. Initially, the Radio Act of 1927 made the Federal Court of Appeals for the District of Columbia responsible for gathering evidence in such regulatory disputes; but in 1929 the Supreme Court convinced Congress that the system would work far more effectively if the federal judiciary avoided direct involvement in the process.[8]

Section 402 (b) of the Communications Act of 1934 directed all challenges of FCC actions to the Federal Court of Appeals for the District of Columbia and vested in it the authority to develop a uniform body of law defining both the legislative and the constitutional limits of broadcast regulatory authority.[9] Except for the occasional writ of certiorari accepted by the United States Supreme Court, it was here that all FCC affirming or remanding opinions were issued, providing a sense of consistency and continuity in the administration of broadcast law. However, this system of broadcast legal administration worked efficiently only as long as the FCC remained actively involved in the regulatory process by investigating and ultimately providing a comprehensive evidentiary record that the Federal Court of Appeals could review solely in terms of its legal implications. Now, with the FCC's regulatory activities diminishing, litigation may no longer flow as naturally through this single, experienced, and centralized channel of adjudication and review. Instead, with the commission continually asserting the independence of electronic mass media from all but federal regulatory standards, actions in this field have already commenced in federal district courts across the nation by media owners and operators challenging every state or local law that limits their autonomy. Cases of this type already have been decided in a number of federal district courts. In *Home Box Office v. Wilkinson* 531 F. Supp. 987 (D. Utah, 1982), for example, a federal judge held that a Utah statute prohibiting the dissemination of indecent material was abridging the constitutional rights of that state's cable subscribers to receive cable-delivered pay-TV service. The following year a Florida federal district judge, in *Cruz v. Ferre* 571 F. Supp. 125 (D. Florida, 1983), was even more emphatic in upholding the right of a local cable system to carry the Playboy channel. He declared that *Pacifica* was not controlling in this situation because, unlike broadcasting, a cable subscriber must affirmatively elect to subscribe to the system, choose to receive the pay-TV service in question, and make monthly payments to continue the service. Thus, the court reasoned, although indecent broadcast programming could be prohibited because it was freely available to all, a voluntary decision to receive a cable-delivered pay-TV service was a personal communication choice that could not be abridged by public law.

Similarly, other federal district courts have begun to undercut the right of local governments to regulate cable through an exclusive franchise agreement. The courts have held that in the absence of some physical limitation on the capacity of existing facilities to carry an additional cable system's trunk or feeder lines, the denial of a second cable operator the right to compete for subscribers is an abridgment of both the operator's and the public's freedom of expression.[10] Unless the United States Supreme Court, in the *Preferred Cable* case now before it, overturns or at least qualifies the application of this lower-court decision, municipalities will no longer be able to use their most effective bargaining technique to gain the broadest possible cable communication rights for their citizens.

In the one case where the Supreme Court recently granted certiorari to make a definitive statement about cable TV, a unanimous court held in *Capital Cities v. Crisp* 104 SC 2694 (1984) that a state cannot require its cable operators to delete liquor advertisements from broadcast programming imported into the state. In distinguishing this case from an earlier decision in which the Court allowed a state to police out-of-state broadcast advertisements receivable within its borders, Justice Brennan noted that although the FCC in the former case had enacted no rules relating to such broadcast practices, its cable-TV broadcast-signal importation rules were so extensive as to clearly preempt the states from any regulatory authority in the field.[11]

The FCC's direct authority over cable TV, which was granted in the Cable Communications Policy Act of 1984, strengthens the capacity of the commission to use preemptive federal authority in order to diminish the role of state and local governments in the field of cable regulation. Now that this foundation has been prepared, there is every reason to expect that it will be used not only by the FCC but also by countless cable and pay-TV operators and by satellite-dish retailers and owners, who can claim under the act the same rights in order to attack a broad range of state or local operating restraints in the federal courts.[12]

Unwilling to consider any justification for governmental supervision of media content other than "scarcity of spectrum space," the federal courts have quite predictably been unsympathetic with state or local efforts to impose standards on their nonspectrum cable-TV systems. At this point, only broadcasting itself, by virtue of its spectrum usage, remains subject to this type of content regulation.

To what extent are FCC deregulatory policies likely to undermine this "spectrum" base for future programming rules; and if this foundation for control should collapse, how effectively will the federal judiciary be able to resolve the many significant controversies about the nature of this mass-cultural content — controversies that have been settled in the past within the regulatory process?

Projecting Future Deregulatory Patterns

Predicting the future course of broadcast deregulatory trends is relatively simple because the options available to Congress and the commission are quite limited. Electromagnetic spectrum space must continue to be allocated among various rival communication users and allotted in a manner consistent with regional and international telecommunications accords. The FCC's authority over nongovernmental channel space could be transferred to the National Telecommunications Information Agency, but this decision would be bitterly opposed by private users concerned that NTIA's current governmental users might receive preferential treatment under such an agreement. In 1983 alone, for example, the FCC protected its nongovernmental users from some 60,000 governmental applications for frequencies that might have posed technical problems for these licensees.[13]

In addition, some government body will have to resolve continuing conflicts between fixed and mobile, microwave and satellite, public safety and UHF television and countless other user groups seeking spectrum allocation adjustments based on changes in technology, consumer demand, and other equally unpredictable factors affecting need. These controversies can be resolved by auction, lottery, or the flip of a coin; but it is difficult to believe that any of these techniques will be as equitable or effective in realizing the maximum value from spectrum space as even the most uninspired of bureaucratic processes. Making adjustments in frequency bands on the basis of the highest bid is probably preferable to a game of chance in terms of cost effectiveness, except that more than 50 percent of all channel space is claimed by governmental users who seem to have the capacity to outbid virtually any private competitor in the auction process.

Assignment of station licenses could also be based on a lottery or an auction rather than on the basis of ownership characteristics and programming promise and performance as they are today. In fact, the auction approach was advocated more than a quarter-century ago by those who maintained that the spectrum scarcity justifying governmental content supervision was actually artificially created by the licensing process itself.[14] This argument, renewed during the 1970s by a group of prominent media economists, contended that broadcast spectrum space was in short supply primarily because the FCC granted licenses virtually free of charge in return for bare promises relating to program performance.[15] If each license were awarded instead to the highest bidder for that particular channel of spectrum space, no frequencies would be occupied except those that could be used in a cost-effective manner and the public would receive some tangible benefit from the use of its resource rather than only some vague and indefinite program commitment.

As was discussed earlier, the FCC has adopted the lottery approach, with certain credits built into the process to favor minority groups, in granting LPTV and MMDS licenses. At the moment, however, the FCC's radio and television licensing processes still rest upon the foundation of program promise and performance; the agency therefore retains the authority to deny, revoke, or refuse to renew a broadcast license on the basis of program content.

It is here, then, that any change in commission policy will have its most profound impact on the future role of the federal judiciary in the field of electronic mass media service. Modifications in spectrum allocation procedure will affect the federal courts only indirectly; but severing the unique legal relationship between the privilege of a broadcast license and the obligation to provide programming in the public interest will also end any constitutional justification for governmental supervision of broadcast programming.

At present, the entertainment programming of each broadcast licensee is not only subject to basic standards of propriety and good taste, but also must conform to the fundamental requirements of the fairness doctrine. In two recent decisions, the commission has indicated that a one-sided dramatic treatment of a controversial issue such as abortion must be balanced by other programming of the station treating the same issue more objectively.[16] As long as these obligations remain in force and have the capacity to influence the decision to renew or to refuse to renew a broadcast license, the broadcast regulatory process will retain at least the theoretical capacity to make broadcasters responsive to public concerns about programming content. This would be true even if the FCC continually refused to exercise this authority, because the agency's rejection of a valid complaint about programming practices could be appealed to the federal courts for review and remanded to the FCC with directions for appropriate action.[17]

Eventually, however, Congress may well allow the FCC to simplify the broadcast licensing process by awarding or renewing applications on the basis of bid or chance without any regard for promises of programming performance. When this occurs, the broadcast industry, in order to prevent state or local authorities from moving into this area of law vacated by the federal government, will probably persuade Congress to declare that all electronic mass media content control has been federally preempted. But although such a declaration may aid the federal judiciary in determining legislative intention, it is not binding on the courts.[18] Despite what Congress might wish, federal courts decide whether or not such a declaration is consistent in each situation with the Tenth Amendment, which reserves to the states all powers not expressly delegated by the Constitution to the federal government.

However, even if the federal courts are willing to acknowledge the preemptive nature of federal authority over electronic mass media content, this acknowledgment may be limited by certain other factors. Thus, for example, the judiciary may recognize federal power as denying any state or local government the right to exert influence over national network television programming. But at the same time, it could view state or local cable-TV franchise provisions that prohibit erotic or excessively violent pay-TV services as legitimate exercises of state police power.

On the other hand, if Congress decides not to preempt state or local regulation of electronic mass media content when deregulating broadcasting, the only difference in those legal controversies facing the federal courts would be that actions would be brought by media owners who are challenging state or local media controls rather than by state or local authorities seeking to impose such controls. In either case, then, proceeding to the next logical phase of broadcast deregulation will almost inevitably force the federal judiciary from the role of broadcast regulatory overseer to that of primary arbiter in all controversies involving the delivery of electronic mass media service.

Litigation will require the courts not only to draw clear distinctions among the conflicting provisions of the First, Tenth, and Fourteenth Amendments as they apply to various media under differing conditions but also to develop a rational, equitable system for recognizing and weighing public interests in such mass-cultural content in order to fill the void in the area of law created by the deregulation of broadcasting. Unfortunately, the federal judiciary is not structured to accomplish these tasks easily or efficiently.

Every media conflict raising a federal free-speech issue will be removed from the state courts to the nearest federal district court for resolution. This will create an erratic pattern of principles resulting from the efforts of each federal judge to master the intricacies of the unique relationships among media, government, and the public.

As a growing number of federal district courts become embroiled in such electronic mass media litigation, the deliberate pace of each proceeding and the particularized nature of the decision ultimately rendered will certainly not be conducive to rapid or effective resolution of the complex mass-cultural issues these controversies reflect. In fact, the very ambiguity existing in this relatively new and unsophisticated field of law will only encourage further litigation, because in the absence of broadly applicable jural principles, every conceivable theory of law is likely to be tested in each jurisdiction until it is eventually accepted or rejected. Unless the Supreme Court is willing to intervene constantly in this process, the body of law that emerges will lack either uniformity or predictability, because the opinions of one federal court have no binding influence on other federal courts considering precisely the same issues at a later date.

One obvious solution to the problem of increasing mass media case load is for the Supreme Court to adopt a totally absolutist policy with regard to media rights and to declare that it will approve no governmental restraints on any form of mass media communication activity. However, each time the Court has sought refuge in such an elemental formulation of human rights in the past, it has eventually abandoned this position after gaining the sophistication necessary to weigh the relative merits of interests it had previously refused to recognize.

Is this vitally important area of law doomed to go through an era of simplistic analysis and then chaotic uncertainty before the federal judiciary gains the capacity to resolve conflicts between the media and the public in an equitable and consistent manner? Unfortunately the answer seems to be "yes," unless the courts have available at that time a broad enough body of jurisprudential thought to base each decision upon some logically consistent set of media free-speech principles. How realistic, then, is the hope that such a system of legal analysis will emerge by the time it is so desperately needed?

Communication Law: From Soapbox to Satellite

Unlike legislative or administrative rules, common law principles cannot be created on command but must emerge in fragmented fashion from specific concepts employed by the courts to resolve particular legal controversies. Because of this characteristic, defining the dimensions of each principle may demand decades of case law. During this time subtle shifts in judicial emphasis may reshape the law's entire meaning. For example, the simple declarative First Amendment sentence that "Congress shall make no law...abridging the freedom of speech or of the press" was not construed in 1943 as preventing Congress from authorizing the regulation of broadcasting, as we have seen in *National Broadcasting Company v. United States*, 309 U.S. 190 (1943), and was

not interpreted as including motion pictures within its protection until
Burstyn v. Wilson, 343 U.S. 495 (1952).

In reality, the Supreme Court's first effort to establish some system
of priorities among various legal interests in conflict did not occur until
1919; its recognition of a federal free-speech right protected against
state interference dates only from 1925, and its initial consideration of
the validity of state content controls being imposed on an unregulated
form of mass entertainment did not occur until 1952 in the *Burstyn* case
noted above.[19]

More significant, perhaps, is the fact that the range of the federal
judiciary's experience in dealing with electronic mass media and their
special qualities of pervasiveness and accessibility has been extremely
limited even during this period of time. The court has been relegated to
a secondary role of reviewing congressional public-interest standards it
had not designed. Denied this firsthand experience, American jurisprudence still lacks the capacity to draw even the most obvious of
distinctions at law between types of communicators, forms of communication, and dimensions of communication influence.

To put this lack of legal sophistication in proper perspective, it is
useful to remember that although communications law is essentially an
invention of twentieth-century American culture, most other elements
of our jurisprudence extend back in time through several centuries of
legal thought and analysis. Both tort and contract law, for example,
were formally recognized by English courts more than 700 years ago,
and American treatises in both fields were studied in law schools
throughout the United States from 1820 onward. Through the intervening centuries, constant judicial interpretation of the relative priority
that should be accorded various legal interests in conflict led in the case
of tort from crude, strict liability to the concept of degrees of causal
negligence; and contract law led from rigid formalities to questions of
intention and mutuality.

Any newly conceived social interest requires several decades of
judicial consideration before its various elements can be incorporated
effectively within the existing case-law system. As late as 1923, for
example, the United States Supreme Court found itself compelled to
strike down a labor-relations law that sought to set minimum wages for
women and children hospital workers, because such governmental
standards constituted an "unconstitutional interference with the freedom of contract" between workers and employers.[20] Constrained by
precedent and the sensible concern it reflects for the rights of those
relying on the stability of law in making their long-range plans, the
judiciary attempts wherever possible to lessen the impact of change
through the use of analogy. Thus, rather than create an entirely new

field of interests and rights known as mass communication law, the courts have tried, through reasoning by analogy from traditional "soapbox-orator" and "printing-press" decisions, to preserve certitude and the precedents that provide this sense of predictability. The problem with this approach, of course, is that its effectiveness in resolving conflicts in an equitable manner depends on whether or not the relevant characteristics of the historic model match those of the legal entity whose rights and responsibility the model is meant to define.

With American mass communication law still at a relatively primitive level of development, such subtle distinctions as the difference between speech and mass-entertainment marketing or political commentary and pornography are beyond the competency of the judicial system.[21] The equating of the media conglomerate with the orator, for example, is strikingly similar to the Supreme Court's reasoning in the 1920s that viewed the modern relationship between a corporation and its employees as being analogous to the master-apprentice guild arrangement of early England. In time the Court saw the obvious differences that made this analogy inappropriate, but adding this understanding to American common law ultimately required more than three decades of litigation.[22]

Similarly, less than a quarter-century ago, it was still extremely difficult for private citizens to convince the American judiciary that their legal interests in protecting the quality of the physical environment that surrounded them should be accorded a higher priority than the property interests of corporations polluting that environment.[23] Those who made such arguments were often viewed as being a threat to their community's prosperity and generally were considered to be un-American as well. Thus, it is not particularly surprising that those who now urge protection for our cultural environment have difficulty convincing a court of the merit of their position and are attacked as being anti-American, fascist "book-burners," or censors by the media they threaten.

Once again American jurisprudence is lacking the intellectual development that only judicial experience or extensive legal thought and analysis can provide. The federal courts need time to come to an understanding of the difference, in cases where such a distinction is relevant, between the communication rights of the creative artist and the simple property rights in communication that are claimed by those who merely commission, process, and market the mass-entertainment product. Public law in most advanced nations recognizes a *droit moral*, or moral right, of the creative artist to prevent works attributed to that artist from being altered or mutilated in any way by a mass media marketer, who might damage the integrity of the work or the artist's reputation. In American law the recognition of this creative right by American law would be at least a first step toward drawing a more precise distinction between the legal interests of an individual communicator and those in the business of merchandising such communication.

In a broader sense, this type of focused analysis will ultimately allow American jurisprudence to differentiate, in terms of legal and social consequences, among vastly divergent forms of activity now all vaguely classified as *communication*. Law is, after all, a process of categorization that ascribes rights and obligations based upon specific attributes of entities or actions that bring them within a particular definition of statute or common law. Thus, a legal system incapable of distinguishing between the humble orator in the park and CBS or, for that matter, between a topless dancer and a poet remains intellectually undeveloped. If the federal court system is to mediate effectively and equitably among conflicting mass-cultural interests and values, it must be able to incorporate within this definitional approach distinctions in classification based upon such attributes as degree of individual or artistic access, range of competitive choice, extent of audience coverage, and other factors that cause electronic mass media to be so dissimilar from personal communication in our society.

Law, unlike philosophy, must be sensitive to differences in scope or scale that may have a significant effect on the nature of an existing legal classification. Thus, for example, although unauthorized, uncompensated copying and usage of another's creative effort may be wrong under any circumstances from a philosophical standpoint, law has distinguished between personal use and commercial piracy of videocassette recordings primarily on the basis of the magnitude of the damages caused by each action.

The judiciary's inability to modify or to create new categories in response to the changing dimensions of a traditional institution or process has retarded development of several areas of American jurisprudence. As we have seen, labor law was impeded in this way for more than a quarter-century by the Supreme Court's refusal to abandon the legal fiction that United States Steel Corporation and the medieval tradesman stood in the same type of contractual relationship with employees. It was ònly when the Court realized that the size of U.S. Steel might make it somewhat less likely for a water boy in the smelter plant to bargain at arm's length with J.P. Morgan than for his counterpart in the Middle Ages to deal with his master that federal interference in state legislative efforts to adopt minimum standards for wages and other working conditions finally ended.

The legislation of the various states and its interpretation by those states' courts have played an extremely important role in the development of nearly all areas of federal public law during this century. Unfortunately, congressional and FCC preemptive policies seeking to free all electronic mass media from any type of public accountability will deny American jurisprudence the benefit of such state or local legislative and judicial experience in the search for the proper legal balance between mass media and individual rights in our society. As Supreme Court Justice Oliver Wendell Holmes declared, such federal arrogance is generally as unwise as it is inequitable; it prevents those "social experiments that an important part of the community desire, in the insulated chambers afforded by the several States." Holmes said he would favor those social experiments "even though the experiments may seem futile or even noxious to me and to those whose judgement I most respect."[24]

In abolishing in 1973, a single, nationwide federal standard for defining obscene content, Chief Justice Warren Burger wrote,

> It is neither realistic nor constitutionally sound to read the First Amendment as requiring that the people of Maine or Mississippi accept public depiction of conduct found tolerable in Las Vegas or New York City. People in different States vary in their tastes and attitudes, and this diversity is not to be strangled by the absolutism of imposed uniformity.[25]

On the basis of this Supreme Court decision recognizing the right of citizens across the nation to have varying levels of toleration for obscene films, magazines, and books, it would seem only logical to grant even broader discretion when the content in question is delivered for display on the family television set. In theory, however, even the power to ban obscene electronic mass media services can be denied state and local governments if the federal courts find that the FCC has exclusive authority to regulate all programming delivered by these media.

No lower federal court has taken this stance. In truth, such a stance has been unnecessary because the lower courts have been able to strike down, without resorting to such risky challenging of Supreme Court analysis, any local cable and pay-TV ordinances that operators contend attempt to control content.

It is important to realize, however, that the federal judiciary, not Congress, determines whether or not a regulatory program is actually so pervasive in scope or so national in its orientation that any state or local law relating to the subject must be preempted.[26] A congressional agency such as the FCC may claim that this is the case, but legal analysis goes beyond the claim to consider whether or not such state or local government activities truly interfere with federal regulatory objectives. Thus, simply staking out a claim to an entire regulatory field is not enough to guarantee the claim's judicial recognition. This is particularly true if the federal agency seeking such exclusive jurisdiction does nothing to indicate its intention to exercise the authority it demands.

At this point the FCC has been recognized by the Supreme Court, in its only recent decision dealing with this issue, as having such preemptive power over regulation of television signals imported for cable carriage.[27] If this decision foreshadows a long-term judicial policy of denying states and local governments any authority in this field, the results of such a federal position in the long run can be extremely damaging for the public, for free-speech principles in general, and even for the media this policy has been designed to protect.

One obvious consequence of preventing the states from exercising any significant degree of control over electronic mass media operating within their domain will be to deny the federal government the valuable source of legislative and judicial experience so desperately needed to develop more sophisticated principles and processes in this field. Another consequence of this policy, less obvious but potentially more damaging, is that the policy may encourage citizens who are denied any public process for making media accountable for their programming practices to seek private, more repressive means to achieve these same objectives.

Balancing Human Interests in Mass Culture

At the moment, all traditional legal channels of federal broadcast and cable-TV control remain in operation even though the flow of process through these channels has become more sluggish during the past few years. The Communications Act of 1934 is still a part of federal law, and its scope was actually expanded in 1984 by provisions for the first time granting the FCC direct authority over cable TV. Broadcast stations continue to be required to obtain and renew licenses, and the fairness doctrine and political-access obligations of section 315 of the act bind licensees as they have in the past.

If anything, broadcast networks have actually become more sensitive and responsive to possible criticism during this era, fearing that some serious miscalculation in gauging public sentiment about programming practices could suddenly erode the political support they have been gathering during the past decade for complete deregulation under federal protection. Under these circumstances, then, the specter of American mass media being totally unresponsive to public criticism seems rather remote and unreal.

Yet, as we have seen, in the absence of public law intervention, the mass-entertainment industry's natural tendency has been to minimize expenses by abandoning all but the most popular, and therefore most lucrative, forms of cultural fare. The segments of our society that lack sufficient economic demand to be considered in mass-cultural marketing efforts will not only receive no services tailored to their interests but will likely be overlooked to the same degree in the cultural world of media features we share. Thus, the young, the old, the poor, and all others without sufficient affluence will lack not only service but identity in mass-cultural programming, which is oblivious to the very existence of these marginal media consumers. On the other hand, these same media will probably become overly subservient to the demands and desires of the affluent and will offer for jaded tastes the exotic and erotic, which will color the cultural environment that surrounds us all a garish shade of "blue."

What remedy will be available during a deregulated era to those who feel that their society's traditional values are being debased simply to satisfy an incessant urge for instant self-gratification? What forum will exist to consider the complaints of those who feel degraded and humiliated by insulting media stereotypes of their sexual, racial, or religious identities? What process will respond to the concerns of parents about the excessive violence in programs accessible to their children and to women who bitterly resent being portrayed as willing participants in their own brutalization?

Some have argued that no forum, process, or remedy should be offered to such individuals, because the choice of a media service should be a personal one and subject to no societal criticism or constraint. Unfortunately, however, modern electronic mass media seem far less personally limited in the scope of their societal influence than is the book, magazine, or even the newspaper that preceded them. Thus, as in the case of atmospheric pollution, although every homeowner within a community may have the personal right to burn soft coal in the family furnace, the cumulative effect of such personal choices makes the air unfit for all to breathe and thus infringes on the rights of those who do not burn such coal but who are denied any choice about the quality of the environment in which they are forced to live.

Perhaps the situations are not totally analogous, but it is likely that the level of frustration and indignation will be equally high in either case where an individual is powerless to protect against the despoiling by others of something precious and cherished. To prevent this anger and concern from erupting spontaneously in chaotic fashion across a wide range of media systems and services, it would seem useful to channel each type of media criticism through some public law channel capable at least of encouraging open debate and negotiation rather than private threats and secret deals. Allowing state and local governments to participate in this effort will be extremely helpful, because the wide variety of approaches that can be tested simultaneously in this fashion could soon provide all governmental bodies with an invaluable pool of information for refining the functions of this unique process.

Decisions about the structuring of this process, the nature of its role in media disputes, and its availability to state and local governments will certainly be significant ones in determining how successfully this system of media mediation will operate. In the last analysis, however, the most crucial factor indicating the system's degree of effectiveness will be the quality of those legal principles the process applies. It is here, then, in this relatively rudimentary area of jurisprudence, where intensive study and thought are essential if this objective is ever to be realized.

American law already recognizes a number of societal interests that will be accorded a higher priority than communication when these interests are in conflict. Beyond the obvious prohibition against shouting "fire" in a crowded theater or making bomb jokes in an airport's boarding area, we ban cigarette advertising from television and allow states to prevent the names of rape victims or juvenile offenders from being revealed to the public. A recent communication law text lists 18 other examples of such public content control that we accept as a matter of course. And these do not even consider such aspects of private censorship as broadcast network program guidelines issued by its program producers, textbook racial-balance requirements, or sexually neutral pronoun standards of scholarly journals such as the APA, which rejects as a matter of policy any manuscript deviating from its approved he/she format.[28]

Even Supreme Court Justice Douglas, the most absolute of the free-speech absolutists, in speaking for the court, declared in *Hannegan v. Esquire*, 327 U.S. 146 (1946), that constraints on U.S. postal officials delivering certain types of printed materials were not unconstitutional because "the validity of the obscenity law is recognition that the mails may not be used to satisfy any tastes, no matter how perverted." Unfortunately, these efforts to define the proper limits of freedom of expression within the context of other societal values on which they may infringe have been only subjective and intuitive and have lacked any broadly based, systematically arranged foundation of logical analysis.[29]

Decades of broadcast industry self-censorship have inhibited the development of a body of law capable of drawing the distinctions that are essential if the unique attributes and special societal consequences of mass communication are to be understood and evaluated in their own right. In no other way, for example, will American law have the capacity to consider whether or not, under certain circumstances, a closely interlocked mass-entertainment marketing structure is operating to limit artificially public mass-cultural choices through a coordinated effort to restrict writers and directors to a narrow set of marketable concepts and themes.[30] If the media distributors themselves are viewed as the communicators, it will obviously be impossible for them to suppress their own free-speech rights. Precise analysis of this situation, however, should reveal that the public's interest in the communication efforts of these writers and directors is being infringed on by the media themselves; in this context, to view the media as communicators is to confuse the role of the artist with that of the patron who merely commissions the work or, even more accurately perhaps, with the censor who dictates its final shape and form.

Similarly, the contrast between the degree of influence that even the most persuasive orator or pamphleteer can exert on national values and the effects achieved by the most innocuous of network television's situation comedies is such that no analogy from the era of the soapbox and printing press seems fully appropriate in defining societal interests in such electronic mass media programming. The power of the media to implant any issue in our minds, to relegate to oblivion any issue they choose to ignore, to shape our sensibilities about others around us, to color our vision of the values we share, seems too awesome to be recognized as being absolute. How this absolutism might best be tempered through law will undoubtedly be one of the most important questions faced in the field of American jurisprudence during the next decade. Until now, however, it has been a question few have dared to raise.

Those who support the position that American media should be shielded from legal obligations to the public tend to be lionized as "experts" or "scholars" by the media, while those whose views diverge in the slightest from this dogma are labeled "critics" or "censors." In fact, it could be argued that one of the clearest illustrations of the media's effectiveness in dominating American thought is the way they have conditioned us to feel so ashamed about harboring socially unacceptable feelings concerning media responsibility that we must preface any statement even mildly suggestive of such a sentiment with the self-conscious disclaimer, "Of course, I don't believe in censorship, but."

The word *censorship* has been invoked skillfully by media supporters during the past few decades to silence opposition as effectively as the word *heretic* did during the period of the Spanish Inquisition. Historically, *censorship* applied only to governmental actions directly or indirectly discouraging the exercise of free speech. Recently, however, media advocates have expanded its context to include the actions of organizations, such as the Moral Majority or the PTA, that seek through private negotiation to achieve changes in media content.

This could be a perilous argument for media supporters, however. If any private interference with the creative efforts of others is actually considered censorship, what fits within this definition more completely than the action of the media themselves in altering, modifying, cutting, padding, or simply mutilating the artistic work they commission solely for the purpose of enhancing its marketability? It is probably wiser rigorously to limit the use of the word *censorship*, for as was true with the words *fellow traveler, pinko*, and *Commie* during the McCarthy era, *censorship* is an emotional, pejorative word used to stimulate anger without inspiring thought.

Instead of such abstract, acrimonious dispute, what is most essential at this time is careful consideration of the various public policy alternatives that may be used to augment the marketplace as the determinant of all electronic mass media service characteristics. Although it is true that current Supreme Court precedents, if unaltered, will severely restrain any governmental efforts to shape media content, it is important in this sense to recall how other areas of common law have evolved in response to changes in societal conditions.

The most logical place to begin this consideration of policy alternatives is at the local and state levels of electronic mass media supervision. Here, various approaches to public access, community communication services, and citizen review of performance are already in operation. At present, cable TV is the only medium subject to such supervision, because it alone requires municipal easements, which legally justify conditions to be imposed upon its service. As we have seen, however, the range of such community controls over cable has been steadily diminishing since the federal government began more than a decade ago its campaign to free cable from these franchise requirements.

Rather than to seek to abolish this last remaining vestige of community orientation or local service in the field of broadcast regulation, it appears far more sensible to permit supervision at this level to flourish not only to provide policy experience but also to continue this single type of citizen access and accountability promised but not provided by either the Radio Act of 1927 or the Communications Act of 1934. At the same time, it seems equally sensible to extend the right of community supervision to include MMDS, LPTV, STV, and all other electronic media delivery systems that by the conditions of their spectrum assignments operate primarily within the boundaries of a single municipality. Because these recently authorized delivery systems interact in many ways with existing cable-TV systems in the communities, the general authority of community supervision would allow local governments to develop comprehensive policies to include all alternative services within a single community-oriented plan for access and other public communication benefits. To contend that such an extension of local jurisdiction is an unconstitutional infringement on the free-speech rights of these media is simply to say that as of the moment the courts have not yet developed the capacity to evaluate the conflicting interests of the communicator and the community to an extent where a sophisticated assessment of their relative rights in these situations is possible. In this regard, it is useful to remember that only after two decades of litigation did the Supreme Court finally recognize the right of states and municipalities to establish community standards for feature-film exhibition. Perhaps, as in *Miller v. California*, 413 U.S. 15 (1973), these standards will be required to conform to minimum federal guidelines in order to ensure their constitutionality. It is difficult to believe, however, that a judiciary that allows communities to supervise the content of films shown in a theater would deny to those same communities the right to supervise the content of locally operated media delivering their product into the home. Recognition of positive rights such as citizen access may come more slowly than recognition of police-power authority over communications content; however, as judicial principles evolve, it may be possible to find another legal basis for government supervision of media service to the public that extends beyond spectrum scarcity to reflect legal responsibility based on the actual degree of influence these services exert on our society.

In that regard, the major television networks may eventually be categorized at law as having a fiduciary relationship with the audiences they serve, much as the public-service broadcast organizations of other industrial democracies are viewed as trustees for the public interest because of reliance placed on the integrity of the service they provide. If our federal courts come to this view, this categorization will raise a number of additional questions requiring immediate answer. How such a trusteeship shall be structured, what societal interests shall be recognized as deserving of protection within its review process, and what remedies may be made available in the absence of voluntary compliance are some of the questions we should consider now if we hope to provide the judiciary with the type of philosophical foundation necessary to develop the jural principles required to resolve complex conflicts between media and society in a logical and consistent manner.

Some may deny law any place in this process and claim that the legal system lacks the capacity to make sophisticated assessments about communication content. Such contempt for the legal process may seem surprising from media advocates who have gained so much from the law's past forbearance, but those who voice this objection contend that to suppress smut today is to suppress Shakespeare tomorrow. What this argument overlooks, however, is that law has progressed from the days of the Star Chamber and trial by ordeal and is now entrusted with some of the most complex and sophisticated questions our society can raise. If a legislature can define and a court or jury can decide at what point fair use becomes copyright infringement, at what point similarity in story or melody line becomes plagiarism, at what moment the aborting of a fetus becomes the murder of a human, or at what level of mental capacity an individual can be held accountable for the attempted assassination of a president, surely this same legal system will be competent to distinguish between experimentation and exploitation in dramatic form.

Despite all this, it is premature to advocate any specific process or set of principles for future public policy in the field of electronic mass media. All that is being advocated here is the need to begin to think the unthinkable. We must abandon the clichés of the noble orator and the brave printer if we are ever to understand our media as they actually operate within our society today. Law must be capable, when necessary, of distinguishing between the creative interests of the artist and the property interests of media in such communication efforts. Law must also be able to consider the plight of those whose status in our society is being undermined because the particular stereotype that humiliates them has proven marketplace appeal. Although the subtle balance between safeguarding these interests and repressing creative thought will be a difficult one to establish and maintain, it is precisely this role of weighing relative rights in conflict that law is best equipped to perform in our society. To refuse to recognize such a right will not be a neutral act but a statement of law in itself, declaring that our media may, with impunity, degrade women, ridicule racial or religious minorities, or manipulate culture values in any way that seems most popular and profitable. Unlike any other communication relationships of the past, however, American society has become so dependent upon electronic mass media for its orientation and common experience that a public-trust relationship may well exist at law and may obligate these media to be responsive to, if not responsible for, the consequences of their acts.

It is still possible, of course, that the totally deregulated era of electronic mass media in the United States will never arrive. The American political process seems to have a sense of when to retreat from a radical change in traditional practices, and this sense may prevent the full-scale retreat from regulatory responsibilities the FCC now envisions or the total emasculation of states' rights in the area of media supervision. Even in the absence of such a political response, industry trade groups may themselves realize the need to create a private policy process capable of responding to individual citizen critics before these individuals mobilize into partisan groups to exert political and economic pressure.

What does not seem possible, however, is for a broadly diverse and truly competitive marketplace of ideas to emerge naturally from the new delivery channels being developed to serve American audiences. The dependence of each new system on the same tightly clustered group of mass-entertainment suppliers will not operate to expand production to any significant extent but simply to increase the competitive demand for such productions to a point where the least efficient delivery systems will be forced out of the market.

Although public policy never had the capacity to alter this pattern of mass-entertainment dominance over electronic mass media service, it did provide a limited degree of accountability, if not balance, through the broadcast regulatory process. To look on telecommunications technology as a solution to the problem of media social responsibility is thus a sadly mistaken viewpoint. In reality, this technology is capable only of eroding the traditional legal justification for public participation in the process and does not offer the promise of a truly competitive mass-cultural environment, which may compensate for losing this sense of participation.

At the moment, though, the greatest problem is not that our law has no answers to questions about the relative rights of individuals and electronic mass media in an unregulated field of operation. Rather, it is that we have not yet begun to ask the questions that will allow us to choose the most appropriate answers. To do this, of course, we must be willing to face the wrath of those who feel the public has no rights in media service except those for which they pay and who have at their disposal the dreaded term *censor* to stigmatize all those who dare disagree with them.

Communication: The Global Perspective

Even if this threat is sufficient to stifle domestic debate about the legal obligations of American media, it will not be capable of discouraging worldwide criticism of our commercial mass-cultural policies. What it will do, however, is make it virtually impossible for us to communicate usefully with those who feel the marketing activities of our mass-entertainment industry must be countered by some of importation restriction.

Viewing free speech as an article of faith, we tend to react to such policies as a missionary reacts to a heathen ritual, hurling invectives such as *authoritarian* or *repressive* at those who dare to restrict the "right to know" or the "free flow of information." By investing what is essentially an issue of foreign television or film marketing with the qualities of a religious crusade, we simply manage to diminish the effectiveness of our arguments that are more validly aimed at such repressive practices as jamming or outlawing the reception of international shortwave broadcasts or restricting the coverage of news events by foreign television crews.

Because our philosophy of freedom of expression is still so basic in nature, we lack the capacity to distinguish between national policies that simply seek to protect domestic cultural values from being perverted by American mass-appeal tastes and those that are truly designed to prevent citizens from becoming aware of the world around them. Thus, we lash out at a French cultural policy with the same vigor we employ when denouncing Russian news censorship. This attitude only reveals our immaturity in weighing relative human interests.

What most Americans fail to realize is how parochial our viewpoint concerning the legal responsibilities of mass media has become since our jurisprudential system began to invest our First Amendment with its absolutist qualities a half-century ago. This nation obviously stands apart from the Communist bloc or Third World in the privileged treatment accorded media, but it also has ranged far beyond most of the world's industrial democracies in its defense of media rights.

Unless we are aware of this degree of divergence between our own media law tradition and that of most West European nations, for example, we are likely to react in anger if several of these nations attempt to stem the tide of American mass-appeal programming pouring out of the new cable-TV and satellite systems being developed in that region of the world. Only if we develop a greater degree of sophistication in our own system of communication law analysis, allowing us to distinguish more precisely among the relative social values of various types of media service, will we be able to understand that different priorities accorded these same services by other legal systems may be perfectly valid reflections of their own legal and cultural traditions rather than ugly manifestations of anti-Americanism.

What is inhibiting our efforts in all international deliberations about communication and telecommunication service today is the superficiality of our legal conceptualizations in this field. We cannot communicate, much less negotiate, effectively because our communication law principles are little more than dogma and are useful only in dealing with those who already share these beliefs as a matter of faith.

It may well be that careful consideration of our current positions will lead us to exactly the same conclusions that we already reached through subjective insight. However, such deliberation will at least provide a rational basis for those assertions that must be defended in a world that has not intuitively adopted our philosophy of media free speech.

If we value our freedom of expression as highly as we have always claimed to do, it now seems essential to refine and, if necessary, to redefine the meanings of this commitment so that law will have the capacity to protect and preserve its intrinsic values both for our society and for others in the world so deeply affected by the influences of our media services.

Notes

1. During the past 50 years, the FCC denied an application for the issuance or renewal of only 118 broadcast licenses, an average of slightly more than 2 per year. Closer analysis of this figure makes it even less awesome in terms of actual regulatory threat because less than 20 percent of these 118 actions were based on any aspect of broadcast programming. Federal Communications Commission, *49th Annual Report* (Washington, D.C.: Government Printing Office, 1984).
2. Barry G. Cole and Mal Oettinger, *Reluctant Regulators: The FCC and the Broadcast Audience* (Reading, Mass.: Addison-Wesley, 1978), 134–43.
3. Ibid., 262–88, for a detailed discussion of the use of this tactic by the FCC during the campaign for better children's programming during the 1970s. For a description of a failure of the FCC to achieve its desired policy through negotiation, see Erwin Krasnow, Lawrence Longley, Herbert Terry, "Commercials: How Many Are Too Many? Who Says?" *The Politics of Broadcast Regulation*, 3d ed. (New York: St. Martin's Press, 1982), 192–205.
4. *National Broadcasting Company v. United States*, 319 U.S. 190 (1943), 213, 215–17.
5. This rationale was proposed as a basis for regulation during hearings conducted in 1977 regarding the rewriting of the Communications Act of 1934.
6. *Federal Communications Commission v. Pacifica Foundation*, 438 U.S. 726 (1978) in which the court observed that "of all forms of communication, it is broadcasting that has received the most limited First Amendment protection."
7. *Southwestern Cable v. U.S.*, 392 U.S. 157 (1968), while affirming FCC authority over cable use of broadcast signals, emphasized the derivative nature of that authority. The court's grudging approval of program origination by a 5–4 vote in *United States v. Midwest Video*, 406 U.S. 649 (1972) certainly suggested the clearly defined limits of such secondary authority. As if to make this abundantly clear, *Midwest Video Corp. v. FCC*, 571 F.2d 1025 (8th Cir., 1978) struck down commission efforts to extend this derivative jurisdictional control to include such cable-TV requirements as mandatory access, minimum channel capacity, and minimum technical standards.
8. In *General Electric v. FRC*, 31 F.2d 630 (1929), the United States Supreme Court pointed out to Congress that in granting this court of appeals the power to gather and consider new evidence in adjudicating broadcast-

regulatory appeals, the Radio Act of 1927 transformed a review court into a trial court and limited the Supreme Court's ability to supervise its activities. A year later Congress amended the radio act (46 Stat. at Large 844), sheltering the federal judiciary from any further responsibilities as a regulatory body.

9. The uniformity of a single court is not quite as great as it seems here, because this court of appeals consists of eleven different judges, from which a panel of three generally decides each case on appeal. However, certain judges, such as Bazelon, Tarr, and McGowan, have generally been assigned appeals from FCC decisions because of their expertise in this particular area of administrative law. It also should be pointed out that although licensing matters are appealed in this court, issues involving rules, orders, or rule changes of the commission are argued in the first instance at the federal district court level.

10. See, for example, *Cable Holding of Battlefield v. Cook*, D. Ga. 11 (1985) and *Telecommunications of Key West v. FCC*, 755 F.2d 1330 (1985).

11. This earlier case in which the state's police-power rights over broadcasting had been recognized was *Head v. New Mexico*, 374 U.S. 424 (1963). Although the court might have chosen at this point to base its decision on the greater degree of protection given commercial speech since *Bigelow v. Virginia*, 421 U.S. 809 (1975), it expressly declined to do so; thus, in effect, it gave greater emphasis to the FCC's preemptive powers in the field of cable TV as the ground for this decision.

12. The right of TVRO owners to receive satellite transmissions was recognized under the Cable Communications Policy Act of 1984, and the FCC recently announced its intention to attempt to preempt local zoning laws that limit the installation of such equipment.

13. Federal Communications Commission, *49th Annual Report/Fiscal Year 1983* (Washington, D.C.: Government Printing Office, 1983), 79–80.

14. In 1951, Leo Herzel, "Public Interest and the Market in Color Television Regulation," *University of Chicago Law Review* 18 (Spring 1951): 792–836, was perhaps the first major scholar to propose that marketplace principles be applied to the granting of television licenses. The most famous study advocating treating broadcast licenses as property rights to be granted to the highest bidder was Ronald Coase's "The Federal Communications Commission," *Journal of Law and Economics* 2 (Oct. 1959): 12–40.

15. Perhaps the most elaborate analysis of this type, proposing shadow rents, or charges based on a reasonable market value to be used to subsidize public broadcast services, is contained in Harvey J. Levin, *Fact and Fancy in Television Regulation* (New York: Russell Sage Foundation, 1980).

16. In *Diocesan Union of Holy Name Societies*, 28 RR2d 545 (1973), a Catholic organization challenged what it contended was a pro-abortion position adopted in an episode of the situation comedy "Maude." Similarly, in *NBC for Renewal of WRC-TV*, 33 RR2d 245 (1975), N.O.W. intervened to argue that the daytime dramas carried by this television station tended to stereotype the position of women in American society and portrayed them

as homemakers rather than career women, nurses rather than physicians, etc. In both instances, while implicitly accepting the argument that such entertainment programming could come within fairness doctrine standards, the commission found that other programming provided by these stations had satisfied their obligation under the doctrine.

17. In reality such a remand from the Court of Appeals for the District of Columbia with instructions only to conduct "further proceedings not inconsistent with the court's opinion" does nothing in itself to change the FCC's original determination in a case. See, for example, *Citizens Committee to Save WEFM*, 506 F2d (1974). However, by delaying a decision or the enforcement of a policy and by raising the prospect of additional costly and time-consuming litigation, this appeal process does provide at least limited leverage in negotiations that would not otherwise be available.

18. Thus, in *Head v. New Mexico*, 374 U.S. 424 (1963), the Supreme Court held that although the Communications Act of 1934 might be read as reflecting an intention on the part of Congress to preempt state or local regulation of broadcast content, it would not be interpreted by the court as supplanting "all the detailed state regulation of professional advertising practices, particularly when the grant of power to the Commission was accompanied by no substantive standard other than 'public interest, convenience and necessity'."

19. *Schenck v. United States*, 249 U.S. 47 (1919); *Gitlow v. New York*, 268 U.S. 652 (1925). In declaring motion pictures to be a form of communication, the Supreme Court was clarifying, if not reversing, its position in *Mutual Film Corporation v. Industrial Commission of Ohio*, 236 U.S. 230 (1915), in which a unanimous court had upheld an Ohio statute requiring prescreening approval by a state review board before allowing a film to be exhibited in the state of Ohio. The Court declared in *Mutual* that films "are mere representations of events, of ideas and sentiments published and known; vivid, useful and entertaining, no doubt, but...capable of evil, having power for it, the greater because of their attractiveness and manner of exhibition. It was this capacity and power...that induced the State of Ohio...to require censorship before exhibition." However, to put this case in proper legal context, it is important to realize that since the alleged abridgment of free speech was occurring at the state rather than the federal level, the Court was being asked to extend the First Amendment protection against congressional interference with these rights to include state governments as well, a new and radical concept it was not willing to accept until a decade later in the Gitlow case above, where for the first time it held that the Fourteenth Amendment protections against state interference with individual rights included the right of free speech.

20. *Atkins v. Children's Hospital*, 261 U.S. 525 (1923).

21. For a brilliant discussion and description of how these distinctions might in fact be drawn, see Francis Canavan, *Freedom of Expression: Purpose as Limit* (Durham, N.C.: Carolina Academic Press, 1984).

22. Federal judicial intervention to strike down labor-relations legislation as a violation of freedom of contract began with *Lochner v. New York*, 198 U.S. 45 (1905) and did not come to an end until *West Coast Hotel Co. v. Parish*, 300 U.S. 379 (1937).

23. The National Environment Policy Act of 1970, 42 USC 4321, and the creation of the Environmental Protection Agency, also in 1970, posed the first major federal recognition of public interest in the physical environment. Although a number of states had similar laws on the books, enforcement tended to be less than rigorous because of a fear that a major industrial employer harassed in one state would simply move to another. Private citizens sometimes prevailed in an action for damages from pollution, but the general philosophy of state courts was reflected in *Gardner v. International Shoe*, 49 NE2d 28 (1943), in which the court observed that "the restraining of normal industrial activity is contrary to public policy." Even as late as 1970, a New York state court in *Boomer v. Atlantic Cement*, 257 NE2d 870 refused to enjoin industrial pollution because the damage sustained by the complaining party of $185,000 was so much less than the $45 million it would have cost the defendant corporation to resolve this problem.

24. *Truax v. Corrigan*, 257 U.S. 42 (1921).

25. *Miller v. California* 413 U.S. 15 (1973).

26. For an extensive historical analysis of federal preemption and the factors that bring it into play, see *Pennsylvania v. Nelson*, 350 U.S. 497 (1956).

27. *Capital Cities v. Crisp*, 104 SC 2594 (1984).

28. Victor B. Cline, *Where Do You Draw the Line?* (Provo, Utah: Brigham Young University Press, 1974), 7–9.

29. Thomas Emerson, *The System of Freedom of Expression* (New York, Random House, 1970) and Franklyn Haiman, *Speech and Law in a Free Society* (Chicago: University Press, 1981) are two major attempts to establish such a foundation. Each provides useful insights but neither successfully synthesizes the personal communication rights stressed into a broader and more effective system of mass communication legal relationships capable of answering the type of complex and sophisticated questions about the relative rights of individuals, societies, and media in a deregulated environment.

30. Such coordinating marketing practices might easily fall outside present public law prohibitions under the Sherman and Clayton Antitrust Acts, 15 USC, secs. 1–21, if the structure did not operate to limit entry into the field or to set prices for the products to be marketed. Simply acting in concert to dictate the nature of intellectual content does not seem to have been a concern of the drafters of either congressional act. It is important to remember that justice department intervention in the relationship between the television networks and television-program suppliers was not based upon any concern for degree of program diversity, but only on allegations that the networks used their superior bargaining position to deny program suppliers economic benefits from the programs they produced.

Tracing the Patterns: Primary Sources

Most American communication law books can be categorized in one of two ways. Works such as Thomas I. Emerson's *The System of Freedom of Expression* (New York: Random House, 1970) or Franklyn Haiman's *Speech and Law in a Free Society* (Chicago: University of Chicago Press, 1981) treat speech or expression as a single indivisible process, differing in degree of dissemination, perhaps, but resting on a seamless foundation of constitutionally protected rights. The second category of books, generally receiving far less scholarly attention or praise, tends to describe mass media law only in terms of those public law restrictions that inhibit or at least influence mass communication programming and news-dissemination functions. Works in this category would include Donald Gillmor and Jerome Barron's *Mass Communication Law: Cases and Comments*, 4th ed. (St. Paul, Minn.: West Publishing, 1984); Harold L. Nelson and Dwight L. Teeter, Jr.'s *Law of Mass Communications*, 5th ed. (Mineola, N.Y.: Foundation Press, 1986); Harvey L. Zuckman and Martin J. Gaynes's *Mass Communication Law in a Nutshell* (St. Paul, Minn.: West Publishing, 1983); Terry Ellmore's *Broadcast Law and Regulation* (Blue Ridge Summit, Pa.: Tab Books, 1982); Don R. Pember's *Mass Media Law*, 2nd ed. (Dubuque, Iowa: William C. Brown, 1981); and a host of other comprehensive, carefully organized descriptions of public law principles affecting media organization practices.

What is difficult to find among these works are studies that either consider how individual and mass media communication processes may differ in terms of their range of impact on individual and societal interests or how the private processes of media-industry policies and contractual agreements may limit or alter artistic expression. In other words, what we lack at this time are studies that consider in some detail how media should be made responsive to the needs and interests of the society they serve and responsible for their actions to those individuals and that society.

In terms of public access, the pioneering work of Jerome Barron in his *Freedom of the Press for Whom? The Right of Access to Mass Media* (Bloomington, Ind.: Indiana University Press, 1973) has been continually ignored by a federal judiciary rapidly retreating from the implications of the *Red Lion* case and no longer willing to be moved by the brilliant philosophical justifications advanced for the recognition of this public interest.

Two other efforts to develop a more extensive set of public interests in mass communication have met a similar fate. A decade ago, Victor Cline compiled an extremely useful set of essays in his *Where Do You Draw the Line?* (Provo, Utah: Brigham Young University Press, 1974) in an effort to establish a foundation for the recognition of certain societal rights to protect the quality of national mass culture. Although the book may not have been burned, it was ignored by all "right-thinking" media law experts, a mind-set that has also been effective in dealing with Francis Canavan's *Freedom of Expression: Purpose as Limit* (Durham, N.C.: Carolina Academic Press, 1984). Canavan, as Cline, has done the unthinkable — he has suggested that law might be capable of drawing distinctions among types of expression based on the significance of their intended purpose, thus protecting a political debate with greater commitment than the ideas that might be conveyed by the gyrations of a topless dancer.

As Henry J. Abraham clearly demonstrated in his *The Judicial Process*, 4th ed. (New York: Oxford University Press, 1980) and as this author has illustrated in terms of communication law in " 'Freedom of Speech' Decisions and the Legal Process: The Judicial Opinion in Context" (*Quarterly Journal of Speech* 72 [Oct. 1976]: 277–87), effective mass communication law principles can only develop through experience in free or robust debate over the social interests that should be accorded highest priority when in conflict in a legal proceeding. Refusal to consider such interests in the guise of protecting free speech will only hasten the day when such narrow and rigid reasoning will no longer be capable of withstanding those social and political pressures that will assail it.

BIBLIOGRAPHY

Abel, John A., et al. "Station License Revocations and Denials of Renewal, 1934–1969." *Journal of Broadcasting* 14 (Fall 1970): 411–421.

Abraham, Henry J. *The Judicial Process.* 4th ed. New York: Oxford University Press, 1980.

"After 10 Years of Satellite, the Sky's No Limit." *Broadcasting* (9 April 1984): 123–126.

Agostino, Don. "New Technologies: Problems or Solution?" *Journal of Communication* 30 (Summer 1980): 198–206.

Antitrust, the Media and New Technology. New York: Practicing Law Institute, Handbook #137, 1981.

Application of CBS Inc. for Authority to Construct an Experimental High Definition Television Satellite System in the 12 GHz Band. Federal Communications Commission File DBS 81–02, 16 July 1981.

Avery, Robert E., and Robert Pepper. *The Politics of Interconnection: A History of Public Television at the National Level.* Washington, D.C.: National Association of Educational Broadcasters, 1979.

Baer, Walter S. *Cable Television: A Handbook for Decision Makers.* Santa Monica, Calif.: Rand Corporation, 1972.

Bagdikian, Ben H. *The Information Machines: Their Impact upon Men and Media.* New York: Harper & Row, 1971.

Baldwin, Thomas, and Colby Lewis. "Violence in Television: The Industry Looks at Itself." In *Television and Social Behavior*, edited by George Comstock and Eli Rubenstein. Vol. 1. Washington, D.C.: Government Printing Office, 1972.

Barcus, F. Earle, and Rachel Wolkin. *Children's Television: An Analysis of Programming and Advertising.* New York: Praeger, 1977.

Barnouw, Erik. *A Tower in Babel: A History of Broadcasting in the United States to 1933.* New York: Oxford University Press, 1966.

————. *The Golden Web: A History of Broadcasting in the United States 1933–1953.* New York: Oxford University Press, 1968.

————. *The Image Empire: A History of Broadcasting in the United States Since 1953.* New York: Oxford University Press, 1970.

———. *Tube of Plenty: The Development of American Television*. New York: Oxford University Press, 1975.

———. *The Sponsor: Notes on a Modern Potentate*. New York: Oxford University Press, 1978.

Barron, Jerome A. *Freedom of the Press for Whom? The Right of Access to Mass Media*. Bloomington, Ind.: Indiana University Press, 1973.

———. *Public Rights and the Private Press*. Toronto: Butterworth, 1982.

Baughman, James L. *Television's Guardians: The FCC and the Politics of Programming, 1958–1967*. Knoxville, Tenn.: University of Tennessee Press, 1985.

Belz, Carl. *The Story of Rock*. 2d ed. New York: Oxford University Press, 1972.

Bennett, Robert W. *A Lawyer's Sourcebook: Representing the Audience in Broadcast Proceedings*. New York: United Church of Christ, 1974.

Bensman, Marvin R. "The Zenith-WJAZ Case and the Chaos of 1926–27." *Journal of Broadcasting* 14 (Fall 1970): 423–437.

———. *Broadcasting Regulation: Selected Cases and Decisions*. Lanham, Md.: University Press of America, 1985.

Bergreen, Laurence. *Look Now Pay Later: The Rise of Network Broadcasting*. New York: Doubleday, 1980.

Bernstein, Marver H. *Regulating Business by Independent Commission*. Princeton, N.J.: Princeton University Press, 1955.

Besen, Stanley. *Misregulating Television: Network Dominance and the FCC*. Chicago: University of Chicago Press, 1984.

Besen, Stanley, and Leland Johnson. *Regulation of Media Ownership by the Federal Communications Commission: An Assessment*. Santa Monica, Calif.: Rand Corporation, 1984.

Bittner, John R. *Broadcast Law and Regulation*. Englewood Cliffs, N.J.: Prentice-Hall, 1982.

Black, David. "How the Gosh-darn Networks Edit the Heck out of Movies." *New York Times*, 26 January 1975.

Bloustein, Edward J. *Individual and Group Privacy*. New Brunswick, N.J.: Transaction Books, 1978.

Blumler, Jay G., and Elihu Katz. *The Uses of Mass Communication: Current Perspectives on Gratification Research*. Beverly Hills, Calif.: Sage, 1975.

Bobroff, Sara A. *United States Treaties and other International Agreements Pertaining to Telecommunications*. Office of Telecommunications Report 74–26. Washington, D.C.: Government Printing Office, 1974.

Boorstin, Daniel J. *The Image: A Guide to Pseudo-Events in America*. New York: Harper & Row, 1964.

Botein, Michael, and David M. Rice, eds. *Network Television and Public Interest: A Preliminary Inquiry*. Lexington, Mass.: Lexington Books, 1981.

Boyer, William W. *Bureaucracy on Trial: Policy Making by Government Agencies*. Indianapolis, Ind.: Bobbs-Merrill, 1964.

Brenner, Daniel L., and William Rivers, eds. *Free but Regulated Conflicting Traditions in Media Law*. Ames, Iowa: Iowa State University Press, 1982.

Brock, Gerald W. *The Telecommunications Industry: The Dynamics of Market Structure*. Cambridge, Mass.: Harvard University Press, 1981.

Brown, Les. *Television: The Business behind the Box*. Orlando, Fla.: Harcourt Brace Jovanovich, 1971.

———. *Keeping Your Eye on Television*. New York: Pilgrim, 1979.

Brown, Ray, ed. *Children and Television*. Beverly Hills, Calif: Sage, 1976.

Bunce, Richard. *Television in the Corporate Interest*. New York: Praeger, 1976.

Busterna, John. "Diversity of Ownership as a Criterion in FCC Licensing since 1965." *Journal of Broadcasting* 20 (Winter 1976): 101–110.

Canavan, Francis. *Freedom of Expression: Purpose as Limit*. Durham, N.C.: Carolina Academic Press, 1984.

Cantor, Muriel G. *The Hollywood TV Producer: His Work and His Audience*. New York: Basic Books, 1972.

———. *Prime Time Television: Content and Control*. Beverly Hills, Calif.: Sage, 1980.

Carey, William. *Politics and the Regulatory Commission*. New York: McGraw-Hill, 1967.

Carnegie Commission on Educational Television. *Public Television: A Program for Action*. New York: Harper & Row, 1967.

Carnegie Commission on the Future of Public Broadcasting. *A Public Trust*. New York: Bantam Books, 1979.

"CBS Records First to Charge for Music Videos." *Broadcasting,* 1 July 1985, 32.

Chafee, Zechariah, Jr. *Government and Mass Communications*. Chicago: University of Chicago Press, 1947.

Chamberlin, Bill, and Charlene J. Brown, eds. *The First Amendment Reconsidered: New Perspectives on the Meaning of Freedom of Speech and of the Press*. White Plains, N.Y.: Longman, 1982.

Chase, Oscar. "Broadcast Regulation and the First Amendment." In *Network Television and the Public Interest*, edited by Michael Botein and David Rice. Lexington, Mass.: Lexington Books, 1980.

Cherington, Paul W. *Television Station Ownership: A Case Study of Federal Agency Regulation*. New York: Hastings House, 1971.

Christains, Charles. "Home Video Systems: A Revolution?" *Journal of Broadcasting* 17 (Spring 1973): 223–234.

Clift, Charles, III. "Forfeitures and the Federal Communications Commission: An Update." *Journal of Broadcasting* 24 (Summer 1980): 301–310.

Cline, Victor, ed. *Where Do You Draw the Line?* Provo, Utah: Brigham Young University Press, 1974.

Codding, George. *The International Telecommunications Union: An Experiment in International Cooperation*. Leiden, Holland: Brill, 1952.

Codding, George, and Anthony M. Rutkowski. *The International Telecom-*

munications Union in a Changing World. Dedham, Mass: Artech House, 1982.

Coffee, Arthur. "The Top 50 Market Policy: Fifteen Years of Non-Policy." *Federal Communications Bar Journal* 31 (Spring 1979): 303–339.

Cohn, Lawrence. "Majors Step on In-House Production Pedal." *Variety*, 13 June 1984, 5.

———. "Half of Megabuck Pictures Win Maxi B.O." *Variety*, 16 January 1985, 7.

———. "Cable Lights Fire under Made-For Pictures; HBO Theatrical Pace Slowing Down." *Variety*, 29 May 1985, 129.

Cole, Barry G., and Mal Oettinger. *Reluctant Regulators: The FCC and the Broadcast Audience*. Reading, Mass: Addison-Wesley, 1978.

Compaine, Benjamin M., ed. *Who Owns the Media? Concentration of Ownership in the Mass Communication Industry*. New York: Crown, 1979.

———. *Anatomy of the Communications Industry: Who Owns the Media?* White Plains, N.Y.: Knowledge Industry, 1982.

Comptroller General of the United States, Report to Congress. *Selected FCC Regulatory Policies: Their Purposes and Consequences for Commercial Radio and Television*. Washington, D.C.: Government Printing Office, 1979.

Comstock, George. *Television and Human Behavior*. New York: Columbia University Press, 1978.

Cowan, Geoffrey. *See No Evil: Backstage Battle over Sex and Violence on Television*. New York: Simon & Schuster, 1979.

Cox, Kenneth. *Television Network Practices*. Staff Report for Senate Committee on Interstate and Foreign Commerce, Television Inquiry, 85th Cong. 1st sess. Washington, D.C.: Government Printing Office, 1957.

———. "The Federal Communications Commission." *Boston College Industrial and Commercial Law Review* 11 (May 1970): 595–688.

Crane, Rhoda J. *The Politics of International Standards: France and the Color TV War*. Norwood, N.J.: Ablex Publishing, 1979.

Cushman, Robert E. *The Independent Regulatory Commissions*. New York: Oxford University Press, 1941.

Daniels, Bill. "Videocassette Sponsorship Seen as VCR Total Rises." *Variety*, 1 May 1985, 437.

Davis, Clive. *Clive: Inside the Record Business*. New York: Ballantine Books, 1976.

Davis, Kenneth Culp. *Discretionary Justice: A Preliminary Inquiry*. Urbana, Ill.: University of Illinois Press, 1971.

Davis, Robert. *Response to Innovation: A Study of Popular Argument about New Mass Media*. New York: Arno Press, 1976.

Delong, Thomas A. *The Mighty Music Box: The Golden Age of Musical Radio*. Los Angeles: Amber Crest Books, 1980.

Derthick, Martha, and Paul J. Quick. *The Politics of Deregulation.* Washington, D.C.: Brookings Institute, 1985.

Dertouzos, James N., and Steven S. Wildman. "A Study of Economic Issues in the Music Recording Industry." Palo Alto, Calif.: *Studies in Industry Economics*, No. 106, Stanford University, 1984.

De Sola Pool, Ithiel. *Technologies of Freedom.* Cambridge, Mass.: Harvard University Press, 1983.

Diamond, Edwin, et al. *Telecommunications in Crisis.* Washington, D.C.: Cato Institute, 1983.

Dill, Clarence C. *Radio Law: Practice and Procedure.* Washington, D.C.: National Law Book Co., 1938.

Dizard, Wilson P. *Television: A World View.* Syracuse, N.Y.: Syracuse University Press, 1966.

Dominick, Joseph P., and Millard C. Pearce. "Trends in Network Prime Time Television 1953–74." *Journal of Communication* 26 (Winter 1976): 70–80.

Downs, Anthony. *Inside Bureaucracy.* Boston: Little, Brown, 1967.

Efron, Edith. "This Time the Indians Won." *TV Guide*, 22 January 1972, 42–46.

Ellmore, R. Terry. *Broadcasting Law & Regulation.* Blue Ridge Summit, Pa.: Tab Books, 1982.

Emerson, Thomas I. *The System of Freedom of Expression.* New York: Random House (Vintage Books), 1970.

Emery, Walter B. *Broadcasting and Government: Responsibilities and Regulations.* 2d ed. East Lansing, Mich.: Michigan State University Press, 1972.

Epstein, Michael. *Modern Intellectual Property.* Orlando, Fla.: Harcourt Brace Jovanovich, 1984.

Ettema, James S., and D. Charles Whitney, eds. *Individuals in the Mass Media.* Beverly Hills, Calif.: Sage, 1982.

Eyesenck, H. J. *Sex, Violence, and the Media.* New York: Harper & Row, 1978.

Fainsod, Merle. "Some Reflections on the Nature of the Regulatory Process." In *Public Policy*, edited by Carl J. Friedrich and Edward S. Mason. Cambridge, Mass.: Harvard University Press, 1940.

Faulk, John H. *Fear on Trial.* New York: Simon & Schuster, 1964.

Federal Communications Commission. *Investigation on Chain Broadcasting.* Washington, D.C.: Government Printing Office, 1941.

———. *An Analysis of the Network-Affiliate Relationship in Television.* Network Inquiry Special Staff. Washington, D.C.: FCC, 1979.

———. *New Television Networks Entry, Jurisdiction, Ownership and Regulation: Final Report.* Vol. 1, Background Report. Washington, D.C.: Government Printing Office, 1980.

"Fifth Estate's $30 Billion-Plus Year." *Broadcasting*, 30 December 1985, 35–41.

Fink, Donald G., ed. *Television Standards and Practices: Selected Papers from the Proceedings of the National Television System Committee and Its Panels.* New York: McGraw-Hill, 1943.

Fischer, Heinz-Dietrich, and Stefan Reinhard Melnik, eds. *Entertainment: A Cross-Cultural Examination.* New York: Hastings House, 1979.

Francois, William E. *Mass Media Law and Regulation.* 3d ed. Columbus, Ohio: Grid, 1982.

Frank, Ronald E., and Marshall E. Greenberg. *The Public Uses of Television.* Beverly Hills, Calif.: Sage, 1980.

Franklin, Marc A. *The First Amendment and the Fourth Estate.* 2d ed. Mineola, N.Y.: Foundation Press, 1981.

"Free at Last: Cable Gets Its Bill." *Broadcasting,* 15 October 1984, 38.

Friendly, Fred W. *Due to Circumstances beyond Our Control.* New York: Random House, 1967.

Ganley, Oswald H., and Gladys D. Ganley. *To Inform or to Control? The New Communications Networks.* New York: McGraw-Hill, 1982.

Gellhorn, Ernest. *Administrative Law and Process.* St. Paul, Minn.: West Publishing, 1972.

General Accounting Office. *Selected FCC Regulatory Policies: Their Purposes and Consequences for Commercial Radio and TV.* Washington, D.C.: Government Printing Office, 1979.

Gerbner, George. "Communications and Social Environment." *Scientific American,* September 1972, 153–160.

———. "The 'Mainstreaming' of American Violence." *Journal of Communication* 30 (Summer 1980): 10–29.

Gibson, George H. *Public Broadcasting: The Role of the Federal Government 1972–1976.* New York: Praeger, 1977.

Gillmor, Donald M., and Jerome A. Barron. *Mass Communication Law: Cases and Comment.* 4th ed. St. Paul, Minn.: West Publishing, 1984.

Gitlin, Todd. *Inside Prime Time.* New York: Pantheon Books, 1983.

Glatzer, Hal. *Who Owns the Rainbow? Conserving the Radio Spectrum.* Indianapolis, Ind.: Howard W. Sams, 1984.

"Gleam in Fowler's Regulatory Eye." *Broadcasting,* 14 September 1981, 27.

Gold, Richard. "Mounting Costs Zap Distributor Profits." *Variety,* 12 December 1984, 3.

———. "Major Merger Mania." *Variety,* 17 July 1985, 6.

Graham, James, and Victor Kramer. *Appointments to the Regulatory Agencies: The Federal Communications Commission and the Federal Trade Commission 1949–1974.* Report to the Senate Committee on Commerce. Washington. D.C.: Government Printing Office, 1976.

Griffin, Byran F. *Panic among the Philistines.* Chicago: Regnery/Gateway, 1983.

Gross, Leonard. "Television under Pressure." *TV Guide,* 22 February, 1 March, 8 March 1975.

Grundfest, Joseph A. *Citizen Participation in Broadcast Licensing before the FCC*. Santa Monica, Calif.: Rand Corporation, 1976.

Guimary, Donald. *Citizen Groups and Broadcasting*. New York: Praeger, 1975.

Haight, Timothy R., ed. *Telecommunications Policy and the Citizen*. New York: Praeger, 1979.

Haiman, Franklyn. *Speech and Law in a Free Society*. Chicago: University of Chicago Press, 1981.

Hall, Jerome. *Foundations of Jurisprudence*. Indianapolis, Ind.: Bobbs-Merrill, 1973.

Haskell, Molly. *From Reverence to Rape: The Treatment of Women in the Movies*. New York: Holt, Rinehart and Winston, 1974.

Havick, John J., ed. *Communications Policy and the Political Process*. Westport, Conn.: Greenwood Press, 1983.

Head, Sydney W., and Christopher H. Sterling. *Broadcasting in America*. 4th ed. Boston: Houghton Mifflin, 1982.

_____. *World Broadcasting Systems*. Belmont, Calif.: Wadsworth, 1984.

Henderson, Madeline M., and Marcia J. McMacnaughton, eds. *Electronic Communication: Technology and Impact*. Boulder, Colo: Westview Press, 1980.

Hess, Gary Newton. *An Historical Study of the Dumont Television Network*. New York: Arno Press, 1979.

Himmelstein, Hal. *Television Myth and the American Mind*. New York: Praeger, 1985.

Himmelweit, Hilde. *Television and the Child: An Empirical Study of the Effect of Television on the Young*. New York: Oxford University Press, 1961.

Hocking, William E. *Freedom of the Press: A Framework of Principles*. Chicago: University of Chicago Press, 1947.

Howard, Herbert H. "Recent Trends in Broadcast Multiple Ownership." *Client* 4 (Fall 1976): 6–14.

Huntington, Samuel P. "The Marasmus of the Interstate Commerce Commission: The Commission, the Railroads and the Public Interest." *Yale Law Review* 61 (April 1952): 467–509.

Jennings, Ralph, and Pamela Richard. *How to Protect Your Rights on Radio and TV*. New York: United Church of Christ, 1974.

Johnson, Donald F. *Copyright Handbook*. New York: R.R. Bowker, 1978.

Jones, Robert H. *Investigation of Television Networks and the UHF-VHF Problem*. Washington, D.C.: Government Printing Office, 1955.

Jones, William K. *Cases and Materials on Electronic Mass Media: Radio, Television and Cable*. 2d ed. Mineola, N.Y.: Foundation Press, 1979.

Jowett, Garth and James Linton. *Movies as Mass Communication*. Beverly Hills, Calif.: Sage, 1980.

Kahn, Frank J. *Documents of American Broadcasting*. 4th ed. Englewood Cliffs, N.J.: Prentice-Hall, 1984.

Katzmann, Robert A. *Regulatory Bureaucracy: The Federal Trade Commission and Antitrust Policy.* Cambridge, Mass.: MIT Press, 1980.

Kaye, Evelyn. *The ACT Guide to Children's Television.* Boston: Beacon Press, 1979.

Kittross, John M. *Television Frequency Allocation in the United States.* New York: Arno Press, 1979.

————, ed. *Administration of American Telecommunications Policy.* New York: Arno Press, 1980.

Koenig, Allen E., ed. *Broadcasting and Bargaining: Labor Relations in the United States.* Madison, Wis.: University of Wisconsin Press, 1970.

Krasnow, Erwin, and Laurence Longley. *The Politics of Broadcast Regulation.* 3d ed. New York: St. Martin's Press, 1982.

Krislov, Samuel, and Lloyd P. Musolf, eds. *The Politics of Regulation.* Boston: Houghton Mifflin, 1964.

Krugman, Dean, and Leonard Reid. "The 'Public Interest' as Defined by FCC Policy-Makers." *Journal of Broadcasting* 24 (Summer 1980): 381–399.

"The Laissez-Faire Legacy of Charles Fowler." *Broadcasting,* 19 January 1981, 37.

Landis, James M. *Report on Regulatory Agencies to the President-Elect.* Subcommittee on Administrative Practice and Procedure. 86th Cong. 2d Sess. Washington, D.C.: Government Printing Office, 1960.

Lawhorne, Clifton O., *The Supreme Court and Libel.* Carbondale, Ill: Southern Illinois University Press, 1981.

Le Duc, Don R. "The FCC vs. CATV: A Theory of Regulatory Reflex Action." *Federal Communications Bar Journal* 23 (Winter 1969): 93–110.

————. "The Federal Radio Commission in Federal Court." *Journal of Broadcasting* 14 (Fall 1970): 393–410.

————. "Cable Communications: Evolution of Revolution in Electronic Mass Media." *The Annals of the American Academy of Political and Social Science* 120 (March 1972): 127–140.

————. *Cable Television and the FCC.* Philadelphia: Temple University Press, 1973.

————. " 'Free Speech' Decisions and the Legal Process: The Judicial Opinion in Context." *Quarterly Journal of Speech* 72 (Oct. 1976): 277–287.

————. "Satellite Broadcasting and Communications: Transforming Principles into Policy." *Journal of Communication* 30 (Spring 1980): 196–206.

————. "Deregulation and the Dream of Diversity." *Journal of Communication* 32 (Autumn 1982): 164–178.

Leifer, Amy, and Neal J. Gordon. "Children's Television: More than Mere Entertainment." *Harvard Educational Review* 44 (May 1974): 213–244.

Leive, David. *International Telecommunications and International Law: The Regulation of the Radio Spectrum.* Dobbs Ferry, N.Y.: Oceana, 1970.

Less, David, and Stan Berkowitz. *The Movie Business*. New York: Random House (Vintage Books), 1981.

Levin, Harvey J. *The Invisible Resource: Use and Regulation of the Radio Spectrum*. Baltimore: Johns Hopkins Press, 1971.

————. *Fact and Fancy in Television Regulation: An Economic Analysis of Policy Alternatives*. New York: Russell Sage Foundation, 1980.

Levine, Richard. "How the Gay Lobby Has Changed Television." *TV Guide*, 30 May 1981, 3–6.

Levinson, Richard, and William Link. *Stay Tuned: An Inside Look at the Making of Prime-Time Television*. New York: St. Martin's Press, 1981.

Lichty, Lawrence, and Malachi Topping, eds. *American Broadcasting: A Source Book on the History of Radio and Television*. New York: Hastings House, 1975.

Lindey, Alexander. *Lindey on Entertainment, Publishing and the Arts: Agreements and the Law*. New York: Clark Boardman Co., 1983.

Litman, Barry Russell. *The Vertical Structure of the Television Broadcasting Industry: The Coalescence of Power*. East Lansing, Mich.: Michigan State Graduate School of Business, 1979.

Little, Arthur D., Inc. *Television Program Production Procurement, Distribution and Scheduling*. Cambridge, Mass.: Arthur D. Little, 1969.

Long, Stewart Louis. *The Development of the Television Network Oligopoly*. New York: Arno Press, 1979.

Lucoff, Manny. "The Rise and Fall of the Third Re-write." *Journal of Communication* 30 (Summer 1980): 47–53.

McAlpine, D. B. *The Television Programming Industry*. New York: Tucker Anthony & R. L. Day, 1975.

McCombs, Maxwell, and Donald L. Shaw. *The Emergence of American Political Issues: The Agenda Setting Function of the Press*. St. Paul, Minn: West Publishing, 1979.

McFarland, David. *The Development of the Top 40 Radio Format*. New York: Arno Press, 1979.

"Made-Fors Fill CBS Movie Nights as Webs Stop Buying Theatrical Film." *Variety*, 22 May 1985, 47.

Magnant, Peter S. *Domestic Satellite: An FCC Giant Step toward Competitive Telecommunication Policy*. Boulder, Colo: Westview Press, 1977.

Maisel, Richard, "The Decline of Mass Media." *Public Opinion Quarterly* 37 (Summer 1973): 159–170.

"Making Life a Bit Easier; Re-regulation Gets Underway." *Broadcasting* 6 November 1972, 19.

Mander, Jerry. *Four Arguments for the Elimination of Television*. New York: Morrow, 1978.

Marcel, Gabriel. *Man against Mass Society*. Chicago: Gateway Publications, 1971.

March, John, and Herbert Simon. *Organizations*. New York: Wiley, 1958.

Martin, James. *Future Developments in Telecommunications*. 2d ed. Englewood Cliffs, N.J.: Prentice-Hall, 1977.

Mead, Lawrence M. "The FCC as an Institution." In *Telecommunications: An Interdisciplinary Survey*, edited by Leonard Levin. Dedham, Mass.: Artech House, 1979.

Meeske, Milam D. "Black Ownership of Broadcast Stations: An FCC Licensing Problem." *Journal of Broadcasting* 20 (Spring 1976): 261–271.

Melody, William. *Children's Television: The Economics of Exploitation*. New Haven, Conn.: Yale University Press, 1973.

Mendelsohn, Harold. *Mass Entertainment*. New Haven, Conn.: College and University Press, 1966.

Metz, Robert. *CBS: Reflections in a Bloodshot Eye*. Chicago: Playboy Press, 1975.

Meyrowitz, Joshua. *No Sense of Place*. New York: Oxford University Press, 1984.

Miller, Randall M., ed. *Ethnic Images in American Film and Television*. Philadelphia: The Balch Institute, 1978.

Minow, Newton. *Equal Time: The Private Broadcaster and Public Interest*. New York: Atheneum, 1964.

Mitnick, Barry M. *The Political Economy of Regulation: Creating, Designing and Removing Regulatory Forms*. New York: Columbia University Press, 1980.

Montgomery, Kathyrn. "Gay Activities and the Networks." *Journal of Communication* 31 (Summer 1981): 49–57.

Morgenstern, Steve, ed. *Inside the TV Business*. New York: Sterling Press, 1979.

Mosco, Vincent. *Broadcasting in the United States: Innovative Challenge and Organizational Control*. Norwood, N.J.: Ablex Publishing, 1979.

"NAB Lifts Radio Advertising Codes." *Broadcasting*, 15 March 1982, 45.

"NBC Breaks Ranks; Settles with Justice." *Broadcasting*, 22 November 1976, 21.

Nelson, Harold L., and Dwight L. Teeter, Jr. *Law of Mass Communications*. 5th ed. Mineola, N.Y.: Foundation Press, 1986.

Nesson, Ron. "Now Television's the Kingmaker." *TV Guide*, 10 May 1980, 4–6.

Neustadt, Richard M. *The Birth of Electronic Publishing: Legal and Economic Issues in Telephone, Cable and Over-the-Air Teletext and Videotex*. White Plains, N.Y.: Knowledge Industry, 1982.

New York State Senate. *Cable Communications and the States: A Sourcebook for Legislative Decision-Makers*. Albany, N.Y.: 1975.

Noam, Eli, ed. *Video Media Competition: Regulation, Economics, Technology*, New York: Columbia University Press, 1985.

Noll, Roger G. *Reforming Regulation*. Washington, D.C.: Brookings Institute, 1971.

Noll, Roger G., et al. *Economic Aspects of Television Regulation*. Washington, D.C.: Brookings Institute, 1973.

Office of Telecommunications Policy. *The Radio Frequency Spectrum: United States Use and Management*. Washington, D.C.: Office of Telecommunications Policy, 1975.

Osborn, J. Wes, et al. "Prime Time Network Television Programming Presumptions." *Journal of Broadcasting* 23 (Fall 1979): 427–436.

Othmer, David. *The Wired Island: The First Two Years of Public Access to Cable Television in Manhattan*. New York: Fund for the City of New York, 1973.

Owen, Bruce M. *Economics and Freedom of Expression: Media Structure and the First Amendment*. Cambridge, Mass: Ballinger, 1975.

Owen, Bruce M., and Ronald Braeutigam. *The Regulation Game: Strategic Use of the Administrative Process*. Cambridge, Mass.: Ballinger, 1978.

———. "Structural Approaches to the Problem of TV Network Dominance." Durham, N.C.: Duke University Graduate School of Business Administration, Paper No. 27, 1978.

Paletz, David L., et al. *Politics in Public Service Advertising in Television*. New York: Praeger, 1977.

Paley, William S. *As It Happened: A Memoir*. Garden City, N.Y.: Doubleday, 1979.

Passman, Arnold. *The Deejays*. New York: Macmillan, 1971.

Peabody, Robert L., et al. *To Enact a Law: Congress and Campaign Funding*. New York: Praeger, 1972.

Pekurney, Robert G., and Bart D. Leonard. "Sticks and Bones: A Survey of Network Television Affiliate Decision Making." *Journal of Broadcasting* 19 (Fall 1975): 427–437.

Pelton, Joseph N., and Marcellus S. Snow, eds. *Economic and Policy Problems in Satellite Communication*. New York: Praeger, 1977.

Pember, Don R. *Mass Media Law*. 2d ed. Dubuque, Iowa: Brown, 1981.

Pennybacker, John. "The Format Change Issue: FCC vs. U.S. Court of Appeals." *Journal of Broadcasting* 22 (Fall 1978): 411–428.

"Pershuk Disqualified in Children's Ad Proceedings." *Broadcasting*, 6 November 1978, 34.

Peterson, Richard, ed. *The Production of Culture*. Beverly Hills, Calif.: Sage, 1976.

Plotkin, Harry M. *Television Network Regulation and the UHF Problem*. Memorandum prepared for Senate Committee on Interstate and Foreign Commerce, 84th Cong., 1st Sess. Washington, D.C.: Government Printing Office, 1955.

Practicing Law Institute. *Communication Law 1984*. New York: PLI, 1984.

——— *The New Era of CATV: The Cable Franchise Policy and the Communications Act of 1984.* New York: PLI, 1984.

President's Task Force on Communications Policy. *Final Report.* Washington, D.C.: Government Printing Office, 1968.

Privacy Protection Study Commission. *Personal Privacy in an Information Society.* Washington, D.C.: Government Printing Office, 1977.

Quaal, Ward L., and James A. Brown. *Broadcasting Management.* 2d ed. New York: Hastings House, 1976.

Quinlan, Sterling. *Inside ABC: American Broadcasting Company's Rise to Power.* New York: Hastings House, 1979.

Randall, Richard S. *Censorship in the Movies: The Social and Political Control of a Mass Medium.* Madison, Wis.: University of Wisconsin Press, 1967.

Read, William H. *America's Mass Media Merchants.* Baltimore: Johns Hopkins University Press, 1976.

Reel, Frank. *The Networks: How They Stole the Show.* New York: Scribner's, 1979.

Reeves, Michael G., and Tom W. Hoffer. "The Safe, Cheap and Known: A Content Analysis of the PBS Program Cooperative." *Journal of Broadcasting* 20 (Fall 1976): 549–565.

Research and Policy Committee of the Committee for Economic Development. *Broadcasting and Cable Television: Policies for Diversity and Change.* New York: Committee for Economic Development, 1975.

Rice, David M., et al. *Development and Regulation of New Communication Technology.* New York: Communication Media Center, 1980.

Righter, Rosemary. *Whose News? Politics, the Press and the Third World.* New York: Times Books, 1978.

Rivkin, Steven R. *A New Guide to Federal Cable Television Regulations.* Cambridge, Mass.: MIT Press, 1978.

Robinson, Glen O., ed. *Communications for Tomorrow: Policy Perspectives for the 1980s.* New York: Praeger, 1978.

Robinson, Thomas P. *Radio Networks and the Federal Government.* New York: Columbia University Press, 1943.

Roper Organization, Inc. *Trends in Attitudes towards Television and Other Media. A Twenty-Five Year Review.* New York: Television Information Office, 1984.

Rosen, Philip T. *The Modern Stentors: Radio Broadcasters and the Federal Government, 1920–1934.* Westport, Conn.: Greenwood Press, 1980.

Ross, Leonard. *Economic and Legal Foundations of Cable Television.* Beverly Hills, Calif.: Sage, 1974.

Routt, Edd, et al. *The Radio Format Conundrum.* New York: Hastings House, 1978.

Rowan, Ford. *Broadcast Fairness: Doctrine, Practice, Prospects.* White Plains, N.Y.: Longman, 1984.

Sadowski, Robert P. "Broadcasting and State Statutory Laws." *Journal of Broadcasting* (Fall 1974): 433–450.

Schmeckebier, Laurence F. *The Federal Radio Commission: Its History, Activities and Organization.* Washington, D.C.: Brookings Institute, 1932.

Schmidt, Benno C. *Freedom of the Press vs. Public Access.* New York: Praeger, 1976.

Schramm, Wilbur, and D. F. Roberts. *The Processes and Effects of Mass Communication.* Urbana, Ill: University of Illinois Press, 1971.

Schwartz, Bernard. *The Professor and the Commission: Its History, Activities and Organization.* New York: Knopf, 1959.

Seiden, Martin H. *Who Controls the Media? Popular Myths and Economic Realities.* New York: Basic Books, 1974.

"Settled at Last; ABC and Justice Come to Terms." *Broadcasting,* 25 August 1980, 31.

Shapiro, Andrew O. *Media Access: Your Rights to Express Your Views on Radio and Television.* Boston: Little, Brown, 1976.

Sharp, Steven. "Can the Broadcaster in the Black Hat Ride Again? 'Good Character' Requirements for Broadcast Licensees." *Federal Communications Bar Journal* 32 (Spring 1980): 173–203.

Siepmann, Charles. *Radio's Second Chance.* Boston, Mass.: Little, Brown, 1946.

Sigel, Efrem, ed. *Videotext: The Coming Revolution in Home/Office Information Retrieval.* White Plains, N.Y.: Knowledge Industry, 1980.

Simmons, Steven J. *The Fairness Doctrine and the Media.* Berkeley, Calif.: University of California Press, 1978.

Smith, Anthony. *The Shadow in the Cave: The Broadcaster, His Audience and the State.* Urbana, Ill.: University of Illinois Press, 1973.

Socolow, A. Walter. *The Laws of Radio Broadcasting.* New York: Baker Voorhis, 1939.

Spalding, John W. "1928: Radio Becomes a Mass Advertising Medium." *Journal of Broadcasting* 8 (Winter 1964): 31–44.

Squire, Jason E., ed. *The Movie Business Book.* Englewood Cliffs, N.J.: Prentice-Hall, 1983.

Stanley, Robert. *The Celluloid Empire.* New York: Hastings House, 1978.

Stein, Ben. *The View from Sunset Boulevard.* New York: Basic Books, 1979.

Stein, Robert. *Media Power: Who Is Shaping Your Picture of the World?* Boston: Houghton Mifflin, 1972.

Steiner, Gary A. *The People Look at Television: A Study of Audience Attitudes.* New York: Knopf, 1963.

Sterling, Christopher H., and John M. Kittross. *Stay Tuned: A Concise History of American Broadcasting.* Belmont, Calif.: Wadsworth, 1978.

———. *Electronic Media: A Guide to Trends in Broadcasting and New Technologies 1920–83.* New York: Praeger, 1984.

Stern, Robert H. *The Federal Communications Commission and Television.* New York: Arno Press, 1979.

Stinchcombe, Arthur. "Bureaucratic and Craft Administration of Production: A Comparative Study." *Administrative Science* 4 (Winter 1959): 168–178.

Stokes, Geoffrey. *Starmaking Machinery.* New York: Random House (Vintage Books), 1976.

Stone, Alan. *Economic Regulation and the Public Interest: The Federal Trade Commission in Theory and Practice.* Ithaca, N.Y.: Cornell University Press, 1978.

Stuart, Fredric. *The Effects of Television on the Motion Picture and Radio Industries.* New York: Arno Press, 1976.

Tannenbaum, Percy H., ed. *The Entertainment Functions of Television.* Hillsdale, N.J.: Lawrence Erlbaum Associates, 1980.

Tebbel, John. *The Media in America.* New York: Crowell, 1974.

Technology and Economics, Inc. *The Emergence of Pay Cable Television.* Washington, D.C.: National Telecommunications & Information Association, 1980.

Tedford, Thomas L. *Freedom of Speech in the United States.* Carbondale, Ill.: Southern Illinois University Press, 1985.

Television and Behavior: Ten Years of Scientific Progress and Implications for the Eighties. Washington, D.C.: Government Printing Office, 1982.

Toll, Robert C. *The Entertainment Machine: American Show Business in the Twentieth Century.* New York: Oxford University Press, 1982.

Tuchman, Gaye, Arlene Kaplan, and James Benet, eds. *Hearth and Home: Images of Women in the Mass Media.* New York: Oxford University Press, 1978.

Tunstall, Jeremy. *The Media Are American: Anglo-American Media in the World.* New York: Columbia University Press, 1977.

Turow, Joseph. *Media Industries: The Production of News and Entertainment.* White Plains, N.Y.: Longman, 1984.

Tynan, Kenneth. *Show People: Profiles in Entertainment.* New York: Simon & Schuster, 1979.

U.S. Congress. House. *Regulation of Broadcasting: Half a Century of Government Regulation of Broadcasting and the Need for Further Legislative Action.* 85th Cong., 2d Sess., 1958.

———. *Option Papers.* 95th Cong., 1st Sess., 1977.

———. *Telecommunications in Transmission: The Status of Competition in the Telecommunications Industry.* Report by the Majority Staff to the Subcommittee on Telecommunications, Consumer Protection and Finance. Washington, D.C.: Government Printing Office, 1981.

———. Committee on Interstate and Foreign Commerce. *Network Broadcasting.* Report of the FCC Network Study Staff. House Report 1297, 85th Cong., 1st Sess., 1985.

Vaughn, Robert. *Only Victims: A Study of Show Business Blacklisting.* New York: Putnam, 1972.

Waldrop, Frank C., and Joseph Borkin. *Television: A Struggle for Power.* New York: Morrow, 1938.

Wasko, Janet. *Movies and Money.* Norwood, N.J.: Ablex, 1982.

Webb, G. Kent. *The Economics of Cable Television.* Lexington, Mass.: Lexington Books, 1983.

Weber, Max. *On Law in Economy and Society.* New York: Simon & Schuster, 1954.

Weiss, Frederic, et al. "Station License Revocations and Denials of Renewal 1970–78." *Journal of Broadcasting* 24 (Winter 1980): 69–77.

Wilson, John Q., ed. *The Politics of Regulation.* New York: Basic Books, 1980.

Winn, Marie. *The Plug-In Drug: Children and the Family.* Baltimore: Penguin Books, 1985.

Withey, Stephen, and Ronald P. Abeles. *Television and Social Behavior: Beyond Violence and Children.* Hillsdale, N.J.: Lawrence Erlbaum Associates, 1980.

Wood, Donald N., and Donald G. Wylie. *Educational Telecommunications.* Belmont, Calif.: Wadsworth, 1977.

Zuckman, Harvey L., and Martin J. Gaynes. *Mass Communication Law in a Nutshell.* St. Paul, Minn.: West Publishing, 1983.

INDEX